Arkle Beck

Hurst

VA

Beck

Riddings

Reeth

Healaugh

Fremington

m

Harkerside

Grinton

Cogden

River Swale

Marske Beck

Garlic Woods

Richmond

Rhubarb

Ellerton Abbey

The Forebears of E. J. Pratt

The Silent Ancestors

The Silent

McClelland and Stewart Limited
Toronto / Montreal

The Forebears of E. J. Pratt

Ancestors

Mildred Claire Pratt

The Canadian Publishers
McClelland and Stewart Limited
25 Hollinger Road, Toronto 374

Printed and bound in Canada by John Deyell Limited.

To the men of the Pratt family
from Thomas of Grinton and all who went before him
to Edwyn James of Newfoundland and all who will
come after him

And did those feet in ancient time
Walk upon England's mountains green?
And was the holy Lamb of God
On England's pleasant pastures seen?

And did the Countenance Divine
Shine forth upon our clouded Hills?
And was Jerusalem builded here
Among these dark Satanic mills?

Bring me my bow of burning gold!
Bring me my arrows of desire!
Bring me my spear! O clouds, unfold!
Bring me my chariot of fire!

I will not cease from mental fight,
Nor shall my sword sleep in my hand,
Till we have built Jerusalem
In England's green and pleasant land.

William Blake

Acknowledgements

So many people have contributed to this book that it is impossible to thank all of them. There are a few key people, however, that I would like to mention for, without their help, the essay might not have been written at all. I want to thank Miss Dorothy Thompson for making it possible to find the family in New Zealand, Dr. Ernest Haworth for doing the spade work in Yorkshire, Mrs. Margaret Batty and the Rev. C. B. Bardsley for making their records available, and Mrs. J. W. Ball and Mrs. Charles Colechin of New Zealand for sharing their memories, letters, and diaries. Special thanks are also due my cousins Jack, Ewart, and Calvert Pratt for their generous help in the publication. To all my family, both living and dead, I owe a debt of profound gratitude, and if there are errors or omissions I hope I shall be forgiven and also that these same may be pointed out to me. The work is but half done and should it attract any members of the family not represented I shall be more than happy to be able to include them on the genealogical tree.

Mildred Claire Pratt

CONTENTS

The Search for Joseph

There is a letter that contains a comment, expressed in the biblical terms of earlier days when the poetry of the Bible still exercised considerable influence on the lives of men. It reads: "The coming generation knows not Joseph. They are not particularly interested to hear of the 'pit from which they have been digged.' Family ties are becoming vague." In this nostalgic statement of Christopher Pratt to his cousin Arthur is embodied the universal sadness of the passage of time, the inevitable sinking beyond the horizon of the ships from which we have been launched.

With the widening of the gaps between successive and proliferating generations it cannot be otherwise. To remember Joseph is not altogether possible nor, indeed, perhaps altogether desirable. And who, in any case, is Joseph? Arthur and Christopher were seeking him out and in their correspondence were attempting to identify him by means of the maddening, exciting, elusive pieces of jetsam still rising, though with increasing rarity, from their common past. Joseph for these two third cousins seems to have been one James Pratt, born around the year 1750. He appeared on a chart, simply, with no elucidation, prepared by Christopher's older brother Leonard, based on some long-vanished information to which Leonard, no longer living, had had access. But what of James's Joseph, and Joseph's Joseph? Earlier generations must have known earlier Josephs who in turn could look back and again back to the very day-spring of our being, now in the mind's darkness.

And what is it to know Joseph? What is it to enter the pit from which we have been digged? It is to lose the present, the comparative physical ease of the twentieth century and return to a rougher, simpler, and in some ways happier time, to claim kinship with the toilers of the earth. It is to become acquainted with the suffering, the darkness, the spontaneous and irrepressible gaiety that breaks through the darkness, and the love that have fashioned and shaped us into the creatures we have become. It is to reach back in time and take hold of the ages as they in their endless variety keep faith with the circling seasons, ringing the changes from birth to death, from death to birth again.

My search is by no means over. As far as family histories go my story is meagre indeed, and I am well aware of its short-comings. It is unenlivened by family legends and the tall tales that are part and parcel of most family chronicles. I have had to rely on cold records and few of them, and on the hazy memories of the living, many of whom cannot or do not wish to remember.

My purpose in writing is to preserve as much as possible, before any more of it sinks into the darkness, of the background of an ordinary family whose descendants now cover the earth and are doing all manner of things – a family who according to the evidence that I can find was a particularly warm and close-knit one, living simply and in poverty, now completely forgotten in the very village in which its members had lived for over a century.

The Singing Land

In the North Riding of Yorkshire there exists a dale that is as unspoiled and beautiful as any in all England. To visit it for the first time, especially if your forebears have come from there, is to be imprinted with a bit of splendour touched with an ancient melancholy that, combined, tell the history of man on the earth, his remarkable suffering and his no less remarkable triumph.

Swaledale, or the "romantic dale," as it is known to distinguish it from the wider and kinder "pastoral dale" of Wensley to the south, rises from each side of the river Swale, in varying degrees of moors or uplands between the village of Keld at the source and the ancient castle town of Richmond at the foot. The green and purple moors are characterized by the dry stone walls that have stood for centuries, despite the winds and the habit of the younger dalespeople of sitting on them and rocking to and fro. The walls, like the moors themselves, are as changeable in mood as the weather, gentle and protecting under the sun, but there are times when under a sombre sky they writhe like serpents in black and sinister patterns stridently goring the moor; while the moors appear to brood over the callous role assigned to them by nature and by man. Upon their backs sheep graze, for their surface is not hospitable to cultivation. Nor are the sheep friendly, but huge, horned, and very woolly with wool darkened and grimy from much peat-rolling. The sheep wander all year over the dark fells, with dye marks on their sides or rumps to indicate to whom they belong.

Along the narrow flats straggle the villages, small clusters of grey stone that seem themselves to have sprung from the earth, so natural do they appear in their landscape. These are the simple homes of the one-time lead miners, laid out in a natural beauty, snugly, with thick grey walls jealously wrapping their wards against the elements.

It has been said that the road from Richmond to Reeth is the second most beautiful road in England, exceeded only by that from Reeth to Richmond. Whoever first thought of it could not have gone beyond Reeth, for the entire thirty-odd miles along the

11

valley of the Swale is a series of breath-taking delights. To enter the valley is to take part in a mystery, and for the first few miles the road winds about among wooded hills with the sparkling river frisking along first on one side of the road then on the other until a blanket of white blossoms deep in the dappled trees issues an invitation to a feast of wild garlic. A little farther on around a winding hill is a patch of rhubarb with leaves so large that one is reminded of a drawing by Hokusai in which rhubarb leaves are depicted as useful umbrellas for the inhabitants of the village when it rains. Here the valley widens out and to the right of the road are some ruins known as Ellerton Abbey, occupied by the Cistercian nuns in the thirteenth century, and by some Pratts in the nineteenth.*

The first village the road runs through is Grinton, the old and central parish for the entire dale, and from now on the traveller is treated to a conglomeration of names so harshly picturesque as to make him believe he has dropped into an old Norse saga. To the southwest is Harkerside and over the bridge to the north is Fremington, then over another bridge that spans the river Arkle is Reeth, the largest village, slithering gracefully off the foot of Mount Calva. A footpath leads off to the right toward Riddings and then the road ambles through Healaugh, in which there is a pretty cottage where "minerals"† are for sale, and crosses Barney Beck. Off the road to the right is Kearton, a village once inhabited by miners, many of whom were Pratts, but it is hard to find much of Kearton now except its sign. Birk Park and Park Hill, in the early days the homes of John of Gaunt where he is said to have entertained Chaucer,[1] are also on this side road but if there is a sign to them it is well hidden. Next is Low Row, a straggle of cottages on either side of the road. It does not take long among the parish records before one is faced with the confusion of a dozen names for the vicinity of Low Row (spelled variously and phonetically Law Raw): Feetham, Blades, Smarber, Riddings, Brockabank, Pick Hill, Whitaside, Wood End, Park

*Among these were James, husbandman and molecatcher, who, after the death of his wife Catherine, took care of his three small children, but no relationship with our Pratts has been established.
†To a traveller west of the Atlantic, this promised to be a geological museum.

Hall, Melbecks. Most of these names have passed into disuse, but there are others such as Isles and Crackpot that have stubbornly refused to give up their identity.

Gunnerside, four miles along to the west, is also dignified by an assortment of names: Heights, Dike Heads, Barffside, Barf Head, Barfend, Lodge Green, Winterings, High Modesty, Low Modesty, Bents,* Ivelets, Calvert Houses, Spring End, Satron. These refer to small dwellings that surround the village proper, which is situated about a hundred yards from the Swale and is divided by the Gunnerside Ghyll which flutes and purls its way down Melbecks Moor past the Anglican Church, the Institute, under the bridge that is the village gossip corner, and past the Methodist Chapel to join the turbulent Swale. Seven miles still farther west is Muker, an ancient medieval hamlet in which records have been kept for the division of Grinton parish known as Melbecks since the sixteenth century. Over the moor of Whitaside is the charming village of Askrigg in Wensleydale, which has been associated with Gunnerside and Low Row since Methodists used to trek the six miles over the moor to attend service at Gunnerside. At the far end of the dale the valley rises steeply and narrowly over the hill of Kisdon through Thorns and into the hamlet of Keld, remote and pretty, with an even remoter waterfall.

It was Gunnerside that was the mecca of our journey and we arrived there the first time silent and dizzy with beauty. This is not a travelogue and no place to describe in detail a traveller's impressions, but all the people I have ever met whose roots are in Gunnerside speak of it with an affection that trembles on the lip and with a softness in the eye that borders on a tear. It nestles at the foot of the moor facing a few acres of low-lying pasture land beside the river. Halfway up the moor behind it are the Modestys and other cottages anciently known as Potting, Bents, and Barfend, while far up at the source of the ghyll lies Winterings,† all of these to be reached by a footpath only. Off to the left is the Corpse Way leading to and beyond an almost

*Named for the coarse grass commonly growing on the moor around.
†A small settlement where miners originally could stay over the winter and not have to go so far to the mine. Later it became a year-round dwelling.

inaccessible little settlement that goes by the name of Calvert Houses, hanging precipitously on the edge of the hills. It is impossible to pass through and not linger in a straining effort to believe.

From time out of mind, until the middle of the nineteenth century, Swaledale has been mining country. The mines were ugly, open sores on the face of the earth. Courage went down into them and returned to the compensation of the eternal hills that enfolded them. The character of the dalespeople has been written of, their stubbornness, loyalty, simplicity, depth. John Wesley described them as an "earnest, loving, simple people." Their lives were such as would not admit of any nonsense. But they were ripe for Wesley and even he was aghast at their own need of him. The solace he gave them rivalled the solace of the hills, and the democratic brotherhood he preached mirrored the spaciousness of the great sky and liberated them from the cramped quarters to which they had been assigned body and soul. For if humanity was war, nature was peace, and nature was all around them. From the comparative warmth of the village, in the glow of noonday and in the darkness of nightfall, they could raise their eyes unto the mountains that were at once their liberation and their bondage.

The moors cannot be described by pen, but must be seen and felt to be believed. Travelling about upon their vast rolls and layers, there would seem to be nothing else in England besides them. They are startling, purple, grey, green, black, stark, immense. Driving up toward the sky for endless miles sometimes it seems the car will not make it but must remain clinging forever under a dizzying expanse of sky or hurtle down to the valleys far below. On the top is flatness, and sheep, and that is all – sheep staring in hostility and disgust. From time to time there arises what appears to be a sea of stone but is in reality numerous stone walls. In some places there are no walls at all. Occasionally a human form occurs, with dog and crook, startlingly in this natural landscape, to herd his sheep, bobbing along like a cluster of dishmops. Sheep-raising and lead-mining, these comprised the eternal business of the dales until in mid-nineteenth century the lead mines, which had operated since the time of Claudius, were closed.

14

Call them and listen
on black heather blowing
the footsteps of ghosts.

The mine in which the Pratts worked was known as "Old
Gang,"* a three-and-a-half-mile walk dawn and dusk up Melbecks moor, to the threshold of Arkengarthdale, through which
flows the river Arkle, the most likely of all the dales as a setting
for a Grimm's fairy story. On a bad day its purple heather looks
as though it would gladly commit murder which might be easily
silenced under the still beauty of the moon landscape. On the
other hand, there is a remote luxury about the place in the way
that the castle of a fairy king might glimmer in a cool clearing
among darkling forests.

The wild moor, the chilly stars, the sparkling Swale and rippling ghyll, low clouds over dark stone walls and rising hills, the
humble miner's cottage and this my origin, planted the seed of
my search. There was not much to go on. Of John Pratt, my
grandfather, neither his children nor grandchildren knew much.
In 1916 a tablet was unveiled at Grand Bank, Newfoundland, in
memory of a lonely man, little known, little understood.

IN MEMORIAM

Respectfully dedicated to the Reverend John Pratt.
Born at Barnard Castle, England, 1840.† Died at
Grand Bank, Nfld, March 15, 1904.
President of Conference 1901. He alone was destined to fall
at his post of duty during the first century of Methodism.
He was a fearless preacher and a faithful pastor.
He being dead yet speaketh.

I never knew him. What I learned of him I learned from his
children, of whom my father was third. Their memories of him
were of a stern, uncompromising father, of Sabbaths so strictly
kept that the youngest daughter remembered standing at the

*From the Old English *gang*, a road.
†He was born in 1839. The discrepancy brings up an interesting point
in heredity. My father allowed his year of birth to stand at 1883 rather than
1882, thus conveniently discarding a year of his age. Similarly is the grave
of John Pratt's brother Metcalf marked with the date 1828, in variance
with the parish records which give it as 1826.

15

window of their house, waiting for the sun to set.

What were John Pratt's thoughts as he saw his children reacting to the religious practices that had been his great solace as a boy and the solace of all of them on the shining Sabbaths by the Swale, that Jordan of rivers, when thoughts of the pick and shovel were put away for twenty-four whole glorious, song-filled hours, and miners allowed the Holy Spirit to flow freely within them? How did he feel when he saw his family unable to share the ecstasy, or appreciate the rarefied path to salvation spread out before them?

It was not until recent years that I learned of the softer side of his nature, and wondered how it was that the harshness of his character had remained so strong in memory. A letter had turned up, one of a scattering that have been found existing in his hand, written to his daughter Charlotte who was away at school in St. John's. It is headed Grand Bank, and is dated Jan. 28th, 1902:

My very dear Lottie,

I must drop you a few lines this time and not let Mother have all the joy of writing you. We got your painting by W. Lake, & we are delighted with it. I took it & the other with the cows in the water & had them in a nice gilt frame each & they look splendid. We have no pictures in the house I like so well. I am charmed with them & show them to nearly every body who comes in. Mr. Wheatly was almost in raptures over them.

You must have your white dress but you must have it lined so as to be warm. Whatever you do do not put on the cold garments so as to be cold going from or coming home from college.

I want you to take all the care possible of your health and not get laid up with a cold.

We had charming letters from Mr. and Mrs. Coates. They got the Portrait we sent & also a handkerchief case from Mr. Coates & tray cloth you worked for Mrs. Coates. Mrs. C. went off into exstasy over your and Mother's work. Mr. Coates tells me to give you a kiss & a good hug for him, calling you my clever daughter. They got the parcel on Xmas Eve – was not that nice?

Get into class when you can. Best love to Jim and Aunt Sophie.

Your affec. father *J. Pratt*

I have written Mrs. Milligan in condolence.

16

Altogether five letters in the pen of this prolific epistolarian have been gathered up, four of them to Charlotte and all written in the spring of 1902, the year of his last trip to England. The next one is dated March 10th:

Dear Lottie,

I must drop you a line this time. I have written ten letters this morning & must write you now. We are so thankful that you are keeping well. We shall enclose the money you ask for.

I want you to make the best painting you can for home & we will have it framed for another advertisement for you. But don't let it be a *winter* scene. I don't like winter scenes. Let it be spring, summer, or autumn, or some natural, home like, or rough romantic view. I like winter very well on land in season, but I do not like it on canvas. We hope to live where it will be always summer or spring and let us have an image of it on the walls of the parlour.

We are having a good work of grace going in Grand Bank. 5 souls seeking on Saturday night & three last night in the Church. We hope to have a good week. Nellie told me yesterday she had got saved.* I asked her when. She said one night in the prayer meeting. Dear little body, she is bubbling over with love all day long.

You should hear Florie read the Bible morning & night. You would be surprised to hear her. I was first time I asked her to read.

Mother had Nellie Harris, Jane Patten, & Maria Buffett to tea on Saturday night. Two of them were in to dinner. I expect you will get a lot of pupils for needle work, music & drawing or painting when you come home. I have advised Mother to drop it altogether because so few pay her. It is not worth the trouble. You will make them pay you when you have taught them. When I come on I intend to get a lot of bill heads printed for you to send out payment in advance like the schools here.

Give my love to James and Aunt Sophie. It will soon be time to come on again. My health is splendid, though working hard.

Your loving father
John Pratt

*Nellie then was not quite six years old.

Nellie has come in in great glee saying she has to be put into second class A.

On May 6th he wrote:

My darling Lott,

I must drop you a few lines tonight. We all have been as busy as possible of late. We have had the painter in the house & out of it for most of a fortnight & it is not done yet. Your bedroom was finished nearly the first. New carpet, [- - - - -], & new border round the paper. It looks first rate for you when you come home. Lizzie has washed off the whitening of the roof in the dining room & painted it.

We have not got any potatoes in yet, but today commenced to get out the manure & soon will get in the potatoes.

Don't get any more of your paintings framed in St. John's. We can get them framed here cheaper. I hope you will have some good ones for us. We are sending on payment for College Bill to Mr. Fenwick this time. Learn all you can with music, painting & everything else during the short time you now have. I see the committee in St. John's have appointed me to speak with Dr. Carman at the Coronation Service during the Conference.

I preached at Fortune last Sunday & Mr. Wheatley was at Grand Bank. Calvert went with me & spent the day with the young Kings. I took dinner with Mrs. John E. Lake. Mr. Lake was away. They enquired after you and James.

Give my love to Aunt Sophie. Remember me to Aunt Annie & Uncle Edwin when you see them. Ask Aunt Annie if she intends to go out to China as a missionary, & if the China men in St. John's are going to teach her their language. They say it is a very hard one to learn. I hope it was very good tea John Chinaman gave her. Tell her to keep a little of it to give me a cup when I come on to Conference. Has Miss Coyle gone home yet? I have heard nothing of her for a long time.
Your loving father
John Pratt

And then on May 24th:

My darling Lottie,

Mother will write you soon. I have written Arthur and Eddie & must drop you a line too. I feel like writing you all when

I start. I shall leave for District meeting by next boat & will
spend a week or so at Burin & then get on to St. John's, I
suppose about the 20th of June. I have told Eddie & Arthur that
as College will close some time before Conference closes, I
don't see how they can remain in St. John's as they will all have to
clear out of the Home. So I expect they will have to come home.

You, of course, will not come home until my return. I shall
have to trouble Aunt Sophie again for a bed, but tell her she
must not give up hers but put me in Grandpa's bed or somewhere
else. But she must not give up hers. Tell her I will try & not
get sick this time & so avoid giving her the trouble I gave her
before.

I expect Mother will try & get on to St. John's some time after
Conference when you can be at home & keep house.

Poor Mrs. Eli Harris died today. She made a good end & is
gone to heaven. How important is life as a period to prepare
for heaven.

We are all well. Calvert has gone to Fortune on a message,
also to see the football match between Fortune & Grand Bank
young men. It is good that the two places can be brought
together even in fight. It is better than cold distance as they have
been in so many years.

Nellie & Florie are splendid.
Your loving father
John Pratt

In these letters the vision of a stern Victorian father certainly
fades into a very human, loving one. Nevertheless he was a
staunch guardian of the faith and strict in the ways of salvation.
Intent was John Pratt upon it. So zealous was he that he was
known, on meeting a parishioner in the street who was smoking
a cigar, to pluck the offence from between the man's startled lips
and crush it on the road beneath his feet. Remembered also by
friends and family were his fiery sermons and wild revival
meetings, singing, tears, and testimonies. And the great fire that
swept St. John's in 1892. The Rev. John Pratt had just received a
new charge at Cochrane St. Church, and the first sermon he
preached there was on the Sunday after the fire. The church had
been ransacked, so that added to the loss of furnishings and
records by fire was loss by looting. Boanerges took possession of

the pulpit that Sunday, and the looters were so filled with fear or shame or both that quietly in the night, one by one, back came the stolen goods to the church, including a piano one music-loving thief had lugged away. But there were other tales as well, transmitted down the years by the people of Newfoundland themselves, by his parishioners and by those who had known him. Tales of human warmth and kindness to neighbours and his flock, of sensitive sympathy in the face of suffering, especially to those who had sacrificed their menfolk and their children to the Newfoundland seasons and to the cruel sea.

The vision and mysticism of those early Methodists in Swaledale were no more evident than in the dying of John Pratt. Again and again my father referred to it in wonder. The cause of his death was undiagnosed, but he died in great pain. As the claws of his disease sharpened upon him he would exclaim and cry out in an ecstasy to which he could give no words. As the claws momentarily released their grip, allowing him to spread into the soft nimbus around him, he would try to describe the visions. With an immense effort he would strive to form words around the blinding light, the incandescent colours, the shapes, flowing, curving, and rising triumphantly in great shafts of pulsing glory. If only he could persuade Fanny and their children that the pain was just a catalyst, and that beyond the contortions, the humiliating and pathetic illusion that was so hard for them to bear, lay the holy radiance. He could only tell them it was so; he could not show them.

He loved his family, and if he must have wished painfully for his dear ones in England, so remote and distant to his wife and family, never mind. These in Newfoundland were his own. Hard as their life may have been – and it was – he had saved them from the desperation of nineteenth-century England, the lead mines he had known in Yorkshire and the coal mines and cotton mills over the Pennines in England's industrial heartland. He had saved his daughters from the twenty-four-hour slavery of service in the homes of those smug ones who could afford to pay a few pounds a year. As the colours swam around him in their glory, carrying him with them, he would think of the Kingdom of God, fettered on the dark moors back home, which he had done his best to release through his own life and that of his children. His children! Still in their first youth, his sons, he hoped, would be channels of that freedom. Many-faceted were they. Among them were business heads – shrewd and careful – scholars, and visionaries – artists through whom the glories of the spirit would be unleashed, through whom the song he had heard so long ago on the Yorkshire moors, muffled, would be delivered in the harsh, clean beautiful air of Newfoundland. He must have longed for a few more years.

A great whirlpool of intolerable, exhilarating pain, and again would come the colours and the angels. And sounds human ear had never heard. This must truly be the music of the spheres, bearing him up on its silver wings, as angels, or was it the angels come in the form of unclouded sound?

He knew he was nearing the end. He looked pleadingly over to where his son Jim was sitting. James Charles Spurgeon, named for his great friend, the evangelist, whose ringing sermons at Metropolitan Church in London had been one of the strongest influences on his own ministry. They had called him Spurgie, and his daughter now possesses the family Bible given to him at twelve years old with the inscription "Presented to Spurgie Pratt by his Pa." Spurgie he remained until he went to school when one of the boys tipped him off to give his name as Jim.*

John's frail transparent hand moved aimlessly over the sheet. He would like to preach again. He had so much still to say, about the heavenly kingdom. And he loved his flock. And there was so much yet to do for them. He *would* preach to them, once more.

He called Jim over to him, and asked him to get pen and paper, and when the young man had done this, he began to dictate, pausing, trailing, breathing with great difficulty. Three days later John Pratt was dead.

From the pulpit of his church in Grand Bank, on Sunday, John Pratt's last sermon was delivered:

To My Congregation: –
My dear Christian people: –
This is my last word to you in the land of the living. I had hoped to have preached the Gospel again since the last Watchnight Service, when my subject was "Man is grass, and the glory of man as the flower of the grass, the grass withereth, and

*He seems to have become "James" to his father, judging from the letters, whose diminutives for his boys appear to have been confined to "Eddie."

the flower thereof fadeth, but the Word of the Lord endureth forever." However, God has designed it otherwise and I am going to Heaven, having spent the greater part of four years amongst a people I so much love and have loved. I die a sinner saved by grace, and I hoped to have seen many more souls saved than I have seen.

I have requested the presence of the Chairman & Secretary of the District, to conduct a memorial service here, along with Brothers Wheatley & Harrison, who have been such a help to me during my illness. After the service in the Church, my body will be brought back to the Parsonage, pending the arrival of the Steamer, when it will be conveyed to St. John's and interred in the General Protestant Cemetery family plot.

My sufferings during the past two months have been very great, but the rapture and joy have been quite as great.

I want you to draw freely from the glorious fountain of God's written Word, as I have done, and to the extent that I have never done before. I hope that there will be a great ingathering of souls in Grand Bank shortly, and I want to meet in Heaven hundreds of souls for whom I have seemed to labour in vain.

I wish to express my sincere thanks for the many instances of kindness shown by the people of Grand Bank.

Good-bye until you meet me in Heaven, a subject of the saving grace of God, who died in full and certain hope of a resurrection to eternal life.

It was the coldest March on record, and the only time in living memory that the ice did not break up in Placentia Bay. The age-old superstition against carrying a corpse on a ship had to be disregarded, for John Pratt had willed that his body be buried in St. John's and there was no way of carrying it over the blowing snow-drifts of the island. Three miles from shore the ship chugged to a stop. The signals were sent out: *The "Home" stopped by ice off the Harbour. The body of the Rev. John Pratt is aboard.*

For twelve anxious days the item appeared in the St. John's *Daily* to be read by relatives and friends of the passengers on board. And twelve times came the signal: . . . *the body of the Rev. John Pratt is on board.*

On the boat the passengers were no less agitated. Food was

running short. Fear was mounting. Here was a Jonah the people loved. One man in fright heaved himself overboard and began the three-mile trek over the ice – shaggy ice in slippery mounds and treacherous ridges. The following day a dark gulf opened and the "Home" was safely piloted into the harbour.

These facts exist, and we know about them. Newfoundland is contemporary. But the early years in England are mantled in a thick mist that has all but obliterated the Pratt memory.

One might well wonder why this is so. All families have letters, photographs, possessions, remnants of productive lives to provide clues to those lives. But not this family. In this family there were none, for they had all been destroyed by fire: books, sermons, photographs, letters, mementos, all burned, by a daughter whose inherited zeal had its outlet in housekeeping. As well as these, among John Pratt's treasures were an autographed photograph of Charlotte Brontë and a large part of the sermons of Charles Spurgeon. These possessions also went the way of the flames. That he had been given the sermons by Mrs. Spurgeon has been attested to in a letter from that lady to John Pratt at the time of her husband's death, a letter that mercifully escaped the holocaust. The picture of Charlotte Brontë remains, probably forever, a mystery.*

Scrapings and gleanings from family oral traditions had yielded the following sparse facts.

John Pratt was born at Barnard Castle in 1839 and had gone to Gunnerside at the age of three. He had been at the younger end of a large family (thirteen, I had been told) and had gone as a little boy into the mines with his father. He arrived in Newfoundland in 1873 as a Methodist missioner at the age of thirty-four. It was known, too, that he had made two trips home. In 1893/4, after he had been appointed to Cochrane Street Church in St. John's – the only time his salary ever reached a thousand dollars – he made the first trip. Then in 1902, two years before he died, he returned on the famous visit for which it was remembered that the family had come from various parts of England, even as far as Cornwall, on bicycle, on foot, to the great reunion at, one supposed, Gunnerside. But who these people were no one remembered.

*For a possible explanation, see p. 128.

In 1924 his son and my father, Edwin John Pratt, on his only trip to England, went to Barnard Castle to see what he could find of the family traces: On June 10, from the King's Head Hotel, he wrote home to my mother:

". . . It is now half past eight and I am a bit sleepy and tired after a very long walk. The last two or three days since coming here have been somewhat full of incidents. As soon as I arrived I looked up a man whose name was Pratt, the only person in this little town of 4000 who possessed that name. He was no relative at all but he gave me the name of a man here – Sunter, who he claimed knew all the old inhabitants. As soon as I told Sunter who I was, he almost fell upon my neck, crying out, 'Are you actually Johnny Pratt's son?' He took me into his house and told me that my father and all the Pratt kin had removed to a little village called Gunnerside about seventeen miles from Barnard Castle, and he doubted whether any of them might be found there as the old folks were dead and the young ones had moved out. However, yesterday morning I started off at 9 a.m. to walk over the beautiful hills and dales to Gunnerside. It took me until 5 p.m. to reach the place, all tuckered out, but all the inhabitants made a great fuss over me when I disclosed my identity. They took me to the house where he was brought up,* a house made of stone (in fact all of the houses here are made of stone) and over one hundred and fifty years old. I met Miss Coates, a lady of more than 80 years who knew not only my dad but his dad, James Pratt. She was a sister of Calvert Coates, Father's friend and namesake of Cal. I went inside of the Church where dad used to hold forth, visited the cemetery where the Pratts for generations were buried, chatted to several indigenous nonagenarians, and did all kinds of queer stunts, getting back to Barnard Castle about an hour or so ago. I will not walk that distance any more. Five miles a day is enough for me, after this. . . .

". . . I want to get to the Yorkshire Coast sometime as well. This Yorkshire country, especially these dales are so beautiful that they cannot be described. I never beheld any village more charming in its situation than Gunnerside. On the way over

*Now demolished.

24

today I plucked one leaf of holly, one forget-me-not, and one blue-bell and am enclosing them in this letter."

So this is how we knew of Gunnerside. The date 1842 was not mentioned and is still to be resolved.

On my first pilgrimage in 1964 I learned a great deal. I learned that my father's brother, who had lived his adult life in England, had made some attempts at discovery in 1947. Some invaluable material turned up and was mercifully saved, jealously hoarded, and carefully filed. In 1964 I assimilated the bare bones of what the correspondence revealed, but it was not until 1968 that I had the opportunity to sufficiently examine it. Inquiries had been made at the parish church of Barnard Castle, which had yielded knowledge of the baptisms of Anthony, Sarah Ann, and John in 1835, 1837, and 1839 respectively, to James and Sarah Pratt (labourer). Here were three of the thirteen children I had heard about and it would serve as a beginning. After that my uncle had applied himself to the pen. The correspondence with Christopher Pratt of Bradford was especially fruitful, for this family had established a flourishing furniture business, and Christopher himself had written a history of the firm for its centenary in 1940. In his letter of 1 October 1947 he wrote:

Dear Arthur:
Your letter dated 13th Sept. has been in my thoughts since it arrived. – I have been doing my best to determine whereabouts in the "PICTURE" you appear. My Father no doubt could have placed you fairly readily but he has been gone for some 20 years. I have turned up a family tree compiled by my Elder brother many years ago – He died some 5 years ago – I enclose a very rough copy of part of this tree. – We all seem to spring from James Pratt – who was my gt. gt. grandfather & possibly yours as well.

The letter continued to explain that Christopher had also had a brother James who married Hannah Coates, went to the United States and helped found the town of Dubuque where he established Methodism and a sixty-thousand-pound business. There had been a sister Ruth who married her cousin William Pratt;*

*This seems to be inconsistent with the records which state that Ruth married her cousin George, and William married another Ruth Pratt.

25

the James/Thomas group who had become involved in New-foundland and New Zealand; and Benjamin Pratt who had been a missionary in Hyderabad and had died a few years before in British Columbia.

"My father used to speak of John Pratt who was a Methodist minister in Newfoundland – I am enclosing a photo which I think my Father said was of Rev. John Pratt. – You of course can verify this! . . . . When at Gunnerside did you see Ann Terry who lives in the Square. – You will see from the tree that her grandfather was Thomas Pratt bro: of Christopher Pratt.

I am sorry I cannot be more helpful. – Quite recently 2 deaths have occurred – William Pratt of Low Row & John Pratt of Reeth. – The last 2 of a family of 8 Arthur & all local preachers. – William was a schoolmaster – had spent much of his life at Sabden in Lancashire. – He retired to his native dale in a house in Low Row. – He was the "historian" of the dale & would no doubt have been able to tell you of your forebears."

One of the characteristics of a hunt like this is that it always seems to be just a little too late to find the buried treasure. Each of the scattered gems, however dust-covered and rusty, must be stored and saved against the day when it can be properly polished and placed into the mosaic.

On 11 January 1948 Christopher wrote again to Arthur:

Dear Arthur:
Thank you for yours of the 4th inst. & for your kind wishes. The book re E. J. Pratt arrived a few days later – I am extremely obliged for this. I have been particularly interested in Chapter 1 – "Life in Newfoundland." It appears that the Pratt family has its literary giants as well as its businessmen. It was one of the gang who introduced Pratt's Petrol, & I have already mentioned James Pratt a brother of my grandfather Christopher who founded Dubuque, a considerable town in America. – I will write to E.J.P. as you suggest & thank him for his book.

With regard to the firm of Christopher Pratt & Sons, Ltd of which I am Chairman of Directors & Secy: In 1940 which was the firm's centenary year I wrote up a History & gathered together photographs with the idea of printing a centenary booklet, but the war commenced & prevented this. I have however, handed the manuscript to some duplicators & have asked them to run off a number of copies. As soon as these are ready I will send you a copy. . . . My father would have been most interested in all this.* He attended some years ago a Methodist Ecumenical Conference in Toronto & wouldn't he have been pleased to meet your brother there.

On that visit in 1964 I met Basil, another brother of Christopher's, who later supplied me with a copy of the Pratt family circles that had been printed by his brother Redvers. In the corner was a legend abbreviated from the selfsame tree that Christopher had sent to Arthur upon which I found my grandfather who had gone to Newfoundland and a brother of his who had gone to New Zealand. For the New Zealand brother two daughters were named. The rest of the chart was vague.

The next family to be sought out by Arthur Pratt was that of his father's great friend, James Calvert Coates, for whom one of his sons was named. After a considerable amount of writing to London, Arthur came into contact with James Calvert's son, Lewis Coates of Kent, and David Coates of Gunnerside. Arrangements were made to introduce Calvert Coates Pratt, Jr., on his honeymoon in England, to Mr. Lewis, and Calvert and Mary recall a very pleasant evening spent with Mr. Coates at his club. Arthur's first letter to David Coates explained his reason for writing, "that we are taking a fortnight's family holiday at Bushy Park Farm, Marske . . . and look forward to visiting Gunnerside where my Father spent his early life." The answer from David Coates is, unfortunately, lost but we know he did reply with an "interesting and informative letter."

Owing to ill health, Arthur was unable to have the holiday in Gunnerside, but his wife Maud and daughter Eleanor went. On this remarkable and improbable visit they came across the Burnley Methodist Choir, in which they found relatives descended from John Pratt's sister Sarah Ann. From these relatives they

*One's father, it always seems, would have been interested and one continues to regret that it is too late. How often have I wondered what the early members of the family now at rest in the Swaledale earth would think if they knew of our attempts to resurrect them. It is the rare person still living who is willing to divulge his knowledge and it is not until he goes that the survivors mourn the loss.

learned of still others living in Burnley, grandchildren of another brother William, whose daughter Dorothy had married and become Mrs. Driver.

By putting the scraps of the above information together I had at the end of that first visit the following chart:

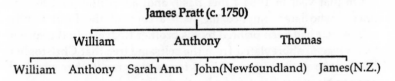

CHART A

James Pratt (c. 1750)

| William | Anthony | Thomas |

William   Anthony   Sarah Ann   John(Newfoundland)   James(N.Z.)

Of my grandfather's family I now knew of his grandfather James,* his father whose name on the chart was Thomas but according to the parish records was James, and of four of the thirteen siblings of which I had heard.

While chatting over coffee in his Ripon home, Basil told us of a cousin of his who had gone at the age of fifteen, with one dollar in his pocket, to Canada, and had settled in an obscure sleepy little place in Alberta. "You'd never have heard of it," he said. "It was just a tiny little place, called Okotoks."

Okotoks! Of all the sleepy little places in Alberta, it was Okotoks where my mother's aunt had also settled years ago and where her one remaining daughter still lived.

Armed with this sketchy and somewhat surprising knowledge, I set about, upon our return, to widen it. Mother wrote her cousin in Okotoks, and received a full and enthusiastic answer that included a letter from one of her neighbours who had known the Pratts well. "Harold was our neighbour," she wrote, "at Dad and Mother's farm, just 5 miles south of Okotoks. He owned ½ section, I guess, from maybe 1908, and was such a good kind friend to all of us. . . . Harold Pratt often came to aid Mother – chop wood, find the cows, etc. He and I often enjoyed pleasant rides and talks. Con, the sister, R. N., came from England to Harold's, maybe in '14 or '15. She and I also rode about often. Con nursed at Gwen's birth in Uncle Bell's home – Big Brick house."

*This was his greatgrandfather, I discovered later.

28

The letter continued with much helpful information. Their daughter, Jean, graduated from the University of British Columbia in chemistry and married a university professor. They lived, she thought, in Toronto. Their son, Christopher, was "in the Navy, and stayed with the Sea." She had read that he was now Commander of one of the large ships.

With the help of this piece of information, Basil's family circles, and the university directory, we soon found Jean Pratt, now married to James Milner – another, so we discovered later, old Gunnerside name. As it happened they lived around the corner, and over they came, with photographs and books on the Christopher Pratts, and more particularly on Christopher's son Benjamin, Harold's father, who as the black sheep in a family of furniture-makers had left the business to go as a missionary to India.

Now I remembered a young woman who, some years before, had introduced herself as a relative. We had met and she had told me of her grandfather who had come from Cornwall to southwestern Ontario and whom she had recalled reminiscing about a cousin of his who had gone to Newfoundland. It would be easy, I thought, to get some information on this branch of the family, especially since Laura was a lawyer, married to a lawyer, and in practice. She was the one to delve into it. The more we chatted, however, the more confused we became and this seemed to be another case of it being too late for correct facts.

One day at the office, out of the blue, came a call from a twig on another Pratt tree. She could help me, she was sure, as I might help her. She tried for some time to relate us both to the Duchess of Richmond, until I told her I doubted it, as our people were labourers from the north of England, wherewith she bid me a polite goodbye and I never heard from her again.

There were letters to many Pratts of various family lines. Dr. Charles M. Pratt, of Saint John, N.B., wrote that his forebears had come to England in the seventeenth century and that, although they had been traced back six generations, the first knowledge he had of them was in Boston. The Pratts are strong in New England to this day. Those of us who were brought up on Longfellow may or may not be aware that the Village Blacksmith, whose shady chestnut tree now stands beside a fine restaurant and shades a plaque to him, was a Pratt. In the portrait of Dr.

Joseph Pratt that hangs in the Pratt Institute of Pathology in Boston is a strong resemblance to the Pratt features, despite the many other lines into which all the branches of the family have in the course of events married. Father McGivern, S. J., a noted genealogist, has traced his ancestry back to William Pratt (1562-1629) of Herefordshire, whose son William emigrated to New England and died at Saybrook, Connecticut.

Major A. M. Pratt of Winnipeg, also a scholar in genealogy, has noted the decided dolicephalic shape of the Pratt head, rather reluctantly, as he favours the view that the Pratts were ancient Britons* standing firm against the onslaught of Saxons, Jutes, and Angles that bore down on the fringes of Cornwall and Wales in a vain attempt to subdue the Cornish and Welsh. There is, indeed, evidence that the Pratt name existed in England before the Conquest. Lefwinus Prat, henchman of the outlawed patriot, Hereward the Wake, had a prominent role in the stubborn defence of the Isle of Ely against the forces of William the Conqueror.

The Pratts in southern England, from all accounts, were more favoured by fortune than their cousins in the hard north. Emerging into the light of recorded history, they are less anonymous, less buried in the obscurity of ages gone, than the unlettered lead miners of the northern counties. Devonshire was the home base of the most illustrious family of Pratts. It was here where Sir John Pratt lived, who was chief justice of the King's Bench in the reign of George I. In 1762 his son Charles† (Earl of Camden) was appointed Chief Justice of Common Pleas and was given a knighthood, shortly after which he was proclaimed one of the great "maintainers of English constitutional liberty."

Another line was found among the Mormon Brotherhood of Salt Lake City. Some correspondence with one member of the Pratt clan in Idaho brought nothing definite, and since then many Pratts have been discovered among the Latter Day Saints, including Governor Romney of Michigan who is the grandson of Parley Pratt, one of the numerous descendants of that early

*Brett, Barrett, Parrott, Pratt.
†It is interesting to note that the name Charles never appears among the Pratts of Swaledale, but is very common among those of Devonshire. Cromwell, no doubt, had his pocket of followers among the parishes of the poor in the north.

30

family of Saybrook, Connecticut, mentioned above.

Yet another family was reached, in the person of W. Mac-Gillivray Pratt, Q.C., of Listowel, Ont., whose mother I had met in the west in 1939 and whose sister I had known years ago before the war. Mac wrote, "My preliminary inquiries indicated that family attachments appear to have been negligible, and no one kept track of any of the others." How like them all! And how true to those hard-time families of all countries whose roots, though deep, had to be severed for good at the painful forced crossing of the hated ocean to a land that offered some hope in the New World.

The real scoop came from New Zealand. The papers there refused to publish my letters on the ground that they would be classified as advertising, but with the help of an interested friend, who had a small item printed in the Christchurch *Times* asking about a family of Pratt, and a piece of great good fortune, I began to receive letters, the first from one of the Charleses who had emigrated from Devon in 1908. Finally, quite a long time after the last epistle had come, there arrived in the mail a letter – a remarkable letter in the light of the fact that the New Zealand brother had had no sons and the name had died out and that the two daughters mentioned on the legend had been childless. It read:

Dear Miss Pratt:

My cousin, Mrs. Sarah Colechin, and I have been interested in your inquiry for a family of Pratts.

My grandfather, Thomas Pratt, came to New Zealand from England with his wife and four daughters about 1878.

He had a brother John, who went to St. John's, Newfoundland, as a minister in the Methodist church. He was later President of the Methodist Conference of Newfoundland. He returned to England for a visit, but died in Newfoundland. . . .

Here was the missing brother, whose name turned out to be, not James, but Thomas, born in 1843, and the youngest of the family. The first of the four daughters was his stepchild. The fourth was the only one to have borne him grandchildren, one of whom was the author of the letter. John Pratt's birth certificate from Somerset House revealed his father to have been in fact

James, indicating that the names had been reversed on the legend.*

In the meantime the existence of another brother had been discovered in the United States. Some years ago, a family friend visiting there had, on seeing a Pratt likeness on the streets of San Francisco, exclaimed to her companion, "Doesn't that look like Jack Pratt!" The figure, turning around, answered "I am Jack Pratt!" As is the case when one is not on the hunt, no follow-up was made. Now a letter was discovered clipped from the pages of the *Methodist Monthly Greeting*, St. John's, Newfoundland, from Parson John Pratt upon the death of his brother Metcalf, struck by a railway train in Nevada the day after Christmas 1891. (See p. 128). Descendants of this brother, at an hour so late that changes have had to be made in proof for this book, were finally discovered.

New Zealand proved a fruitful source.† Cut off at such a distance, the family were deeply interested. Thomas's daughters, no longer living by this time, had kept diaries and had paid two visits home in the early 1900s. Immediately, I began a fascinating and continuing correspondence with his granddaughter, Mrs. Ada Ball. As though this were not riches enough, the Mrs. Colechin mentioned in the first letter turned out to be none other than a daughter of Mrs. Driver who had been living in New Zealand all her adult life. With her, too, a warm and informative correspondence began. Having spent her early years in England, she could remember a great deal of her grandfather William and his family and of those who had lived in – and this was the first I had heard of it as a home town of the Pratts – Burnley, Lancashire.

Ancestors silent
while the voice of the curlew
screams over the moor.

To rouse the sleeping then became my purpose. Against their will I would resurrect my ancestors but I would never have believed they could sleep so soundly. Every fact I discovered in-

---

*My father's letter was not discovered until later, but reports from Art Pratt's investigations, as recalled by his wife, had had his name James.
†A visit there in 1969 enriched my knowledge of William and Thomas Pratt and their branches of the family.

creased my guilt at disturbing their much deserved rest, yet I could not let them sleep in peace. An old Swaledale epitaph expresses what must have been the dearest wish of some of them:

Don't weep for me now,
Don't weep for me never;
I'm going to do nothing
For ever and ever.

Immortality for such may be the least desirable of gifts, yet they are immortal and if their earthly lives may have seemed meaningless, significance will be given them by their resurrection. This they owe to their descendants as we owe them remembrance.

My second trip to the Yorkshire dales was made in 1967 and I was able to spend two weeks there, copying with the noble help of my mother and cousin names from tombstones; baptisms, marriages, and burials from parish records; and births and deaths from the county office. One afternoon spent at the Public Record Office in London yielded many more names from the early nineteenth century directly connected with my Pratts. Armed with a file of approximately a thousand names I set out to sort them into families. They fell roughly into two main branches: the Gunnerside Pratts and the Low Row Pratts. To the best of my knowledge I have had access to all the records kept by the Church of England and the Methodist Chapel, whose records commenced in 1796. From this evidence the Pratts would seem to have come to Gunnerside around 1750, the date that appeared on the chart of the Bradford family. From that time on the names Anthony, James, Thomas, and William occurred with monotonous regularity in Gunnerside; John and Michael in Low Row. The earliest mention of Gunnerside among the records is found in the baptism of Anthony, son of James Pratt. This simple entry, puzzling as it was among many Anthonys and Jameses, was important because of the combination of James, Anthony, and Gunnerside, and was filed away. By constant looking at the files, matching, and pestering the sources, it began to be evident that James was not the father of my great grandfather James but his grandfather. A clue to the search was the almost invariable practice of a man to call his firstborn after his own father. Since the second James had called his firstborn Anthony, as the records had revealed, it was reasonable to suppose that his father had been Anthony and not James. This meant that the ancestor we had supposed to have been John Pratt's uncle was in reality his grandfather. A generation had been skipped. The revised chart now read as follows:

CHART B

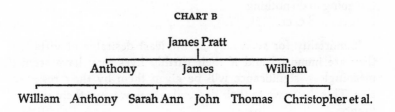

It was now established that great great grandfather Anthony was born to James Pratt in Gunnerside and was baptised 24 June 1769. The marriage records must now be looked to for a clue to Anthony's mother. There was on 4 July 1768 a marriage between a James Pratt and an Elizabeth Raw. Although no place name was given, there is no other record of a marriage for James Pratt near that date, and since the timing is deadly accurate it seems safe to assume that these are the ancestors we were looking for.

This, however, is as far back as the Gunnerside records go. Did James himself originate in the valley, or was he an emigrant from the west or some other part of Yorkshire? In *Yesterday Our Ancestry* Leonard Pratt* suggested that one day a tired family had arrived in Gunnerside, having tramped all the way from Derbyshire. The Enclosures Act of 1760 had caused many people to become mobile and Gunnerside was fairly prosperous at the time. "Hitherto," wrote Leonard Pratt, "the villages of England had been closely knit communities and lived in comparative isolation. But by the turn of the century men were trying to better themselves. Earlier, any man who uprooted himself to seek a livelihood elsewhere would have been frowned upon by his neighbours.† But this no longer obtained. Otherwise James Pratt might never have left his Derbyshire home for the better

*The "Elder brother" referred to in Christopher Pratt's letter, p. 25.
†This still maintains to a certain extent.

prospects which Swaledale offered an ambitious and energetic man. And it is evident that prospects were better there than in Leeds, Bradford and Halifax through which he would pass on his journey north."[2]

Before I read this, I had made an exhaustive survey of the Grinton records prior to 1769 and had concluded that the family had probably been entrenched in those eternal hills for many generations. I cast my lot with the dale. Many records, to be sure, are missing, for not only are burials recorded of infants for whom there is no baptismal record, but a second, third, or even fourth William or Anthony would be born to one family with no record of the deaths of the previous children. In any case one must consider first the evidence at hand.

Who in that ten-mile radius might James's father have been? Since his first-born was Anthony it is reasonable to assume he followed the traditional practice in naming. A search through the files revealed James Pratt, baptised on 17 May 1747, son of Anthony of "Feetholme." Married on the twentieth anniversary of his baptism. Feetham. Settled earlier than Gunnerside, at least by Pratts. In want of other evidence we might assume Feetham to be the birthplace of our first James.

The farther back in time the thinner became the Pratts in this region. Anthony, father of James, had three daughters before a boy was born to whom he gave the name of William. Sure enough, an Anthony was baptised 10 April 1698, son of William of "Healah," two or three miles east of Feetham. One William only was left among the records, early enough to be the father of Anthony, and he born still a few miles east of Healaugh and south over the Swale River in Grinton to Thomas Pratt, and baptised 11 August 1667. And since Thomas's first child was born in 1651 and the earliest record is 1639, that is the farthest back we are able to take the Pratt family in the parish of Grinton.

The publication of Leonard Pratt's book has sent me in search of the Derbyshire Pratts. So far, nothing has revealed itself. Certainly if James Pratt was a newcomer to the Swale valley he came as a bachelor or a newly-wed, for the baptisms of his children are recorded in Grinton parish. Until more conclusive evidence is reached I shall assume that Thomas Pratt of Grinton was our first known ancestor.

Seeds in the Mist

Dawn.
Out of an ancient saga,
out of the mist.

The family of Pratt seems to have had its origins among the
Vikings, although there is also evidence of an Anglo-Saxon
beginning. Of the Anglo-Saxon derivations is the Old English
praett, a "trick," or an adjective meaning "astute" or "cunning."
The tactics of Lefwinus Prat during the defence of Ely, mentioned
above, were described as "Astutus quod ab inimicis saepe captus
caute evaserit."[1] Another, still of Anglo-Saxon provenance, is a
reference to buttocks, from which our present word "pratfall"
is derived. This latter sense would indicate that the earliest members of the family may have been acknowledged as the village
clowns at the dawn of Saxon Britain.

Family tradition has it that the Pratts were, however, not of
Saxon but of Scandinavian origin, and here again one of two
paths may have been taken. The first is possibly related to the
Saxon word praett, for the Bradford branch of the family believe,
and this is supported by many north country people, that the
word is derived from the Norse and means "crafty," not in the
sense of trickery, but of following a "craft" or working with
one's hands. The other source is of Latin origin, applied to the
Scandinavians who settled Normandy early in the tenth century
under one of the Norse kings who bore the name of Ragnvald.
To these folk who settled down on the gentle meadows of western France was given the name of de pratis by the rulers who
practised the Latin tongue. Later, a crest was granted Edward
Roger Murray Pratt of Ryston Hall, Norfolk, with the motto
Rident florentia prata ("the flowery meadows smile").[2] It would
take a lifetime of study into the complicated migrations of the
Scandinavian peoples in the ninth and tenth centuries to make an
even educated guess at the route by which the Pratts found their
way to the lead mines of Swaledale. In the ninth century the
Vikings held nearly all of northern Europe from Ireland to

36

Russia. Their gracefully curving ships ploughed the seas with the pride of pirates, and their legacy has been one of terror for the raids they are reported to have carried on.

"From the fury of the Northmen, O Lord, deliver us" was the desperate prayer common on the lips of all Europe, and indeed no one can refute the evidence of history. Yet not all the Norsemen of that era were Vikings. "To go viking" was the phrase used of a man whose lust for adventure prompted him to leave his hearth and take off with the pirate explorers in search of high romance, and who might return, sickened or wearied by the rapine and murder that were all part of the game. Be that as it may, small colonies of peaceful and peaceable settlers established themselves in the lonely outreaches of Britain. There is no evidence of anything other than friendliness among the Scandinavians who were looking for new lands to inhabit, and this is borne out by the fact that the Norse colonies from the west were confined to the unsettled regions of the inhospitable moors of west Yorkshire. Preferring the wild freedom of the hill country to the more fertile plains where the Angles and Danes had taken up farming, they gravitated to the northern dales where they patterned their living after the ancient and familiar manner they had known among the fells of Norway and later Ireland.[3] It is possible that it was at this period that Gunnar the chieftain brought his little band to the valley of the Swale and settled them into the small grey village of Gunnerside. The stone walls and buildings of the dales bear resemblance to those in Norway. As in other parts of England, the walls are dry walls, that is, no mortar has been used to secure the stones in place. The walls of the dales, however, are further distinguished by having one, two, or sometimes three layers of flat stones spaced at variable distances for further security against tumbling.

The earliest attacks from Scandinavia on Britain are unrecorded, and little care has been taken to distinguish between the Danes and Norwegians in all cases. The first activity of which we know was the attack in 795 by Danes on Ireland during her Golden Age when she was rich in learning and intellectual vigour as well as prosperous in material wealth.[4] The Danes were quickly followed by the Norsemen who continued to plunder and settle the land, gradually supplanting the Danes. By 834 the Norse chieftain Thurgeis proclaimed himself king of Ulster[5] and in

37

853 Olaf the White chased out the Danes and set himself up as ruler of Dublin. The Danes, outdone, admitted their defeat gracefully by withdrawing to Britain[6] under Ivar the Boneless who had made a covenant with Olaf by which peace was established. On the bleak hills surrounding York, the Boneless set about establishing his kingdom, subduing the native tribes and organizing the Danelaw, the land that had been given the Danes in the north country by Alfred the Great.

The strength of Irish culture proved too rich for the blood of the Norsemen, and in the late ninth century the Scandinavians who had resisted assimilation into it began to emigrate to the shores of Scotland and western England, and in the early tenth century a large invasion of Norsemen from Ireland arrived in the mountains of the Lake District and moved eastward into Yorkshire.[7]

In the meantime, it is supposed, the meadow people of Normandy were settling peacefully into their new environment and by the middle of the tenth century comprised no threat to their Gallic neighbours.[8] It is not unreasonable to believe, however, that some of these people may have been recruited for further Viking raids, for some parties did set out from western Europe, to raid England, during the first part of the century. And later, after the Conquest in the eleventh century, they may have been brought over as settlers by the homesick Normans, or as servants to the settlers. These Pratts, if Pratts were among them, are more likely to have been the ancestors of the families originating in the south. Nevertheless, the names prevalent in the dales include some of Norman origin. Such are Cherry (from *chéri*) and Raw (from *roux*). Pratt, itself, in Yorkshire lore, is said to be from Du Prat or Du Pré. If this is so it is quite possible that some of the Norman folk made their way northward to work the lead mines of Swaledale in the future shire of York.

Throughout the tenth century wars and skirmishes took place in and around York and Northumbria. It was at the time of the moulding of Saxon Britain, and Edward, son of Alfred the Great, having unified southern England, moved north against the stubborn Northumbrians who were heavily reinforced by their Scandinavian allies. After a fierce struggle, in 954 the last of the kings of York, Erik Blood-Axe, fell to the Saxons and was deposed.[9] Unease continued throughout the next hundred years, and in

1066 Britain came under Norman control. The Conquest at first made little difference to the tribes of the north. In 1069 some Scottish exiles together with some Northumbrians and newly arrived Danes marched on York, took the garrison, and put its three thousand men to the sword. By this brash act they succeeded in arousing the wrath of the Conqueror of Britain as it had never been aroused before, and he vowed to break the people across the entire region. Christmas of 1069 saw William, geared to cruelty such as he had never practised before nor was ever to practise again, victorious in York. The season of peace that year heralded the bloodiest and cruellest action ever perpetrated by him as William spread desolation from York to Durham so extravagantly that at the time of the Domesday Survey in 1086 the term *wasta* appears more often on it than could be counted. For nine years there was no sign of man or of his habitation in the country round about York and Durham.[10]

The lands least affected by this devastation were the remote Yorkshire dales, lying west of Richmond along the River Swale. The Domesday Survey, which covered most of England, stopped at Grinton, short of the wild and inhospitable area beyond. It is possible that the lead mines of Swaledale did not even close down throughout the period although one wonders what the market could have been at that time.

The Swaledale mines had been discovered early in the game. Hewker Mill, on the slopes of Kisdon along the first stretches of the Corpse Way, and Hurst, high on the eastern slopes of Arkengarthdale, claim the remains of the earliest mines. A verse, more informative than poetic, is still recited among the dalespeople:

When Julius Caesar was a king
Bowes Castle and Hurst and Arkendale
Mines was a famous thing.[11]

A pig of lead was found at Hurst with the inscription stamped on it: "Adrian 117–138." Another, found slightly to the south, bears the stamp of the Emperor Claudius, with the date 49 A.D. Pliny writes of the large amount of lead brought from Britannium to Rome for water pipes.[12] There is evidence of more than one revolt on the part of the early dalespeople, or Brigantes, against the Romans, and in A.D. 155 coins were struck in celebration of a Roman victory over them. Roman control was, however, greatly weakened, and by the middle of the second century the penal camps passed out of existence and the mines began to be operated by natives of the district and by freed slaves.[13] By the time that area was settled by the Saxons in the sixth and seventh centuries the mines upon whose ancient scars the heather was again blooming were referred to by the dalesmen as "t'owd man." "T'owd man" and newer veins of ore were worked by a method known as "hushing," whereby water was collected and dammed at the top of a hill and then let flow at full force, thus washing away the earth from the lead. Deep grooves from the hushing neatly seam the steep moors to this day and are sometimes brightened by a narrow ribbon of trickling water. Lead in the early days was melted in "bayles," or circles of stone built about two feet high on low hills facing the prevailing winds. Within the circle, fires of peat and brushwood were started, upon which lead ore was melted to be carried away in a trough.

A variety of people composed the personnel of the mining community. At Hurst was a penal colony to which Romans sent their prisoners who undoubtedly were set to work among the mines. Then came the Saxons, then the Norsemen, and later in the eleventh and twelfth centuries the Normans. Between Grinton and Harkerside are the remains of a peculiar construction known as the "Maiden," where dalespeople were executed for the most trifling of crimes. One wonders how many Pratts may have been among the victims of this forbidding shape upon the dark slopes of Harkerside. The rich mines of the dale had a black reputation for cruelty, as throughout the centuries they yielded Britain invaluable returns at the price of human suffering.

It was into this milieu that the Pratt family moved in the far distant past, either as the craftsmen of the north, the meadow people of the south, or as Saxon clowns.

We first hear of them in the century of Geoffrey Chaucer. Indeed, Chaucer may have been known to them when he used to visit John of Gaunt at his summer house of Birk Park near the old priory at Healaugh. The Gaunts were early owners of land in Swaledale, as Henry I in the early twelfth century had "confirmed the gift of the church of Swaledale by Walter de Gaunt."[14]

The "Forest of Helagh" was a poacher's paradise. On Wednesday, 13 October 1316, in the ninth year of the reign of Edward II, William Hay "came poaching in the forest of Helagh Carr with bows & arrows & he is a confirmed poacher in the forest, and Adam Crabbe was in his company both before and after." For this misdemeanour, surrounded with an aura of green glades and Robin Hood, William was fined, Adam outlawed.[15]

Nor was the poaching restricted to the poor. Thirty-five years earlier, in 1279,

"Gilbert de Gaunt, being summoned to answer to the King on a plea of *quo warranto* as to his claim to a *free chase in Swaledale*, free warren at Helagh and wreck of the sea at Hundmanby, says, that he and all his ancestors have held a free chase there from time immemorial; that as to the warren at Helagh, he claims it because it is within Swaledale where his free chase is, and he and he [*sic*] ancestors have always had it. He does not claim any wreck of the sea, except a whale, if that can be called a wreck. He claims a whale, with the exception of the head and tail belonging to the King, because he and his ancestors have always had it. His claim is allowed and he is quit."[16]

Which stands to illustrate that the rich shall inherit the earth.

In the reign of Edward III John Pratt makes his appearance, not in Swaledale, but in the forest of Pickering, where he, along with William Smart, was fined two shillings for "not producing Thomas de Pickering, tenant of part of the lands which formerly belonged to Alan Malcake, one of the verderers, of the forest."[17] For not appearing on the first day of the Eyre, Agnes Prat was pardoned because she was poor, but John Pratt was fined.[18]

In Healaugh Park stood the Augustinian Priory of St. John the Evangelist. The priory claimed lands as far as the valley of the Wharfe with its pleasant meadows and groves and waters which it shared unwillingly with poachers, both high and low. In the year 1331 a quitclaim was signed at Tadcaster by William Barker and Agnes his wife, who was the heir of Nicholas de Hederslaw, giving up "the claim of ourselves and our heirs, forever, to the meadow of Haggandeby in the wood and plain, to the house of St. John the Evangelist of the park of Helagh, and to the canons of the same place, inasmuch as neither we nor our ancestors ever had, or could ever have any right to it." The inquisition, held by John de Shirburn, Steward of Henry Percy, was under-

41

taken at Tadcaster by twelve jurors, including Robert Pratt, who swore "by their sacred oath that the prior of Helagh Park and his ancestors had a fishery in Wharfe as the lands and meadows of Haggandeby butt on the aforesaid fishery at the aforesaid place from time out of mind until John de Saltmarsh hindered them in the first year of the reign of King Edward III."[19]

If one Robert Pratt was acting as juror in a legal case at Tadcaster, another was getting into mischief at Scawby. He turns up in a plea to the master attorney of the Duchy of Lancaster by one aggrieved Henry Parker who wished to remind "your good Maistership" that he had

"graunted unto your seid suppliaunt a passage or gateley called Furewode withyn the seid parisshe of Scawby for xl^s by yere, the whiche he hath occupyed peasible by the space of oon hool yere accordyng to your graunte and hath paide truly his duete for the same, And so it is [he continues] that oon Robert Pratte hath entred into the seid ferme and the same gadreth by the commaundement of Roger Chomley [sic] as he sayeth, your same Oratour standyng contynually charged to your maistership for the payment of the Rent therof, hit may therfore please your good maistership to direct a commaundement downe to the seid Robt Pratte dischargyng and commaundyng hym that he ne noon other that dooth occupye under hym from hensforth do not medle in the seid passage nor the gadryng therof, but that your seid oratour may have it accordyng to your seid graunte, And that the seid Robert and suche as occupye under hym may content and pay to your seid oratour all suche money as they have gadred for the seid passage, And that also your seid Oratour may have either wryting therof that he may surely occupye it, or els that he may be lawfully discharged of the same, and your seid Oratour shall pray to God for the preservacion of your good maistership.

"Also please it your good maistership to understande that it hath been accustomed of long tyme that the Freholders there shulde kepe a Court every three weke, so it is now, because that the same freholders will not suffer Roger Cholmley to put in newe officers and put out olde officers at his pleasure, the same Roger wolde not suffer them to kepe their Court on Saterday was sevenyght, but there came Richard Dotton, Robt

Pratte and William Court in the name of the said Roger Chomley as they saide, And drave awey the Stuard, the Cryer of the Court and all other that were there, besechyng you therefore to provyde suche remedy that they may kepe their Court peasible as they have doon in tyme past."[20]

Although there were Pratts in the North Riding of Yorkshire in the thirteenth century, and although there is one associated with Healaugh Priory in the Hederslaw case, no evidence that I have been able to find admitted them in the Middle Ages to Swaledale itself. This, of course, proves nothing, as it is not easy to learn much about individual inhabitants at that time, and it is likely that the Pratts were mining lead from the hills of Swaledale time out of mind of man.

With the coming of the Renaissance in England, lead mining reached a new zenith. Lead from beneath the darkly heathered moors had supplied England during her medieval wars, and in the twelfth and thirteenth centuries had been used to the glory of God in the building of great abbeys and cathedrals. Now in the "spacious days of great Elizabeth" England's empire was reaching new heights and the time was not far off when under Oliver Cromwell her strong ships, manned by strong men, would be making her mistress of the seas. As with China, Russia, and all the mighty empires of the past, so it was with England: greatness battened on human misery.

From time to time surveys were taken of the mines. Those of Harkerside, Whitaside, Grinton, and Fremington were assessed in July 1650 – "late of Charles Stewart King of England" – by the Parliamentary Survey undertaken by the Parley Commissioners. At that time all "Mines & veins of Lead lying & being within the fields of Harkerside" were estimated to be worth *communibus annis* twenty pounds; Whitaside twenty-two pounds; Grinton six pounds; and Fremington twelve pounds; making a total of sixty pounds for the area.[21] From 1599 by Letters Patent to Richard Wiseman these ancient mines were leased to certain people for periods of twenty to thirty years. Between 1628 and 1803 they passed consecutively into the hands of Humphrey Wharton, George Tushingham, Reginald Marriot, Edmund Moore, the mayor of Richmond Caleb Readshaw, and John Moore Knighton of Devon. These had "full power to have dig and take the Lead in any part of the said several grounds and fields so as that it be first consented to or agreed upon by the tenants and farmers of the ground and soil in the said Manor or Manors of Grinton, Whitaside, Harkerside, and Fremington, granting and allowing to them and their assigns so much and such sums of money as shall compensate and satisfy them for the injury and damage which they shall or may receive by reason of the digging or mining within their grounds and pastures. Together with all buildings grounds commons waters water courses and all other rights jurisdictions profits commodities and emoluments whatsoever to the said premises belonging or appertaining or with the same premises or any of them heretofore usually demised leased used occupied or enjoyed."[22]

It is rather nice to know that some compensation was provided, whether or not the amount that might "compensate" or "satisfy" had been always agreed upon by all parties.

Mining remained dangerous, although with each spurt of industry improvements were made in the methods of extracting ore from the earth. New ways of pumping water made it possible to sink the shafts deeper into darkness, and the lead industry boomed. Men went down to the pit in utter black and slaved away the daylight hours. Women also worked at "kibbling," gleaning the bits of lead left in the streams of water and near the openings of the mines. In the seventeenth century a woman received for this work one shilling a week and two flannel petticoats a year.[23] Children, too, became miners as early as eight years, and were carried down the shafts into the night by their fathers, who felt their way as best they could with their children in their arms lest they lose a foothold and hurtle to the bottom.

It was not until the civil registration of vital statistics in 1837 that the causes of deaths were given. It is rare to find one among the parish records, so we do not know how many died by accidents in the mines. Among the Grinton records published from 1640 to 1806 scarcely more than a dozen such deaths are listed. Of these was "Nathan, son of William Pratt of Kearton, killed in Whitaside lead mines." Nathan was fourteen. It has been recorded, also, that a man whose clogs were still damp from the snow when he pulled the door shut as he descended into the dark, slipped and fell to the bottom; and a boy who begged his father not to carry him just once, stumbled and was killed.[24] In 1778 the mines claimed "James Spensley of Smarber, Ralph Spensley of Blades: These was Two Brothers kild in the Lead Mines at Old Gang." These brothers were related to William Spensley, the first host in Swaledale to John Wesley, and father-in-law of Betty Pratt (see p. 56).

The largest cluster of mines was "Old Gang." These mines begin on the east side of Gunnerside Ghyll, and their great scars follow one another up over Melbecks Moor and into Arkengarth-dale. Under the earth the shafts and levels run for four miles, and it was possible for a miner who knew his geography to enter the mine near Gunnerside and reappear in the neighbouring dale.

Ore was smelted in the valleys. Peat was used and hard coal in the smelting furnaces of the mills whose ruins are dotted along the Arkle and around the hem of Mount Calva. After the smelting the lead was taken by packhorse to Richmond and Barnard Castle. Mining and smelting and scraping together a hard living – such was the life of the dalesmen during the making of the British Empire. The small people contributed to the coffers of the rich, and in so doing became poorer, more anonymous, less important.

In the dales the miners were living a life of their own. The people of the valley plodded along in the lengthening shadow of the Church which, with the mines, determined the course of their lives. Life was lived around the parish, and there was little encouragement for Dissenters as no authority other than the Church could administer to their needs. Marriages and burials meant a journey to Grinton throughout the length of the valley.

Until near the end of the sixteenth century, the dead from the west end of the dale had a long journey ahead of them before they could rest in consecrated ground, in the Grinton churchyard. In a wicker basket slung from the shoulders of the pallbearers, for two days the deceased would swing along over the moors following a path known as the Corpse Way. Slabs of stone served as resting places for the basket while its bearers stopped for a glass of ale to refresh their weary bodies. The journey was broken at Riddings where the coffin was left at the Dead House and the bearers put up at the Miners' Inn, now the Punch Bowl, for an evening of cheer while the dead slept alone up on the hill. In

1580 this journey was cut in half, at its longest, with the erection of Muker church.

In the year 1537-8 mention is made of certain common Swaledale names whose bearers lived in the village of Grinton. Among these are Metcalfes, Closes, Kyrtons, and Spensleys.[25] In 1535 Anthony Metcalfe was paid twenty shillings a year for acting as bailiff.[26] In 1575 a survey was made of the Lordship of Grinton in which *"The said Manor of Grinton with members is occupied by the tenants and inhabitants* within named as *customary hold,* paying their fines as is expressed and doing service and hath been by their ancestors *time out of memory of man."*[27] The survey refers to Grinton as a manor. In the first year of the reign of James I, however, which would have been 1603 or 1604, there was some dipute as to whether Grinton was a manor or merely part of a larger manor. Richard Hutchinson, in collecting rent, was brought to court by one Mr. Simpson who maintained that

"The Manor is granted from the Crown and no fee-farm rent reserved, and so he [Mr. Hutchinson] has no privilege . . . and it is not therefore certain that he can have any title . . . in the said Manor, *'if there were any such Manor,'* . . . and the resiants [*sic*] . . . say they *do not know* that the Queen *ever had any* Manor of *Grinton.* . . . They think that Grinton is *either parcel of the great Manor of Midleham,* one of the King's manors, or of the manor of *Heley.* . . . *Grinton is no manor,* but a village . . . and there are *no free holders."*[28]

How much effect these disputes had on the lead miners is doubtful. Grinton continued to be referred to as a manor, the title of which was held until 1622 by Richard Wiseman. In that year it passed to H. Simpson; in 1626 to Robert Hillary; and in 1670 to Roger Hillar[y], who was living there himself at that time. But whether they lived in a manor or a village it is likely that most of them leased a cottage with a little garth* on the slopes of Harkerside or by the river, probably in some cases several branches of one family under one roof. In the time of Elizabeth, among those who leased cottages were the Closes, Brodericks, Spensleys, and Metcalfs, including one Spensley by the name of Ralph, a common forename of the Spensley family for centuries to come. By 1595 Anthony Alderson puts in an

*Saxon for gate, literally, but used to describe a small enclosed piece of land.

appearance in the legal case of *Charlesworth* v. *Broderick*,[29] and some years later the families of Alderson and Wiseman became entangled as the fee farm rent of Somerlodge was conveyed by Richard Wiseman to Anthony Alderson.[30]

The earliest record of any Pratt in Grinton parish is the baptism of Jas Prate, son of Edm. on 1 March 1639. This is in the custody of the Vicar of Muker, toward the west end of the Swale settlements. No place of birth is given. The first burial was that of Elizabeth, daughter of William Prat de Kearton in 1644, Kearton being of the Low Row community. Marriages do not put in an appearance until 1660, when Thomas Pratt married Alice Lonsdale. Again no place name is given, although numerically the Thomases seem to have been gathered at Grinton at that time.

Kearton and Feetham cradled the earliest of the Swaledale Pratts, although the family of Edmund may have lived elsewhere. There are no other records for Edmund, and he probably belongs to a prehistoric branch of whom we can never know. Anthony Prat de Kearton had a large family beginning with Margret, baptised 6 October 1644. The entries for his next two daughters in 1646 and 1647, both called Elizabeth, give his name as Anthony Part [*sic*], Jr., and for the fourth child William in 1649, Anthony Prat the younger. Because of the way in which the dates fall one assumes they are all the same Anthony. Anthony and Frances* of Feetham had two children, Anthony in 1651 and Mary in 1654. Other early Pratts of the dale are James and Mary Pratt* of Kearton (and Healaugh) whose children Alice, Anthony, Agnes, and Margaret were born between 1677 and 1682. There are also burials recorded for two daughters of James of Kearton: Margaret in 1661 and Agnes in 1681. One is tempted to identify the two Jameses despite the fact that Agnes was born on 11 January and was buried on 7 January of the same year. Slips in accuracy did occur, although one cannot rely on mistakes in determining the truth! James, the father of the two girls who died, may easily have been the son of Edmund born in 1639, thus providing a continuing link with the earliest of the records. There was also John of Feetham, father of Elizabeth in 1660, Phillis in 1662, and Michael in 1667, beginning the tradition of John

*Records at this time do not include the name of the mother. This has been assumed from the marriage records of approximately the same date.

47

and Michael in Low Row; John and Elizabeth* of Kearton, parents of James in 1675; Michael of Kearton, father of Elizabeth in 1689, of another Elizabeth in 1699, and of James in 1706; Thomas of Kearton whose children James, Elizabeth, Mary, and William were born between 1657 and 1663; William and Dorothy* of Kearton whose daughter Elizabeth died in 1644; and William and Jean* of Feetholme, parents of Ann, Ruth, James, and Jane, born between 1682 and 1705.

From Grinton to Gunnerside

To a cottage with a little garth
dreams return
to a green time.

As mentioned above, the Pratt movement seemed to have been from east to west, with Grinton, headquarters of the parish, as seat of the first of our known fathers. There is no record of the birth of Thomas Pratt of Grinton. It is likely his advent passed unrecorded, as Grinton parish did not begin its records until after the probable time of his birth. His burial is recorded on 25 October 1689. The first of his children to be baptised was Thomas on 29 February 1651.† From this we would assume that the latest date for his birth might be around 1631, in which case his death would have occurred at the age of fifty-eight or fifty-nine. It is likely he was a few years older than this and his birth might be reasonably placed somewhere around the 1620s.

Grinton is the first of the hamlets along the road from Richmond. Its approach today is marked by entire fields of closely

*See note on p. 47.
†A nice example of the inaccuracy of the records. Either the day is wrong or the year, for 1651 could not have been leap year.

packed buttercups that lend a sunniness to the dreariest of clouded summer days. Perhaps it is the gentle green fields, from which the village derives its name, that set it apart. Perhaps it is the early Norman parish church with its added sixteenth-century tower and its comparatively prosperous-looking grave-yard that make Grinton somewhat more awe-inspiring than the wildly modest little settlements farther along the Swale. It is doubtful whether we can ever know that Thomas was born in this green place, or chose to settle there at the parish centre, but it is unlikely in the latter case that he came from far.

The records of the baptisms of his children tell us nothing, each stating the simple fact: "Thomas, son of Thomas Pratt of Grinton." His first three children were born during the Commonwealth of Oliver Cromwell, the others were children of the Restoration. It is difficult to know where the political sympathies of the miners lay. The common folk of England, whose lives were dominated and paced by the church, generally mourned, during the Commonwealth, for the days when they might enjoy without fear of the eagle eye relief from work in fun and dancing and the celebration of great festivals such as Christmas and Easter. Sir Solomon Swale of Grinton, who along with Humphrey Wharton administered the Swaledale mines, received his knighthood for his motion in parliament calling for the restoration of Charles II.[1] On the other hand, some evidence exists that the men of seventeenth-century Swaledale yearned for the stern freedom of non-conformity. In the early days of the Restoration there occurred in Wensleydale and Swaledale the Kaber Rigg Plot whose aim it was to return the Commonwealth to England. Secret agents travelled the dales and one such is described in the trials afterwards as "the stockinger of Askrigg," so-called for the stockings, hand-knit by Swaledale folk, that were his wares.[2] There is also a noticeable absence of the name Charles among them that would argue that the Bonnie Prince was not as popular as might be. Reference to the ending of the Commonwealth is meagre among the records. The naming of the four and twenty church officials in 1661 is worded thus:

"These are the names of those who were chosen to be the four & twenty according to the ancient custome for the Parish of Grinton. Anno Dom: 1661: upon Tuesday in Easter weeke being

49

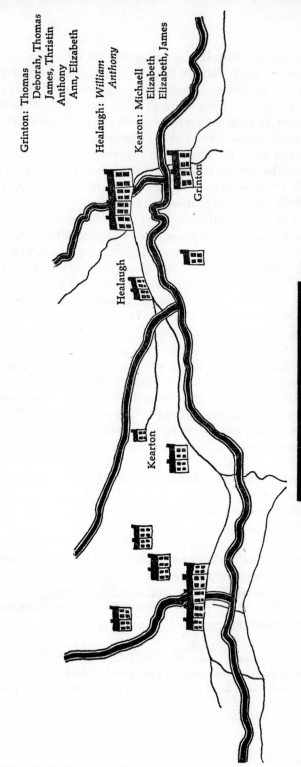

Grinton: Thomas
  Deborah, Thomas
  James, Thristin
  Anthony
  Ann, Elizabeth

Healaugh: *William*
  Anthony

Kearon: Michaell
  Elizabeth
  Elizabeth, James

Grinton

Healaugh

Kearton

Sons of Thomas of Grinton in 1690

the first years of the Restauration of King Charles the Second after the unnaturall Civill Wars (were by the Blessing of God ended) which continued full Twenty yeares"

Had the Non-Conformists in those early years kept records with the foresight of the Church of England – indeed had they the time and volunteers to do so – some interesting stories would no doubt have come to light. Methodism had yet to be born, but there were other associations. Philip Lord Wharton who had a hunting lodge at Smarber, beyond Low Row, had a Chapel built there in 1691, just outside the five-mile limit from the church, and he gave much support to Non-Conformist ministers.[3] First among the Non-Conformist groups of those days was the Society of Friends, commonly called Quakers, which had originated with the preaching of George Fox in 1648 and was formed into an organized church in 1666. There was a considerable Quaker settlement in Reeth and its members became the target of abuse by the Church of England as they were later to become the target of John Wesley. Occasionally, a Quaker joined the Established Church, usually, it would seem, a woman of adult years, which would indicate that the step was taken to please her bridegroom rather than out of conviction, a common reason for "conversion" to this day. Among the "baptizati" of 1677 was "Elizabeth Galloway now yᵉ wife of Daniel Addison. Haveing been formerly brought in yᵉ errours of Quakeing was baptised after she came to woman's estate."

Owing to the dearth of Non-Conformist records, therefore, we can only know of the Pratts who were with the Established Church, or who were recorded therein, and it seems that Thomas duly had all his children baptised within its folds. The firstborn Thomas was followed by John in 1654; Anthony in 1659; Michaell in 1661; Isabell in 1663; Ralph in 1666; William in 1667; George in 1669; Elizabeth in 1672.* All the most commonly used names for the Pratt men, with the exception of James, are here. Ralph runs like a single thread to the present generation, and George occurs now and then, especially among the Gunnerside Pratts. Isabel and Isabella are frequent among the women, and Elizabeth is one of the most favourite. There is a burial date for Ralph, son of Thomas of Grinton, for 3 April 1666, thirteen

*For the exact dates, see genealogical tables, p. 196.

days before the baptism of another Ralph, which would lead us to think he was named for his dead brother. George, buried on 24 April 1670, died four months after his baptism.

It is interesting to see names familiarly associated with the Pratts of nineteenth-century Gunnerside that belonged to their Grinton neighbours in that far-off time: Thomas and Francis Place, Christopher Harker, James Wharton, Thomas and Simon Milner, John Simpson, and Ralph Coates, who died a few months after the birth of Elizabeth, youngest child of Thomas Pratt, and a few days before his own son and namesake was baptised, first privately in his own home and then two days later brought to church by his mother, the "Widow Coates." Neighbours in the area, also, were the Kipling family – of whom Thomas of Kearton was among those chosen as "overseers of ye pore" in 1643. The family of Rudyard Kipling were natives of North Yorkshire and his great grandfather was a local preacher in the 1860s when John Pratt preached in Swaledale.

Of Thomas Pratt's children, four at least lived to found their own families. The firstborn Thomas, also living in Grinton, had four children: Deborah, baptised in 1680; Thomas, 1683; James, 1685; and Thristin, 1687. In 1708 Deborah was born, out of wedlock, to Thomas Pratt of Grinton and Mary Blades. It would appear that this is our Thomas, grandson of the first of the Thomases and the second child of his father. There were two families of Blades in Grinton, those of John and of Francis, who were neighbours of the Pratts, but it seems more likely that Mary may have been the daughter of Henry Blades of Whitaside, not far away. There is a marriage for Mary Blades in 1712, to Ralph Scott, which may well have been that of Deborah's mother at the age of thirty. Thomas later had three more children, presumably within the bonds of holy matrimony. These are Thomas, baptised in 1715; Jeffrey, 1717; and Thomas, 1724. Anthony, who also remained in Grinton, was the father of Ann, baptised in 1692, who died at the age of seventeen, and was buried 9 June 1709, and Elizabeth, baptised in 1697, who died at the age of ten and was buried on 10 May 1707. Deaths in infancy, childhood, and early youth were common, and many were the parents of large families who were left childless. Constant childbirth as an ensurer of immortality fought a grim battle against the Black Angel, while desperate parents could do nothing but watch helplessly as their children vanished in agony.

The third son, Michaell, started the westward move by going to Kearton, the village a mile up the hill from Healaugh and off the main road. His family consisted of Elizabeth, 2 March 1689, whose unrecorded death was followed by another Elizabeth, baptised exactly one year later on 2 March 1690. A gap of sixteen years occurs in the records before a son James was born to Michaell of Kearton and was baptised on 9 June 1706. He may not have been a brother to Elizabeth but the son of another Michael of Kearton for whom there is no record. Or he may have come at the end of a long line of unrecorded children who in due course became parents of children whose baptismal records exist to confuse the searcher. Michaell was buried on 8 October 1717 at the age of fifty-one.

The fourth and last of Thomas's sons to found a family was William who, in Healaugh, the pretty village with the minerals on the nether slopes of Mount Calva and at the foot of the hill upon which his brother Michaell lived, became the father of Anthony, baptised on 10 April 1698. Anthony, our four-times great grandfather, was the only child recorded for William.

At Healaugh, ancient seat of St. John the Evangelist and the family of Gaunt, lived James Alderson whose sons were contemporaneous with Anthony. The Sunter family were also well established there, although they were beginning to die out in the village. Old Richard Sunter died in 1692 and his son Christopher in 1699. Christopher had married Mary Pratt, of another line unrelated as far as is known, in 1681, but Mary died in 1689 when their son Joseph was but seven. Danjell and Sarah Sunter, with their two daughters, were also neighbours at the turn of the century. It was at Healaugh where the Pratts may have first become friends with the Spensley family who were to become so active in Methodism a century later. Two couples lived there: Thomas and Dorothy Spensley, and Anthony Spensley and his wife. Their child William, who was buried the day after his baptism, was born the same year as Anthony and may well have been named for Anthony's father.

There was then, as always, a fund for the poor, to which contributions were made by all who could afford them. These seem small by our standards today and surely they did little to lift the poor out of the station in which it had pleased God to place them. Nor were they intended to do so. But when one considers that Henry Parker paid only forty shillings for his "passage" or "gately" of Furewold for the entire year, a few pence probably went further than we realize today. The fund was administered by "overseers of the poore" from different parts of the parish, which consisted of four men chosen at irregular intervals of from one to a few years. In the mid-seventeenth century the following are among those listed as overseers: in 1670 Henry Blades, father of the wayward Mary; George Butterfeild who was to drown later in the River Swale; Thomas Kipling of Kearton; James Clarkson of Crackpot; James Milner of Muker; and James Alderson of Healaugh. Pledges were made on the part of both villages and individuals. "John Peacocke of Harkeyside hath given to the poore £18 to pay 5 on St. Thomas day and 5 on good friday till it be paid."[4] Sometimes the pledges were not honoured. "Robinson of Woodmansey nere Beverley gave five shillings yearely to be paid at Easter yearely by——————Peacocke should pay it but doth not."[5] "Ralph Hutchinson of Ruccroft gave five shillings yearely, to be paid on good friday but hath not . . . since 1618."[6]

It was easier for honest overseers to see that the money was justly paid to the poor when it was left by will, as it often was, distribution to be made usually on Good Friday, or by a deed of property. "Ralph Garth gave £20 to buy Land. The benefitt there of to goe to the poore."[7] And "William Jefferson gave a little close in Grinton feild nere townefeild and ye rent to goe to the poore for ever,"[8] a confident assertion of the permanency of the poor.

In 1708 the X of Thomas Pratt and signature of John Prat stand as witness to one such transaction recorded in the parish records. The poor of "The Three Towns of Grinton Fremington and Reeth" had come in for a share in the interest on £10 bequeathed to them by Thomas Falconbridge, the "Interest thereof to be paid yearly to the Poore of ye said Three Towns." The money had been paid by the executors to the Ecclesiastical Court of Richmond, who lent it to some of the inhabitants of Grinton parish. Chief among these were Ambrose Garth of Blades and his son Ralph who were "Bound for ye paym^t of ye s^d money which s^d Ambrose Garth during his life time and his son Ralph Garth since his Death have duly p^d ye Interest of ye s^d Ten pound till of Late ye s^d Ralph Garth had a mind to pay in ye principall." The bond was nowhere to be found by this time at the Court of Richmond, so Ralph Garth paid the money to the Grinton church in receipt of which twenty-one witnesses signed their names or crosses.[9] By the time the interest on £10 had been divided among the poor of three towns, one wonders how many wretched pence were doled out to each once a year. One wonders also what happened to the principal after Ralph Garth was through with it.

Anthony Pratt, born at Healaugh at the close of the seventeenth century, took another step west and settled in the hamlet of Feetham on the main road a mile or two from his birthplace. At the dawn of the eighteenth century a whole colony of Pratts had taken up residence at Feetham. William and Jean Pratt had died before the advent of Anthony to this spot, but their son James lived there with his brood of nine. There were also Thomas and his family, Michael and Jane Pratt whose children were to be contemporaries of the children of Anthony.

At Feetham also were the Spensleys, Simpsons, Closes, Whites, Cleminsons, Michael Bell, and Thomas Cherry. And nearby, so near that the names of the hamlets become easily confused with each other, were the Sunters and Milners of Melbecks, the Clarksons of Crackpot, the Raws of Low Row and Smarber, and the Coateses and Harkers of Blades. These were the neighbours whose lives for the next century and a half and all through the rise of Methodism were intertwined in friendship and marriage and whose names to this day are juxtaposed in the surviving generations.*

And so lived Anthony, and for the first time a wife is mentioned, although we do not hear of her until her death on 26 August 1788. Her name was Mary and that is all we know of her, our first known grandmother. She outlived her husband by twenty-six years. Their family consisted of eleven children. First three girls were born: Jane baptised in 1730; Sara, 1732; and Mary, 1734. Mary lived to adulthood but it is unlikely that she married for her burial record in 1758 gives her as the daughter of Anthony Pratt of Feetham. A few years later a son was born and called William after his grandfather. He was baptised in 1738, but must have been dead within three years for another William appeared in 1741. Next came a girl, Ruth, baptised in 1744, who lived to be buried at the age of twenty-two. Then followed our forefather James, baptised 17 May 1747; then came

---

*Pratt Cherry is an example, and Metcalf Bell.

Thomas in 1748; and then Anthony, born in or around 1750, for whom we have no record of baptism; and finally Hannah in 1758.

Four of Anthony's sons became fathers of families. For Thomas we have the first of the marriage records to be found among the family. On 15 April 1765 Thomas Pratt became united with Ann Lawson. If this record is correct Thomas was a very young bridegroom. It is possible his age may have been more than seventeen, however, as the date given is that of his baptism, but he could not have been much older without overlapping with his brother James, who was baptised less than a year earlier. Thomas and Ann settled down in Feetham. To them were born ten children between 1766 and 1788: Nanny, Anthony, Betty, Anthony, Mary, Ruth, Thomas, who was buried on the day of his baptism, Dinah, Thomas, and Nancy. Nancy may be a namesake of the first-born Nanny, or Nanny may have by 1788 become Ann, as sometimes happened. Marriages are recorded for two daughters: Betty, on the 3 November 1795, married William Spensley, son of William Spensley of Blades, and Dinah on 23 December 1806 married Joseph Whitfield, both names strongly associated with Methodism. Thomas died on 19 August 1796 at the age of forty-eight.

William, Anthony, and James were the first of the Pratts to live in Gunnerside. The second to be married was the older brother William, who took for wife Mary Clarkson of Crackpot on 5 May 1766. This couple moved west to Barfend, up on the slopes of Lodge Green, leading the Pratts to Gunnerside. In the little living of Barfend was also James Fawcett, whose daughter Ann was born the same year as William's marriage, and George and Ann Peacock, whose son James was born the same year as the first of William and Mary's children.

Between 1767 and 1799 William and Mary had three sons and three daughters: Anthony, Joseph, William, Betty, Jemmy, and Betty. William and the first Betty died in childhood, probably in an epidemic, and were buried on the same day, in midwinter, 14 January 1779. The last two daughters were born at Winterings, the tiny enclosure high on the moor up by Old Gang.

In the Quaker stronghold of Reeth there lived a family of that persuasion by the name of Raw, whose members figured prominently in good works. A Quaker House was endowed in the

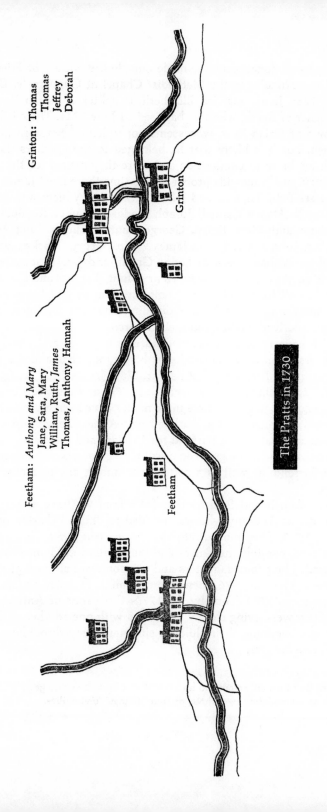

Grinton: Thomas
        Thomas
        Jeffrey
        Deborah

Feetham: *Anthony and Mary*
         Jane, Sara, Mary
         William, Ruth, *James*
         Thomas, Anthony, Hannah

Grinton

Feetham

The Pratts in 1730

village and donations were made outside the Society of Friends, and in particular to the Methodist Chapel at Gunnerside. On 4 July 1768 James married Elizabeth, daughter of Isaiah Raw, a gardener of Reeth, who was baptised 24 June 1744. There is little known of Isaiah Raw, who seems not to have been born in the parish, but it is likely that he belonged to the Quakers. James took his bride to Gunnerside and there they settled for the next century. In Gunnerside proper at this time there lived James and Michael Bell, Thomas and Mary Birkbeck, William and Mary Brunskill, Henry Cantril, Joseph Hodgson, James Reynoldson, William and Mary Story, George Sunter, Thomas and Mary Waller, John Watters, and James White. George Harker was at Potting, William Slack at Lodge Green, and James Spensley at Barfside. At Winterings were Henry Hunt, Thomas and Elizabeth Garth, and John and Jane Thompson. And at Old Gang itself, for there must have been a dwelling near the entrance, were James and Ruth Pedley and their children.

We have records of seven children for James and Elizabeth. The first, Anthony, namesake of his grandfather and the next in our line of Pratts, was baptised in 1769; James, in 1771; Agnes, in 1772; William, in 1779; Isabel, in 1786; and the twins Samuel and Thomas, in 1789. Three place names have been given in their records: Gunnerside for Anthony and Agnes, Lodge Green for James and Isabel, and Barfend for William and the twins. Lodge Green was the name given an area that included both Gunnerside and Barfend, as well as a cottage containing one or more "livings."*

The fourth and final brother for whom we have a marriage record was Anthony who was wedded to Phillis Wharton on 10 April 1775. They moved into Winterings where the Thompsons still lived, possibly the Garths and the Hunts, and Thomas Sunter as well. Their four daughters and one son were all born at Winterings: Mary in 1776, then Nanny, Phillis, Hannah, and finally Anthony in 1789. Thus by the 1770s three sons of Anthony of Feetham were living closely associated with one another at Gunnerside, begetting their children simultaneously throughout the next two decades.

---

*These tiny hamlets amount to no more than one or two cottages, each accommodating two, three, or four "livings" or families.

Until the Harvest

"The kingdom of heaven is likened unto a man who sowed good
seed in his field: but while men slept, his enemy came and
sowed tares among the wheat, and went his way. But when the
blade was sprung up, and brought forth fruit, then appeared
the tares also. So the servants of the householder came and said
unto him, Sir, didst not thou sow good seed in thy field?
from whence then hath it tares? He said unto them, An enemy
hath done this. The servants said unto him Wilt thou then
that we go and gather them up? But he said, Nay; lest while ye
gather up the tares, ye root up also the wheat with them. Let
both grow together until the harvest: and in the time of harvest
I will say to the reapers, Gather ye together first the tares,
and bind them in bundles to burn them: but gather the wheat
into my barn."
Matthew 13:24-30

Throughout the ages the world has been divided between the
rich and the poor. It is only in comparatively recent years and in
our own society that the term "the poor" has gone into disfavour,
as we have learned that one's economic condition is relative and
accidental and not an inalienable state. It was not always so. In
days of yore, the poor had their place and knew it. If they did
not, so much the worse for them. For long centuries, however,
they did know it, more or less. But by the eighteenth century the
process of evolution had reached a time of acceleration that led
straight into what has been termed, for want of a better phrase,
"the Industrial Revolution." As labour-saving devices such as the
spinning jenny and the flying shuttle, the advent of steam and the
inevitabilities of discovery dispossessed "the poor" from their
time-honoured occupations and at the same time thrust them into
the market of cheap labour for the machines, conditions reached
an all-time low.

That any of our ancestors survived the eighteenth century is
justification for a belief in miracles. By the middle of the century
England was sunk in the evils of the gin age. Not yet ready for

revolution but with the seeds of it stifled deep in human wretchedness, in England as in her sister countries of France and Russia, there was little hope for the little man.

His condition was determined by an iniquitous principle universally followed by exploiters since man has had a socio-economic society and that reached its zenith in England during the Georgian period: that the labouring man, in the state in which he existed by divine decree, was a better and cheaper labourer uneducated, and that his children could be an even more lucrative source of labour if given no chance to go to school. History books have chronicled the facts of child labour, and English literature has supplied abundant illustrations of the child-machine, set to work often from the age of five years to work as long as sixteen hours a day, until he dropped dead from exhaustion to be replaced by another replica of himself, with no chance of rescue by his mourning parents (if he had any) who were forced to require his pitiful supplement to the family earnings. The unwanted child, whose pale image multiplied in rat-infested street and wind-chilled moor, was sucked into the workhouse to increase the pool of labour to be used wantonly until it was spent.

The only available anaesthetic was cheap liquor, which was less expensive and more accessible than any food. The gin age had been developing since the late seventeenth century. In 1689 an embargo on imported liquor had steeped the country in cheap home brews. In 1750, the year of the birth of Anthony of Winterings, 506 of the two thousand houses in St. Giles, London, were gin shops that sold gin at a penny a pint. Signs read "Drunk for 1d; Dead drunk for 2d. Free straw."[1] Did Anthony Pratt of Feetham frequent the Miners' Inn* there, established since 1634? It is reasonable to suppose that he did, although he was one of the first to welcome John Wesley to the dales by the middle of the century.†

Throughout the century wages fluctuated from 4s to 12s per week. Children earned as little as a penny a day for the same hours put in as their elders. Nor were costs low. In 1793 a labourer in the south of England, earning with the help of the odd sixpence turned in by his wife 46 pounds per annum, had to fork out £36 8s on bread alone for the year.[2] Food other than bread

*Now the Punch Bowl, Low Row.
†Somewhere it has been noted that John Pratt kept an inn at Low Row, but I have been unable to find corroboration of this.

cost him £16 4s, leaving him in the red £6 12s 8d for all other expenditures.

If the populace was spared death from starvation, it is a wondrous thing it did not completely succumb to death from disease or poison. Nothing was known of hygiene. Milk, cheese, butter, and meat were usually sour, spoiled, rancid, or otherwise infected. To keep bread white, for the British would not eat brown bread, additives were used – alum, lime, and white lead being among the favourites, as well as the ashes of human bones raked from the charnel houses.[3] The irony of this is more deeply felt when one considers that one reason the poor had for not eating brown bread was the fear that it had been made with sweepings. You just did not know what was in it. Pickles were made a beautiful green by verdigrease, a concomitant of acid on copper.[4] Watered beer received its kick from an infusion of picro-toxin,[5] tea its colour from vitriol.[6] The British are a hardy race.

In 1789 James Pratt earned at Gunnerside 4s 4d per week, or £10 to £11 per year, and was fortunate to have sons to help him. In the north of England things were somewhat better than in the south, as people ate less bread and more raw cereal, and they had learned the value of the potato which was not yet accepted in the south. Cheese had become part of the staple diet of the poor,[7] and of the various brands that were being developed it is likely that cheese from neighbouring Wensleydale was enjoyed in the valley. It is possible, too, that the people of the dales may have had access to garden produce at reduced rates, or even have had the use of a bit of garden to grow their own vegetables. In any case, the lot of the people in the country districts never reached the depths to which the city people sank, if only because there at least fresh air was free.

During the lifetime of the first James Pratt of Gunnerside, two great revolutions took place in the western world. Across the channel, France stood on the edge of a new world for the common man. Those in England who carried a broader vision watched in hope with bated breath and a heady euphoria. For Wordsworth "Bliss was it in that dawn to be alive, But to be young was very heaven!" and in so saying he spoke for many. Coleridge, too, was delivered of a great buoyancy, not unmixed with shame.

When France in wrath her giant-limbs upreared,
And with that oath, which smote air, earth, and sea,

61

Stamped her strong foot and said she would be free,
Bear witness for me, how I hoped and feared!
. . .
But blessed the paeans of delivered France,
And hung my head and wept at Britain's name.

But France saw her dream, which was the dream of the world, juggernaut into terror. Coleridge then reported in his ode, "In mad game/They burst their manacles and wear the name of Freedom, graven on a heavier chain!" And freedom-lovers in England watched the crumpling of their dream and turned away in fear and loathing.

But the revolution in France was not the only one that had taken place. By the time it was over, England had lived through the beginnings of a spiritual revolution destined to change the face of the country and initiate reforms that saved her from the bloody carnage that had washed over France.

In the middle years of the eighteenth century there had arisen in England a revolutionary leader whose influence had begun to penetrate, though slowly and painfully, into the conscience of man. The call to arms was not to the sword, nor to the bloody battle, but a rallying cry of the spirit, called by a rider who circuited his country and Ireland on horseback, over hill and dale, swamp and mountain, in fair weather and foul, week after week for fifty-two years. John Wesley had come with his message of salvation through faith, and a promise of a heavenly kingdom for all who held the banner of Christ before them throughout the length of their earthly life. Nowhere in all England was he received with greater hospitality than in the dales of Yorkshire.

It was about this time also that from our hitherto silent ancestors faint murmurs begin to be heard. Although we do not know of Wesley's visits to Swaledale prior to 1761, he had preached in Wensleydale, and there had, no doubt, been those from Swaledale who had crossed the wastelands into the villages there to hear him. In any case messengers of Wesley were bringing word of a new movement into the valley. The earliest of which we know was Jacob Rowell who, with two other "exhorters," formed a small society at Feetham, the Pratts' village, around Christmas 1749. Of this first society were two brothers by the name of Spence who arrived at Blades early in 1750 and put up with relatives who were called Spensley. William Spensley opened up his house for preaching, and it was there in the little hamlet of Blades that the first Methodist society in Swaledale was formed. A cottage adjoining the Spensley house was provided for the holding of services when the weather was too inclement for the preaching to take place, as it usually did, under the thorn tree at Pick Hill. A special room in Low Row was fitted out as accommodation for itinerant preachers, although John Wesley himself made his home with the Spensleys while in the dale.[8]

We do not know exactly when the Pratts first became active in the new movement. At the time of Wesley's first visit in 1761, the four Pratt brothers, three of whom were soon to settle Gunnerside, were young boys between the ages of eleven and twenty. It is almost certain that they, along with their parents Anthony and Mary, had had a part in the entertainment of Wesley,* although Anthony was to die in 1762. Thomas and Ann, whose daughter Betty married William Spensley's son William in 1795, most certainly helped in its growth. And Annas Metcalfe, who was to marry William Pratt, son of James of Gunnerside, in 1799, and himself a local preacher, distinctly remembered hearing Mr. Wesley preach when she must have been a very small girl.[9]

There was a little girl of the Spensley household in whom the leaven of Wesleyanism was early at work. Along with the other folk of the dale, she was accustomed to knit in order to eke out the family's slender living, and with the proceeds of her knitting she bought a table, her own prized possession. On the great occasions when John Wesley visited Low Row, the table was proudly offered as a podium for him as he preached out of doors by the thorn tree. So sweetly did she beg for this privilege that he was greatly touched, called her his little friend, and afterwards made a point of asking for her table. The table was long treasured by the descendants of the family.[10]

In the possession of Mrs. Sarah Colechin in New Zealand are two photographs – one of Mrs. McFarlane, the other of Mrs. Hall† – taken together with a chair which John Wesley in ancient

*In the New Zealand copy of *Methodism in Swaledale* there is a notation opposite the account of the forming of the society which reads "Grandfather's."

†The two daughters of Thomas Pratt mentioned on the Bradford chart.

times had stood upon to preach. This chair was also at Blades and may have belonged to the Spensley or Whitfield families into which the daughters of Thomas Pratt married so long ago. In 1925 Mrs. McFarlane wrote in her diary on Easter Saturday: "In the afternoon we went to see Mrs. Whitfield who is almost a relation, a lovely old dear who knew Aunts Sarah Ann & Bessie. Our cousins are her cousins so we are almost akin." The kinship is obscured now by the haze of distance but undoubtedly both table and chair have been treasured by the descendants of those early hosts to John Wesley at Blades.

The seeds of Methodism fell on fertile ground. To the life of the dalesman, whose nature was characterized by a cheerful lustiness, given to fighting, versifying, and drama, was added the extreme zeal of salvation. In his journal Wesley makes several references to the dales and their people. In 1747 he wrote of his outdoor congregation at Blanchard, twenty miles west of New-castle:

Tues. Mar. 24, 1747. ". . . all the congregation kneeling down on the grass. They were gathered out of the lead mines from all parts. . . . A row of little children sat under the opposite wall, all quiet and still. The whole congreation drank in every word with such earnestness in their looks, I could not but hope God will make this wilderness sing for joy."[11]

Two weeks later he sketched an amusing picture at Stonesley Gate, and one that can easily be imagined by anyone who has visited the north country.

Tues. May 5, 1747. At Stonesley Gate. "They filled both the yard and the road to a considerable distance and many were seated on a long wall adjoining which being built of loose stones, in the middle of the sermon, all fell down at once. I never saw, heard or read of such a thing before. . . . The whole wall and the persons sitting upon it, sank down together, none of them screaming out, and very few altering their posture, and not one was hurt at all: but they appeared sitting at the bottom just as they sat at the top. Nor was there any interruption of my speaking, or of the attention of the hearers."[12]

In 1761 he paid the first of his visits to Swaledale and the Spensleys:

Tues, June 9, 1761. "At noon I preached in Teesdale. Most of the men are lead miners, who a while ago were turned out of their work for following 'this way.' By this means many of them got into far better work; and some time after, their old master was glad to employ them again.

"We had a long stage from hence to Swaledale where I found an earnest, loving, simple people, whom I likewise exhorted not to leave the church, though they had not the best of ministers."[13]

An opiate of the people? Perhaps. But for better or worse England was spared the bloodbath in which France was to be saturated a decade later. And, paradoxically enough, the lot on earth of those who were fed the opiate of a gloryland in the hereafter was made easier to bear than was the lot of those who were promised nothing in the next world.

The following years saw many a lay preacher rise to correct the state of affairs described in Wesley's entry in 1761.

The Rev. Hodgson Casson in 1825 wrote: "The last circuit I was in I visited one place which had long been very low. I went determined to kill or cure; laid on, as some of them said, unmercifully and cracked the pulpit."[14]

Wild and robust must the preaching have been that replaced the "bruising contests" and fisticuffs that were wielded for the sheer love of battle. One dalesman, having licked the champion of Westmoreland in a bruising contest, spent the following week carousing day and night with his former opponent in celebration of their friendship.[15] This energy was now put into the wild fight for souls. So great was the energy that people collapsed from the force of it, and the "exhorter" Jacob Rowell was given the sobriquet of "Fell 'em in the heck" as people in the attempt to escape from his zeal were struck down, like St. Paul on the road to Damascus, in their own doorways.[16] Mr. Wesley himself was appalled:

May 7, 1772. "I took Thomas Cherry* away with me; but it was too late, he will hardly recover. Let all observe that no more preachers may murder themselves; here is another martyr to screaming."[17]

*This is very likely Thomas Cherry, born in 1717 to Thomas Cherry of Feetham, and a neighbour of Anthony Pratt (see p. 55).

It would be hard to exaggerate the far-reaching effects of the Wesleyan movement. In a very different way Wesley was grappling with the same problems that Karl Marx was to tackle a century later. Both men were concerned with the common man and both were enemies of capitalist domination. But where Marx's approach was intellectual, Wesley's was emotional; where Marx avoided contact with the people, Wesley became one of them; where Marx commanded respect, Wesley invited ridicule; where Marx accepted the class war as a means to the ideal community in which there would be neither rich nor poor, neither master nor slave, Wesley pleaded for a change of heart that would recognize the dignity of the individual and the priceless value of every immortal soul. The new society envisaged by Marx in which all would be equal under a dictatorship of the proletariat was seen by Wesley as a human society where all would be reborn to a spiritual prototype.[18] His influence was to appear in the Labour movement in Britain, in the trade union movement of Keir Hardie, and in the numerous welfare societies that arose from a conscience-stricken land.

Wesley's journal is full of accounts that rival the Acts of the Apostles for rioting and jeering. The highways and byways were full of gin-sodden countryfolk. The streets of the cities and towns overflowed with their urban counterparts. At Wesley's approach they would leap out and tear at him, howling and gleeking, drag him through the mud, pelt him, stroke his hair. But invariably those who came to scoff remained to pray. When he preached in the Established Church he was, almost without exception, requested not to return. More and more frequently his sermons took place by the wayside, among the lilies of the fields, on the seashore, among the hills, until his growing numbers of followers opened up their barns, their kitchens, and their humble homes.

For him, life was a ceaseless round of personal visitations. His method was the painstaking formation of innumerable small societies of approximately twelve people, both men and women, who were set to work to tackle the main causes of oppression. Every member was to be a crusader for temperance, justice, equity, popular education, and joyous fellowship. Methodist schools were started in godforsaken places, and members were helped to save, if possible, a penny a week to pay off the public debt and thus keep themselves out of the iniquitous debtors'

66

prison. One can imagine with what joy the clop clop of Wesley's horse was greeted as he rode like a spring wind over the "horrid mountains"* into the valley of the Swale.

Bounding to the sea
on the flooding Swale,
the fallen stars.

By the 1770s, when Methodism had taken root, William, James and Anthony, sons of Anthony and Mary Pratt of Feetham, were living as neighbours in Gunnerside, and undoubtedly frequent visits were paid between them and their brother Thomas, four miles away in Feetham. Their mother Mary was still alive at that time and services would have been held at Blades for some little while until the Gunnerside congregation set itself up. Even then the family met for Sunday observance at one place or the other. Their children, too, it is not difficult to imagine, would be well acquainted with that stretch of the Swale that flows between Rowleth Wood and the slopes of Crackpot and Whitaside as they pounded the route in an exchange of cousinly visits. They were all much of an age. Betty, the little daughter of William and Mary of Barfend, and her cousin Betty of Feetham who was to marry into the Spensley family were baptised the same year, only the first Betty did not live to marry for she died during the hard days of January, just five years after her beginning, and was buried the same day as her eight-year-old brother. Scarlet fever took many lives, as well as diphtheria and other children's diseases against which there was no cure at the time.

In the midst of disease, death, and hard physical labour, the Methodist communities grew. In 1768, the year the first James of Gunnerside married Elizabeth Raw, Wesley wrote: "I have not found so deep and lively a work in any other part of the kingdom

*This was Wesley's description. Daniel Defoe in his journal for 1724 wrote from Skipton: "Looking forward to the north-west of us we saw nothing but high mountains which had a terrible aspect and more frightful than any in Monmouthshire or Derbyshire, especially Penigent Hill. So that having no manner of inclination to encounter them, merely for the sake of seeing a few villages and a parcel of wild people, we turned short north-east . . . . " When one considers that the road to Askrigg was "fit only for a goat to travel"[19] and that the ones into Swaledale were worse, one can scarcely blame either Defoe or Wesley. Yet these were the mountains traversed daily by the miners on foot.

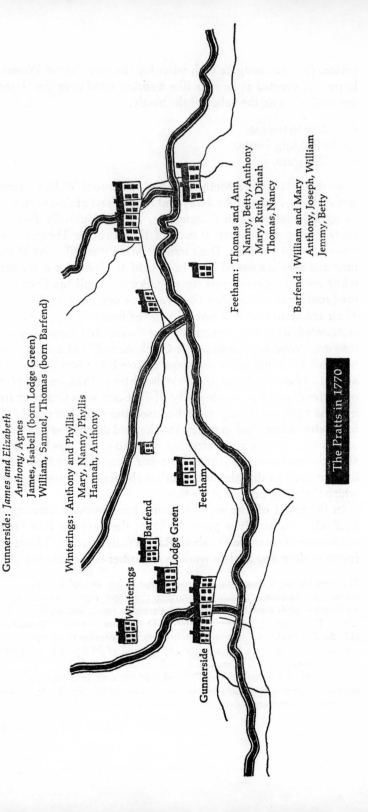

Gunnerside: James and Elizabeth
  Anthony, Agnes
  James, Isabell (born Lodge Green)
  William, Samuel, Thomas (born Barfend)

Winterings: Anthony and Phyllis
  Mary, Nanny, Phyllis
  Hannah, Anthony

Feetham: Thomas and Ann
  Nanny, Betty, Anthony
  Mary, Ruth, Dinah
  Thomas, Nancy

Barfend: William and Mary
  Anthony, Joseph, William
  Jemmy, Betty

Winterings
Barfend
Lodge Green
Feetham
Gunnerside

The Pratts in 1770

as runs through the whole circuit, particularly in the vales which wind through these horrid mountains."[20] That year Blades returned £1.18.6 for the June quarter as compared with Reeth's 8s. 6d. The following year the first chapel for Low Row was built at Pick Hill by the thorn tree under which the Itinerants had preached since their first meeting in 1750. By this time enthusiastic meetings had been held in Gunnerside for three years to which came worshippers from many miles over the dreary fells, in season and out. One woman used to trudge the six miles over the mountains from the market town of Askrigg in Wensleydale to join in the shouting and rejoicing of the faithful as they gathered at the junction of ghyll and river. It was just there to the west of the ghyll where the first Methodist sermon was preached, out of doors, at Gunnerside.

Outdoors in the kinder months of the year was fine, but an indoor meeting house was needed for inclement weather and the early services were held in the home of Deborah Waggett, up on the green slopes of the village, nestling in a row of orderly stone cottages and fronted with colourful gardens. Later the community met at the home of John Brunskill at the eastern end of the town.

By 1788 it was evident that these private homes could no longer accommodate the swelling congregations, and steps were taken to build a chapel – no small task, financially, at that time. Anthony Pratt was then nineteen years of age, James seventeen, and both with their father James working the lead mines. William, at nine, it is hoped, was not yet being sent down to the pit, but it is quite probable he may have had to go for the mines had fallen upon hard days, and the times were perilous. The Child Protection Acts were as yet dreams in the minds of a few visionaries, and the extent to which the Pratts were victims of the unimaginable barbarity of Georgian England is surrounded by an envelope of silence. It may be better so.

At that time Agnes was sixteen. Little Isabel was two, and the twins Sam and Tom not yet born. They would arrive the following year, and by the summer of the next year Elizabeth would be dead and buried, her child-bearing over. The gaps between the ages of the children would lead us to believe that many were the unrecorded births and infant burials.

As for the brothers, William and Anthony, they were in much

69

the same boat. William had been married to Mary Clarkson for twenty-two years. Their son Anthony was twenty-one, Joseph nineteen. Anthony and Phillis had been married thirteen years and had three daughters. When a son was born to them the year after the chapel was built, they were listed as paupers at Winterings. The same year the brothers lost their mother Mary at Feetham, who had been a widow for twenty-six years. The wages for miners were 4s. 4d. per week. The cost of living was high, flour being 7s. a stone.[21]

Nevertheless, by the grace of God and human sacrifice a chapel would be built. Contributions came in from everybody, one of the largest from James Spensley, who may have been a brother of the William who seven years later married Betty Pratt at Low Row. Those who could not afford it contributed what they could, but when all was in, the chapel fund was fifty pounds short of the six hundred needed. The following story has been told and it bears repeating, as an example of the devotion of the faithful when the goal is to be reached through love. William Buxton, a miner of twenty-seven, organized a few miners who with himself agreed to work overtime and give the proceeds to the chapel fund. They toiled and moiled and found no ore and all gave up but Buxton. He worked on alone, in the dark, and found nothing for several more days and finally in the desperation that had long ago driven him into the wilderness,* he fell on his knees in prayer. Soon a vein was recovered with enough metal to push the chapel fund over the top.[22]

The Darkening Hills

"Go, Shepherds, go to Bethlehem and see the wonders of that morn. For Low a Stare Directes your cours on the plains of Bethlehem. I think I hear the Singing Land in the regions of The [- - - -] Such Musick for to Chairm a World upon the plains

*It is said that years before, such was the turmoil of William Buxton that his family and friends had feared for his sanity. At the age of thirteen he was driven by it out onto the moors crying for mercy. There he found peace in conversion.

70

of Bethlehem. Shall we through sin forget such Love which God to Shephards maid so known [- - - -] fulfilled the promise true when Christ appeared in Bethlehem."
Methodist Record Book 1802-1836

The French Revolution had come and gone and Napoleon's star had risen and set during the lifetime of the Gunnerside brothers, at least of James and of Anthony, for we do not know when William died, and Thomas of Feetham was laid to rest in 1796. But civilizations could rise and fall and kingdoms crumble without appreciably affecting the lives of the dalespeople whose days were influenced by two compelling forces: lead mining and Wesleyanism. Toward the end of the eighteenth century when the chapel was built at Gunnerside, the split between the Methodists and the Established Church, which Wesley had tried to avoid, became inevitable. More and more the Church of England refused baptism and burial to the dissenters, and in the year 1796 the names of these began to be recorded in the Methodist registers. Holy Communion being denied them, the followers of Wesley developed the Love-Feast and Watch-Night services which, together with the class meetings, became the centre of the religious and social life of the community and provided the chief outlet for the love of drama, excitement, and artistic expression so characteristic of the dalespeople.

For two and a half decades after the chapel was built, Methodists, although they held their own services there, attended Church and Holy Communion in the Anglican churches as long as they would admit them, so that it was not until 1812 that the first Sacrament was held in Gunnerside Chapel, to be celebrated thereafter three times a year. On that first occasion the wine bill was 7s 10d, nearly two weeks' of a miner's pay, and the collections taken up in the early years were not sufficient to cover the cost of the communicants' wine.[1] In time this righted itself as the numbers of communicants grew.

By 1796 the Methodist community in Gunnerside was large enough to be divided into six classes under the leadership of William Buxton and his wife Alice (who had a class of unmarried girls), Thomas Buxton, Joseph Sunter, William Reynoldson, and John Kearton. To Joseph Sunter's class belonged James Pratt and his daughter-in-law Dorothy. Oddly enough Dorothy's husband Anthony is listed as a member of John Kearton's class. Whether married couples were split up by accident or design we are not told. Ann Pratt, single, is also in this class. She may have been James's unmarried niece Nanny, who would have been seventeen at the time and more likely to have been in Alice Buxton's class, or possibly Nanny, oldest daughter of Thomas and Ann, come from Low Row to worship with her relations. At thirty, it is more probable that Nanny, rather than her cousin from Winterings, would be in this group. In Alice Buxton's class was a young lady of the Pratt family by the name of Elizabeth. The entry is marked on the New Zealand copy of *Methodism in Swaledale* in which the lists are given, indicating that she was known to the daughters of Thomas of New Zealand. The likeliest candidate is the daughter of William and Mary of Barfend, who was christened Betty, one month after her older sister Betty was buried that winter of 1779.

Like the services, the class meetings were held at the homes of the leaders. It was at these where, except for the sacramental collection, which was designated for the poor, money was accepted from the members who were to pay, if they could, a penny a week and a shilling a quarter. At the meetings, the leaders would speak, pray, and read the Scriptures. The meeting was then open for the airing of problems, the giving of testimonies, and to good-natured criticism of one another's faults, the latter of which was kept in the strictest secrecy, giving to the meetings something of the character of a brotherhood lodge.

Once a month the Itinerant arrived, preached in the Chapel, and met with each class, becoming acquainted with the good behaviour or backsliding of each member. Once a quarter he distributed tickets of membership and was paid by the Steward from the funds collected from the members. Frequently his small salary could not be met in this way, and had to be made up by one of the more affluent members. Inspired by Wesley's maxim "Get all you can; save all you can; give all you can" and prompted by their own inborn Yorkshire canniness, those early Methodists in the dales took pride in saving and giving.

The Steward also took pride in his job. From his carefully kept accounts,[2] we can imagine the Quarter Day dinner of 3 April 1809, with Joseph Sunter, sarvent, waiting on the guests:

The Diner on the Quarter Day (which would be for all present)	10s	0d
To Joseph Sunter Sarvent	1s	0d
Ale at the Quarter Day*	2s	0d
Pipes and Tobacco		6d

The Steward's Book is fascinating. Each entry suggests a story in itself expanding upon contemplation into humour or pathos or both. A few of the entries run:

1808	Dec. 3.	Brimstone for the Preacher's Hos	1d
1809	Mar. 7.	To Elezebeth Thompson for Bearing snow of the Chappel sealing	8d
1809	May 2.	John Daykin for Hoars and Cart for fetchen a Cartload of Moarter from Low Row	1s 6d
	May 9	To John Calvert for Reparing the Chappel sneck	1d
	June 30	To Ralph Millner for puting in the Gallery Poasts	1s 0d
	Aug. 14	To John Calveart for 2 Holdfarsts for the Chappel clok	3d
	Oct. 19	To John Calvart for making a Lupe and hinging the Chappil gate	9d
1813	June 2	To Len'd and Chr. Metcalf for waling the courtin wall	18s 6d
1814	Mar. 28	To Ralph Milner for putting in furm feet	1s 2d

During these years we lose all contact with Feetham. Thomas died in 1796 and records for his children have not been discovered beyond the marriages of Betty to William Spensley and Dinah to Joseph Whitfield. William and Betty removed to High Whitaside where their children, Susannah and John, were born in 1806 and 1807. Susannah lived a year, dying a few months before her brother was born. That the Whitfields may have still

*Even devotion to the Methodist cause had not yet made outcasts of ale and tobacco in Gunnerside.

been living at Blades in 1925 is suggested by Mrs. McFarlane's diary (see p. 64).

At Barfend, William and Mary fade out and also their sons Anthony and Joseph, so close of an age to James's Anthony and James, and undoubtedly as close in spirit.

On Anthony and Phillis at Winterings fortune had not smiled kindly. In 1789 Anthony was without work and was listed in the records with no occupation whatever. From this we may deduce that he had either met with an accident in the mines or become too ill to work. There are several burial dates for Anthony Pratt in Gunnerside in the 1820s and 30s, and the date 23 June 1834 seems to fit him. If this is so, and he had become disabled before 1789, he had indeed had a long period of invalidism. In 1810 their third daughter Hannah, at the age of twenty-five, gave birth to a daughter in Gunnerside, to whom, as far as we know, she gave her own name and then disappeared from view. The following year their youngest child and only son Anthony married Ann Kearton and, living on in Gunnerside, this couple had three children: George in 1816, Elizabeth in 1820, and in 1823 Anthony, who died and was buried a year and some months later. There is no indication of what happened to their first daughter Mary, but we do know that Nanny lived to a ripe old age and since she did not marry and her parents lived well into the century, it is reasonable to suppose that Nanny lived with them. Doughty old Phillis lived to be ninety-one and was living by herself in Gunnerside at the time of the 1841 census, when she was eighty-nine years of age. The census of that year does not indicate Nanny's whereabouts, but in 1851 she was a lodger with the Kitchens who were her first cousins. Elizabeth, the daughter of Anthony and Ann, married John Thompson in 1841. In 1837 George married his second cousin Ruth, daughter of William Pratt and Agnes Metcalfe, whose story appears on p. 86.

Of the seven children of James and Elizabeth we know of the three sons of Gunnerside – Anthony, James, and William. For convenience's sake, these sons will be referred to by the nicknames of Anty,* James Doley,* and Willie. Of Agnes, and the twins, there is no trace. Isabel may have married John Pounder on 18 April 1809.

*Anty is probably authentic, as this was the common diminutive of Anthony. James Doley is the actual name of this son, presumably derived from his doleful outlook.

74

Now the murmuring ancestral voices become more distinct. In 1791 Anty, the firstborn, married. He acquired his bride from the beautiful little village with the goatpaths beyond Satronside and Crackpot Common.

In Askrigg there lived a family of carpenters by the name of Chapman. In 1735 one of the sons of this family, called Philip, married Dorothy Horsfeild, daughter of Henry Horsfeild and his wife Elizabeth Ibbot of Kearton. Philip and Dorothy seemed to have lived in Kearton for the children's christenings are all recorded there. At the time of their marriage, however, Philip was listed as belonging to Wensleydale and it was at Askrigg that he died. The fourth of their five children was Henry who took to wife one Elizabeth, and they became the parents of three daughters: Dorothy, Mary, and Aly. Dorothy it was who, on 9 August 1791, became the bride of Anty Pratt. She is mentioned in John Ward's book as being a member of Joseph Sunter's Methodist class (see p. 72), and Hannah McCaffrey has underscored her in the New Zealand copy of the book as her great grandmother. At her marriage she was registered as Dorothy, but thereafter at the baptisms of her children she was simply Dolley, and probably so remained. But she introduced into the Pratt household from the Horsfeild line the name Dorothy which was to become a traditional Pratt name from that time to the present generation.

Anty and Dolley were the parents of eleven children. The first five were born at Gunnerside: James (henceforward referred to as Jimmie), 31 July 1792; Jinny, 22 August 1793; Phillis, 19 December 1795; Harry 23 April 1797; and Nanny, 25 November 1799. At the time of Nanny's baptism, Anty is listed as a farmer. From time to time the miners took on some extra labour, working the farms for those on whose land they lived, while retaining the occupation of "miner," so we suspect this record may have some significance, either that times were bad for miners or Anty may have had the opportunity of tilling his own bit of land. A year later tragedy struck, taking the baby Nanny who was buried 23 November 1800. Anty's farming did not last long for, at Ruth's baptism, 18 February 1802, he is listed as a miner once more. The family had by then moved to Dyke Heads, a mile or two west of Gunnerside, the first westward move made by the family since leaving Feetham. They appear to have stayed at Dyke Heads at least until the last of the children were born. The baptism of the next daughter Ann was recorded on 12 April 1802 but it is reasonable to suppose that the year is an error and should be, probably, 1803. Mary, born in 1806, died in 1812 at the age of six. Alice, born three months after Mary's death, lived five months. Henry and Anthony, we are invited to believe, according to the Christopher Pratt chart, lived and, it is hoped, can be traced with sufficient persistence. On the same chart, against one of the Anthonys, is the notation "deaf and dumb" and it would appear that this son of Anty and Dolley Pratt was he who was so afflicted.

James Doley married Dolly Reynoldson of Gunnerside in 1803. Dolly, born in 1785, was the fifth child of George and Dorothy Reynoldson of Gunnerside. For the baptisms of their six children, four places are registered. The family started off at Barff Head, a small "living" not on the map but presumably a little to the northeast of Gunnerside. Here it was where William was born in 1806. Ann in 1808 was born at Heights; George in 1810 and Elizabeth in 1813 at Gunnerside; and James, baptised at the age of three with his little sister Isabella in 1820 at Lodge Green. To the best of our knowledge it was James Doley who, on 20 November 1822 at the Gunnerside general store, bought a half-stone of sugar for four shillings and, for four and three, a half-stone of soap, an ally enlisted in what must have been an endless battle against the dirt of Old Gang.

Willie, like his brother James, moved around considerably among the gentle grey cottages up on the slopes of Melbecks Moor, beyond Gunnerside. He was married in 1799* to Annas, daughter of Thomas and Agnes Metcalfe. Thomas had been a stonemason, but his miserly inclinations had enabled him to retire into the more genial occupation of pub-keeper and he became the proprietor of the King's Head Inn at Gunnerside.[3] His sons Leonard, Reuben, and Christopher were to continue in the trade. William and Annas moved into Bents House, beyond the Modestys on Melbecks Moor, and proceeded to raise their family of some dozen children, while William went to work in Old Gang. The baptism of their first son, James, was entered for Lodge Green in 1800. At Potting, Betty was baptised in 1804, then Thomas in 1805. There seems to be no record for Thomas

*It is interesting to note that on the marriage certificate William signed his name instead of making his mark, as his nephew James had to do over thirty years later.

but he appears on Leonard Pratt's tree of this family and his descendants are now well known in the dale. Anas, in 1807, was baptised at Winterings. For the next three children the family was once more at Potting: Ruth in 1809, Mary in 1812, and William in 1814. Robert arrived at Heights in 1816, as did Christopher in 1819. In 1821 the family were at Bence Cottage* where Anthony was born; then at Heights in 1823 for Agness and at Gunnerside in 1824 for Jane. By the time William and Annas celebrated their Silver Wedding in 1824, the family had moved into a larger and finer house at Winterings.[4]

What can we know of these folk who, born of and to England's mountains, climbed the backs of Kisdon, Scabba Wath, and Great Shunnor Fell, under huge moving skies, following a strict code made stricter by their own need? We can only know them by their fruits. The "gentle, loving, simple people" of John Wesley exist today in their descendants, both in their memories and in themselves, widely though the paths have diverged. The men and boys who trooped each day up over Melbecks to Old Gang had, without romanticizing, a sensitive nobility hardly in keeping with the rough-hewn image so commonly held of the labouring class. No doubt they, so full of music,[†] sang as they trudged, their male voices and boyish trebles ringing out in the crisp dawns, but more than likely stilled in weariness on the homeward stretch. We do know they shortened the miles by knitting. Wool from Swaledale sheep not only kept the Gunnerside families warm and helped to eke out a living by adding a few extra shillings to the family coffers, but provided a release from monotony on those long morning walks.

What mean these stones
snaking their way over the moor
dark on the grey uplands?

They murmur an old tune
in the wind, of bygone feet
that trod the darkening hills.

*The spelling varied considerably in the records.
†The Yorkshire soprano Janet Baker has suggested that the high percentage of fine voices in Yorkshire may be attributed to the same influences that have produced the broad accent of the Yorkshire dialect – that is, the spacious moors and breadth of landscape of her native county.

While England was at war with France and the United States of America, things were less bad in Swaledale than in other parts of the kingdom, because England had need of lead for the war effort and the mines were kept busy. At this time, between 1793 and 1815, three generations of Pratts lived simultaneously at Gunnerside and worked Old Gang. Judging by the variety of birthplaces for the children of the families, the dwellings beyond Gunnerside up on Melbecks Moor seem to have comprised communal living for James, William, and Anthony, and their sons and grandsons. It is hard for us, their descendants across the world who do not know of each other's existence, to realize how close our forefathers were in that dimly envisioned past. But looking at the map they can be pictured, several hours off from dawn with their lanterns, on the march up the yawning moors; James and his sons – Anty with his sons Jimmie and Harry; James Doley with his son William; and Willie with his son James. Shadowy figures, darkly emerging, they would be joined by other silhouettes with a hearty backslap in the dark frost of the early morning, and perhaps a whimper or two from the little ones as they stumbled out over the gorse until the kind arms of their elders around their shoulders quietened them. The company, setting out from Gunnerside, would collect, as they passed, by ones, twos, and threes, the family and friends at Heights, Lodge Green, Barfend, Potting, and finally Anthony and his son at Winterings. These dwelling places, being comparatively near to Old Gang, were host to many miners, especially during the winter months, so that they would not have so far to go to the mines. It is likely that the crowd swelled considerably at Winterings, with the Hunts, Sunters, Garths, and Thompsons. It is probable also that Anty and his sons would meet the rest near here on their journey from Dyke Heads. A good start in the early morning gloom permitted no stops for a mile or two up the moor until within sight of the levels the troopers might, with their knitting, "sit down for six rows." But no longer, for no one could afford to be late and run the risk of having his pay docked for the entire week.

From their middle years there was little play for children when they returned home at night for it was not until 1819 that the Act was passed prohibiting the exploitation of those between nine and sixteen beyond sixteen hours a day, and even then it

78

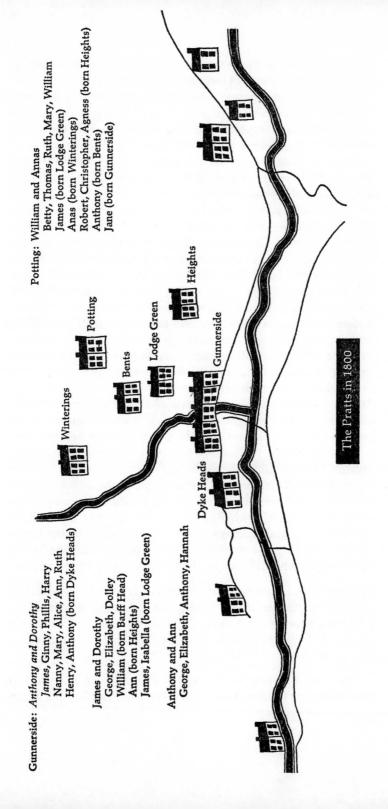

Gunnerside: *Anthony and Dorothy*
James, Ginny, Phillis, Harry
Nanny, Mary, Alice, Ann, Ruth
Henry, Anthony (born Dyke Heads)

James and Dorothy
George, Elizabeth, Dolley
William (born Barff Head)
Ann (born Heights)
James, Isabella (born Lodge Green)

Anthony and Ann
George, Elizabeth, Anthony, Hannah

Winterings

Potting

Bents

Lodge Green

Heights

Gunnerside

Dyke Heads

Potting: William and Annas
Betty, Thomas, Ruth, Mary, William
James (born Lodge Green)
Anas (born Winterings)
Robert, Christopher, Agness (born Heights)
Anthony (born Bents)
Jane (born Gunnerside)

The Pratts in 1800

was easy enough to evade the law. Nearly sightless from fatigue and lead, the small miners were not difficult to put to sleep.

Despite hardship there is every reason to believe the dalesmen loved their lives. There were good times to be had in those close-knit communities, especially if one possessed, as they nearly all did, a love of drama, music, and beauty, and that great saver of souls – a sense of humour. The miners were profoundly interested in their work, proud of their knowledge and skill, and deeply devoted to their valley.

The Sabbath was strictly kept in the true Hebraic manner. Self-denial was a virtue and good for the soul. No work was done on the Sabbath in Gunnerside, neither by man nor wife, son nor daughter, manservant nor maid-servant (of those who had them), ox nor ass nor horse. Hot dinners on Sunday were unknown. No dishes were washed, no cleaning done. No fruit was picked, no flowers. No nails were pared, even if a troublesome one were broken, nor hangnails trimmed. All tools had a rest. No walking was done for pleasure, and certainly no riding for any purpose. Even the Itinerant minister had to watch his step in Gunnerside for fear of rebuke from the local preacher.

The day was completely that of the Lord. As such it was a day for all of them when thoughts of the mine were put away and praises rang throughout the valley. It was spent at services and meetings, sometimes outside when the weather was fine, when the hills lost the tedious aspect of the morning walk and became the dispensers of comfort and wisdom. Then it was that the host of marchers turned their backs upon the mines and their faces toward the Swale and came down over the grassy slopes along the Gunnerside ghyll, past the grey cottages, through the pleasant roads and lodgings of Gunnerside and over the bridge to the Chapel by the sparkling ghyll or, in clement weather, to the riverside. The sight inspired a travelling preacher to write:

"The most flourishing parts of our field of labour are Swaledale and Arkingarthdale. If you were to see the crowds of miners who came pouring down the craggy hills to our places of worship, you would be led to inquire, 'Who are these that fly as a cloud, and as the doves to their windows?' "[5]

The year 1812 saw the first of the Pratts known to us to take an official part in Chapel life, when William Pratt became a class leader. It is not certain which William this is, but narrowing down the candidates the most likely one is Willie of Potting. The same year Gunnerside began collecting for missions, and even before the Methodist Missionary Society was organized in 1816, made its first contributions.[6]

About this time there developed two festivals, held on the winter and summer solstices, at the instigation, it seems, of the women. At quarterly or half-yearly intervals the miners received their pay which was handed out at the "Miners' Arms," a convenient place to spend it. Inevitably, the amount left as housekeeping money for the wives must have been sufficient to cause them to put down their brooms and weep. Accordingly, however, in true Yorkshire fashion they decided to handle the problem which they took to the minister declaring that if a celebration could be staged in the Chapel they, the wives, would put on a spread with which no "Miners' Arms" could compete. They were as good as their word and thus began the Shortest Day and Midsummer Festivals.[7]

On 6 July 1813 the first of Anty's sons, Jimmie, was married to Sally Bell, age sixteen. They were married at Grinton Church, by banns, and with the consent of their parents, by J. Edmondson, Vicar, and in the presence of Metcalfe Sunter and William Watters whose signatures appear, a little uncertainly, at the foot of the marriage certificate. As for James and Sally themselves, their marks are carefully drawn beside their names.

Sally was the daughter of John Bell of Broken Bank, a village near Feetham, named, one supposes, for John Brooksbank, an immensely wealthy and religious philanthropist of London whose death was greatly mourned in the dales. It is very difficult to determine who Sally's mother may have been. In 1864 a John Bell married Elizabeth Sunter, and John and Joseph stood up for them. Joseph Sunter was a pillar of the Methodist Society in Gunnerside. However, in 1793, a John Bell married a Sally Spence, and their marriage was witnessed by William Parkin of Feetham and Ottewell Robinson of Fremington, both places much nearer Broken Bank than is Gunnerside. This marriage would appear reasonable as Sally was born in 1796 and could have been named for her mother. There is only one other entry for John Bell of Broken Bank and that is for 2 December 1792 when Ann was baptised, daughter of Jonathan Bell, who might

81

just conceivably have been John. In this case the marriage is either later than it should have been or Sally Spence married a widower. In 1775 John Bell married Ann Roberts, which makes it logical that Ann may have been born to them, but there is no sign of Ann Bell dying. Until further evidence presents itself we shall have to assume that Sally Bell was the daughter of John Bell and Sally Spence.

Jim and Sally moved into the house at Barfside, and the following year Sally started the first of the childbearing that was to be her steady lot for nearly thirty years. The first child was a son, baptised on 31 October 1814, whom they named Anthony for his grandfather. On 13 October 1816 came John, named presumably for his grandfather Bell, as this is the first John to appear among our Pratts.

The years 1816 to 1820 saw a long depression and in 1818 there was a famine. On 5 February 1819 James and Sally buried their firstborn and their next son, born the same year, they named Anthony after him. On 6 February 1821 James was born and buried seventeen days later. The death dates for John and the second Anthony are lost, but die they did for later brothers were to be given their names.

In addition to the depression and famine there was painful quarrelling in the Methodist society and we are told that "the Chapel was almost forsaken."[8] William Buxton was "filled with deep sorrow . . . and gave himself to special prayer upon the matter. Night after night he repaired to the Chapel with his lantern, to pray without anyone to join him."[9] A few months later a great revival filled the Chapel again to overflowing.

In 1822 old James Pratt at seventy-seven was made a class leader, which post he was to fill for two years before he died on 18 April 1824. Also a class leader was his son James Doley, and in the Society Steward's Book of Accounts for 1824 James Sr. was paid 8.0 and James Doley 2.0 for their services. In 1826 James Doley became Chapel and Society Steward for the Methodists.

James had died on April 18, two weeks before his children, William and Annas, were to celebrate their Silver Wedding. A few days after this event, William, whose health was never robust, died himself, leaving Annas with her dozen children, the youngest of whom was four-month-old Jane. The eldest son,

James, was twenty-four, married to Hannah Coates, and was, presumably, there to help.[10] Betty at twenty was as yet unmarried. Tom had married Ann Calvert six months before his father's death and, living in Gunnerside, was no doubt a stalwart help. Anas had married Joseph Buxton two years earlier. This left Annas with Betty; Ruth, 15; Mary, 12; William, 10; Robert, 8; Christopher, 5; Anthony, 3; Agness, 1, and Jane. Fortunately for Annas, her father was a man of property and, miser though he was, he must have been some help. On one occasion when the rent was due and Annas was unable to pay it, she appealed to her father and was told he would require security. She had a cow and sent Christopher down to the pub with it, where it stayed until the debt to her father was duly paid.[11] Of such are the men of fortune. About 1827 the old man sold the pub and went to live in Bradford where he purchased some land on George Street upon which he had begun a building project. By 1830 the bank had failed, Thomas Metcalfe died of heart-break, and the job was completed by his son Leonard who persuaded Annas that a home would be prepared for her and her family in the city.[12] And so the journey was made, out of the dale. It took two days, crossing into Uredale, down the valley of the Dent, over the moors and out onto the plains into Bradford.[13]

The decade of the twenties was a hard one. The depression deepened with year after year of bad harvests and sheep rot and the epidemics, which are never absent for long but are angrier during depressions – tuberculosis and typhoid fever. It may have been during these years that James and Sally lost their sons John and Anthony.* In 1821-2 they moved back to Jimmie's parental home at Dyke Heads, and on 16 June 1822 their first daughter Dorothy was born there. On 27 September 1824 James was born and named for his dead brother and the great grandfather he had lost five months prior to his advent. On 30 November 1826 Metcalf was baptised and on 24 February 1828, William.

The depression continued; the price of lead plummeted; the numbers of unemployed increased. On 16 October 1830 Edward Broderick of Spring End wrote in his diary: "Now the mines are exhausted, the price of lead is low and miners are forced to

*Since Metcalf and William were named before the arrival of Anthony in 1835 and John in 1839, however, it seems more likely that these children died at a later age.

obtain a living in other countries which they cannot get here. The independence of spirit is gone." The year 1831 saw a nation-wide cholera epidemic that took more than three times as many lives at Lodge Green as usual. A general exodus that must have taken place under great agony of spirit commenced, as families, seeing nothing ahead but a black tunnel spiralling into the dark, packed their belongings and, with a few oatcakes to sustain them on their journey, left the beloved dale that had been home for so many generations. "Emigration was the theme of the con-versation," wrote Edward Broderick in his diary on 3 September 1830, at a meeting at the ghyll head by the high road, "all apparently are for going but few go." In ones and twos, however, families left for America, crossing the hated ocean never to return, some of them settling in Pennsylvania where there was mining and other employment around Pittsburgh. Among these was Henry Hunt, a great friend of James Pratt and perhaps a relative of the Thomas Hunt who married his sister Ruth. An-other was James, son of William and Annas, with his wife Hannah. In 1832, fired with the idea of "becoming his own boss" he left for Ohio.[14] Edward Broderick writes of how he helped the people move, getting up at two in the morning to help them pack their few possessions, so few they could carry them on their backs, and speeding them on their way over the Buttertubs Pass in the early hours of dawn. What we know of Edward Broderick, a comparatively wealthy man, endears him to us. In 1845, in order to relieve the unemployment, he had a bridge built over the Swale near Gunnerside, but Jimmie was not there to help in its building for he and Sarah had taken Dorothy, James, Metcalf, and William (we do not know whether John and Anthony were left behind in the graveyard or not) seventeen miles out of the valley to the bustling centre of Barnard Castle.

Out of the silence
part of a song
borne away on the wind.

Of the Barnard Castle days there is little trace. No baptismal records exist for any children of James and Sally in Gunnerside after 1828 or in Barnard Castle before 1835 when Anthony was born and baptised on 7 May. On 9 March 1837 their second daughter Sarah Ann was born and baptised three weeks later;

and on 2 September 1839 the birth of my grandfather John Pratt, 28 August, was registered in the District of Teesdale by the Registrar, George Middleton, informed by the infant's father James. He was born, according to the certificate, in, of all spots, the Market Place, leading us to believe that, barring an untoward accident, the family must at that time have been living right in town. James's occupation is now "labourer." Since there is no X beside his signature one is tempted to believe he had learned to write at least his name since his marriage, but the handwriting of the signature seems to be identical with that of George Middleton. It is all neatly entered, and one is a bit puzzled as to why the mark was overlooked.

In Barnard Castle was another family of Pratt, Matthew and Mary, whose children, Ann, John, and George, were roughly contemporaneous with those of James and Sally. Matthew was a "weaver," a term loosely applied to factory workers in the towns, and possibly derived from the use put to the coarse yarn that was sent from the dales to Barnard Castle to be woven into carpets.[15] There was not much love lost between the "tammy weavers" and the miners from the dales, and riots were frequent, particularly on Wednesdays when the farmers brought their produce to market. The general animosity is reflected even in the parish records at Grinton, as in one item on 9 February 1768 when Joh Hird of Harkerside was buried and identified as "lazy weaver."

The fortunes of James and Sally are not known in detail, but the going was certainly not smooth, for James seems to have tried his hand at a number of things. In 1835 when Anthony was born, he was listed as a miner; in 1837 as a quarryman, and in 1839 as a labourer. By 1841, at the time of the census, there is no sign of the family, either at Barnard Castle or at Gunnerside. Family tradition has it that they returned to Gunnerside in 1842, when the mines had improved somewhat, and indicating that life in Barnard Castle had not been all beer and skittles. Be that as it may, they were back in their beloved valley by April 1843 when Thomas, the last of their children, was born, across the Swale at Spring End, the homestead of the Broderick family since the sixteenth century, a large stately place surrounded by fine trees.

It is pleasant to think of their homecoming, in which Edward

Broderick no doubt played a considerable role. It is pleasant to imagine the family there to greet them in the valley, welcoming them back after an absence of a decade and a half. And what of the family that had remained in Gunnerside?

In their absence Jimmie's sister Phillis had been bringing up her two fatherless children, Hannah and Anty, born in 1820 and 1822. With whose help, if any, she did this we do not know, but Hannah was sixteen and Anty fourteen when Phillis married Thomas Kitchen in 1836. By 1841 Anty was a lead miner living with his mother and stepfather, and Hannah was working as a servant in the home of John Reynoldson. In 1843, the year Thomas was born at Spring End, Anty married Margaret Neesham who, born at Muker the same year as her bridegroom, was the daughter of Charles Neesham who had succeeded James Calvert as the blacksmith of Gunnerside.

Brother of the cousins who had left for Bradford with the widowed Annas after 1825, Thomas was still in Gunnerside and there also to welcome back the Barnard Castle contingent. In 1842 Thomas and Ann had a family of children roughly corresponding to those of James and Sally. That year Agness would be eighteen, William sixteen, Mary twelve, Nanny nine, John seven, Hannah five, Elizabeth two, with Jane to come in 1843 two months ahead of Thomas at Spring End, and Thomas in 1849.

Annas's daughter Ruth, who was fifteen when the family moved from Gunnerside, went into service in Bradford, and there became the quarry, willing or not, in one of the favourite pastimes of an employer household. In 1833 she was invited to Gunnerside (to her brother Tom's?) to have her son William. There she stayed, and in 1837 married her second cousin George, the son of Anthony and Ann, grandson of Anthony of Winterings and Phillis who at ninety was still living alone at Gunnerside, although she was to be buried at the end of that year on Christmas Day.

The following year Anthony was born to George and Ruth: in 1841, Agnes, who lived but a month; in 1842, James; and in 1844, Mary Ann, who lived into her fourth year and was buried in June 1848, one month to the day after her father was laid to rest. Poor Ruth, full of grief, and with three children to bring up alone, took up millinery, in order to eke out their living. William by this time was fourteen and working in the mines, and quite possibly at eight little Anthony may have had to go too. By 1851, in any case, at seventeen and eleven, both boys were in the mines, and their mother with their help was managing to keep James, at eight, still at school. It is with a sense of relief that one finds on 20 January 1852 Ruth married to Anthony Milner, the originator of the Sunday School at Gunnerside. They had one son, Ralph, before Anthony was drowned while attempting to cross the Swale on horseback.

Uncle James Doley, living up the hill at Modesty, had died in 1839, outliving his son George by two years, and Dorothy his widow was living there with her oldest son William. Elizabeth had married John Watters in 1833 and Isabella, James Lowes in 1840. And James, son of Doley, was living alone in Gunnerside.

On the Bradford family, fortune, with the help of courage and hard work, had begun to smile. Bradford in the thirties was a rapidly growing city of 43,000. Jobs were to be had for those with a few connections, and the Metcalfes were now in a position to provide these. With some assistance from Annas's brother Leonard, employment was found for the older boys, William* and Robert, helping their uncle who was master mason in the construction of a building on North Parade. The younger boys, Christopher and Anthony,* were to continue the schooling begun in Gunnerside,[16] whatever that may have been (see below, p. 92).

Two or three years after Annas had moved to Bradford a small incident occurred that demonstrated the measure of Yorkshire common sense applied to good luck that is the key to success in the business world, and that would seem to have sprung more from the Metcalfes than from the less worldly Pratts. It was when Christopher was about eight and standing with his mother by the curb of a Bradford street. An object glittering in the gutter caught his eye and he stooped down to pick it up. The movement was noticed by a tough character passing by who accosted the little boy and demanded the coin which he said he had dropped from his pocket and which was rightfully his.

"What did you lose, my young lad?" asked Annas, without a moment's loss, "was it a half-sovereign?"

"Yes," the youth replied.

---

*In "Christopher Pratt & Sons" the working brothers are referred to as Anthony and Robert. In the records, however, Anthony was born after Christopher, and it seems likelier that William would have gone to work.

"Well," said she, "this isn't yours." The coin was a sovereign. Christopher, whose chore back home had been to carry lunch to the men working at Old Gang, was chosen for the same task in Bradford. Each day he would bring a basket of tasty food from his mother to his uncle and brothers as they sat among the scaffolding in their noon hour, discussing the virtues and faults of beams and buttresses.[17] His manner and vitality caught the attention of the owner of the enterprise, Joseph Nutter, who offered him a paid job as errand boy.[18] This was the first step taken by young Christopher toward the ownership of a furniture business that in 1940 celebrated its centenary.

Not only did Leonard Metcalfe introduce the Pratt boys to employment suitable for ambitious young men, but he invited them also to worship with him at Eastbrook Methodist Chapel. Nearby sat a family called Cheesborough in which there were a number of brothers, sons of William Cheesborough of Snape in Bedale, who had come to Bradford to work. In 1835, there came from Snape to keep house for them, their little sister Jane, then fourteen. Accompanying them to church one Sunday, she was noticed by a pair of eyes from the next pew that belonged to a tall, handsome youth of sixteen. At some later point Christopher and Jane began walking out together and one morning in the spring of 1842 in the village of Snape they were married.

No doubt there were comments. Although Christopher at twenty-three was a promising young man, he had little education and less money, and Jane had what would have been described in the dales as fantastic wealth. Hers in the bank was the tidy sum of, according to some accounts, forty pounds,[19] according to others, two hundred pounds.[20] Furthermore she had had a "proper schooling."[21] Nevertheless, the comments, if there were any, were forgotten by 1845 when Christopher, having served his apprenticeship under Joseph Nutter, started his own cabinet-making business. In 1850 Mr. Nutter retired, and Christopher, in partnership with Thomas Prince, inherited the firm which became Pratt and Prince on North Parade.[22]

In Swaledale the decade of the forties must have had its ups and downs. The bridge begun in 1835 by Edward Broderick for the relief of unemployment could not be completed, for lack of funds, until 1842 when the mines had begun a partial recovery, bringing back a few of the emigrants, including James and Sally, who had not gone too far away. The recovery proved to be but a friar's lantern and many of those who had returned home began to leave again. The alternative to mining was farming, and land, the few acres of it available, was running out. The Pratts, however, were among those who stayed.

Strong were the friendships formed in the valley. Among those in Gunnerside, a particularly close relationship developed between the families of James and Sally and that of William Coates. Strong, Non-Conformist, and colourful, William Coates became something of a legend in the dale. In 1844 he was appointed Chapel Steward and filled the position with a competence and flair matched by his ability as farmer, undertaker, and carpenter. He acted as decision-maker for the village even when he had to be carried from a sickbed to arbitrate at a meeting.[23] In 1848 he succeeded Jonathan Daykin as local preacher, and on Sundays, unwilling to permit his horse to work, he walked up and down the valley on his preaching missions.[24]

It was William's son James Calvert who became the very dear and lifelong friend of John Pratt, who named his youngest son Calvert Coates after him. The name has survived in the Pratt family in Newfoundland, who bear it with pride to this day.

When a local preacher died he was buried by the Itinerant who was brought to Gunnerside at a fee for the purpose. Otherwise the local preacher himself buried the deceased to the tune of the Swaledale Dirge which was sung at every funeral. This tradition, it is thought, dates from antiquity, traced to a tune sung by the monks and used in the Middle Ages as the funeral procession swung along the Corpse Way. It was important that the singing should be kept up, as, so the ancients believed, the soul might be escorted to heaven without hindrance from the devil. William Coates, who had an ear for music, once heard the dirge being sung off-key from his sickbed and was so irritated by it that he hoisted himself out of bed and over to the window where he bellowed, as loudly as he could, the correct version to the mourners below.[25]

The cousins on the Bell side have been lost to view. That they lived nearby is attested to in a brief entry in Mrs. McFarlane's diary for Tuesday, 26 May 1925:

"A Mrs. Bell was organist. I asked her if she knew Mr. James Bell, my father's cousin. They asked me to go with them, as my hostess was busy. We found him getting his cocoa ready, but he never touched it till after I left. It was a happy hour that we spent as he revelled in going back to the days of his childhood when Dad, Uncle John, & he were boys. Also of Ruth Neesome,* Dad's first sweetheart, & of Rev. Ralph Milner† and others."

On 19 May Mrs. McFarlane had visited Miss Holmes and her father, "a sturdy old Christian of 87. He remembered Dad & Uncle John well & told us the text Uncle John preached from."

By 1848 the James Pratts had moved to Calvert Houses up on the old Corpse Road. That same year Jimmie's son William, age 20, was married to Mary, 19, daughter of George Calvert. In 1850, Sarah Ann was born to these two and in 1851, Isabella.

Life was not becoming easier for this family. James must often have wished he had taken the irrevocable step and accompanied his friends to the New World from which there was no returning. Only it cost money, and required health, both of which were in short supply. His friend Henry Hunt had gone to Pennsylvania, and James had his address near Johnstown. He thought of the life ahead for his children** – Sar'an, John and the baby Thomas now five – and despaired. Going to whoever it was who served as scribe in the village, he asked if he might dictate a letter to Henry. When it had been committed to the post, he settled himself to wait for a reply. Finally, it came, in the neat copperplate hand of the scribe:

To James Pratt
Near Johnstone, Feb 3rd 1849
Dear Friend

I was at Johnstown yesterday & got your letter & was glad to hear from you & that your family were all well; likewise that you were still striving in the good old way for if we all be Faithful we shall soon all meet where there will be no afflictions & partings. We are glad that you intend to come to America in the spring for we think you will do better in this country with your family than you are doing there. If you can raise the

*Another of the bevy of Neesham girls who belonged to Charles the Cobbler.
†This was probably their second cousin, son of Ruth Pratt (see page 87).
**In the 1851 census, there is no sign of Anthony. At this time, however, he would have been but thirteen and probably at home with his parents.

means to get to Philadelphia we can assist you from there to our home. We would recommend some of your friends to make a collection in the society to assist you to get over. You can sail from Liverpool to Philadelphia or New Yourk [sic], the cost is about the same each way, only by New York is 3 or 4 days sooner. But if any of your friends can give you recommendations to any of their friends at Liverpool it will be of great benefit to you. W. Spensly of Reeth recommended us to one Anthony Barnes who treated us like a father but we do not know whether he is living or not. The fare across the ocean is from £3 to £4.10 each person, children half price. We have not heard of Metcalf Bell this 8 or 10 years, as for Galana* we do not know much about it, only it is a great lead mining place. We do not know the exact distance, but we suppose it is between 2 and three thousand miles from here. You can go from here to Pittsburg & then down the Ohio River up which you can go to Galana, but whether it is the best way or not we do not know. We would like to see you come this way. You could get work here, they are making a new Railroad from Harrisburg to Holidas-burg. This distance is 100 miles. From Holidasburg to Johnstown is 36 miles by Railroad. We live 6 miles from Johnstown. We are well known to many as we go every week to market. When you get there inquire for Jonathan Bowing. He is a pious local preacher & he will give you directions. It is generally the best time to come early in the spring, for they open the canals in March. You must write from Liverpool & let us know when you sail & what ship & where you land & whether we must send you money to Philadelphia or engage your Passages. . . . We farm our own we have 134 acres altogether. Between 30 & 40 acres are cleared. We have 2 horses, 6 cows, 9 head of young cattle, 50 sheep & 4 hogs.
Your affectionate & loving friends
Henry & Elizabeth Hunt
Direct as below
Mr. Henry Hunt, near Johnstown, Gar[side] County, Pensilvania, Nth America

    In a rougher hand we can assume to be Henry's own are further urgent messages:

*His first cousin James was there founding the town of Dubuque.

"Please give our love to our Brother Joseph Hunt and tel him if
he intend to come to america he ought to come the sooner
the Bether for Land is sil getin dearer so it will take more money
to buy a farm   please give our love to Johnathan Daykin*
and family and all our friends you met with before you come
over. O had you come along with us you [wouldn't be sick].†
We often thought of you And taked about you and wondered
how you were coming on but when we heard from you we felt
deply For you but I hope the good Lord will open out your
way to this good country. . . ."[26]

Why James and his family did not pack up and leave is anyone's guess, but the good Lord had evidently not opened the way
for them. That they could not raise the enormous figure of some
fourteen pounds was now no obstacle, and the prospect of warm
friends to greet them would have greatly helped relieve the pain
of leaving friends and home. That he was in desperate straits
is evident. Perhaps his failing health had taken a sharp down-
ward turn. In any case, James Pratt stayed with the dying mines.

In 1850 a great Methodist revival heralded yet another wave of
prosperity that was to last, as a faltering swan song, for thirty
years. During this period wages reached an all-time high of 19
shillings per week, but this was not till later on. At the time of
the 1851 census the Pratts had left Calvert Houses and were
living on Mount Pleasant in the hamlet of Lodge Green, in the
row of houses in which Deborah Waggett had had the first chapel
meetings. With them were their three youngest: Sar'an, John,
Thomas. Both boys, eleven and eight, are listed as lead miners.

Up until 1854 education in Gunnerside was in the hands of the
Sunday school, and in those of Mary Storey who, a widow living in Lodge Green, ran a dames school. There was, also, a school
at Muker, endowed in 1678 by Anthony Metcalfe, and during
the nineteenth century it was taught by the vicar every day from
eight-thirty to five, Saturdays included. One wonders when the
poor vicar planned his Sunday activities, not to mention any
weekly commitments. Also, at Muker during the 40s and 50s a
very good school was run by the Methodists. As well as this, in

*The local preacher in Gunnerside.
†An informed guess. It is impossible to make the writing out here.

92

the 1830s up on the slopes of Kisdon charity schools were held for girls and boys and a cobbler gave evening classes in the warmth of his kitchen where miners at the end of the day would grapple with the rudiments of an elementary education.[27]

How James and Sally's children acquired their education is a mystery. We know that the two youngest boys were mining at the ages of eight and eleven. Up until this time they probably attended Mary Storey's dames school. Whatever the groundwork of their education may have been, they were both well-educated, literate men.

In 1854 a dwelling was bought in Lodge Green, part of which was to be a schoolhouse. The Wesleyan Education Committee contributed twenty-five pounds and the school opened in 1855 with 103 children who paid 2d a week. Too late for any of the Pratts.

That same year, Sar'an was seventeen, and had grown into a tall, dark, vivacious, and strong-willed young woman. Like many of the girls in that area, in those times, she was destined to bear her first child out of wedlock. On December 21, Moses came into the world, and was received, if not with joy at first, at least with love. It is long ago, and now the details of Moses' early years have dropped away. It is probable Sar'an cared for him at home, with the help of her mother who, it can't be denied, was used to child-rearing. Then when he was two and a half, Sar'an married Anthony Alderson. Moses stayed with his grandparents, although his ties with his mother remained close. The year after he was born William and Mary had their next child, James, and in 1856, Dorothy.

Mining accidents continued to be numerous, and those who escaped accident only lived to contract silicosis and consumption from the lead in the mines. "Miner's complent" it was called. Men fought for breath, and the descendants of Willie Alderson remember seeing him on his hands and knees, wracked with coughing, as he crawled home up the hill to Modesty.[28] In 1857 Jimmie fell victim and suffered for eight months as his respiration became more and more difficult until on 13 July 1858 he died in Gunnerside, with his son John, aged 18, attending him. Two weeks before his death another granddaughter, Elizabeth, had been born to William and Mary.

Not Thrones and Crowns

"One evening last week I stood by the seashore when the storm
was raging. The voice of the Lord was upon the water; and
who was I that I should tarry within doors, when my Master's
voice was heard sounding along the waters? I rose and stood
to behold the flash of his lightnings, and listen to the glory of his
thunders. The sea and the thunders were contesting with
one another; the sea with infinite clamor striving to hush the
deep-throated thunder, so that his voice should not be heard;
yet over and above the roar of the billows might be heard that
voice of God, as he spoke with flames of fire, and divided the
way for the waters. It was a dark night, and the sky was covered
with thick clouds, and scarce a star could be seen through
the rifts of the tempest: but at one particular time, I noticed far
away on the horizon, as if miles across the water, a bright
shining, like gold. It was the moon hidden behind the clouds, so
that she could not shine upon us; but she was able to send
her rays down upon the waters, far away, where no clouds
happened to intervene."
C. H. Spurgeon, Sermons

In 1861 there were in Gunnerside James Pratt's aunt Dorothy,
widow of James Doley, who lived with her son William; his
nephew and niece, Anthony and Margaret, with their daughters
Hannah, Margaret and Phillis; his cousins Thomas and Ann with
their children and Thomas's son John, who had married Mary
Sunter in 1859 and whose first child Thomas was one year old;
his cousin Ruth, now married to Anthony Milner; and Anthony
the son of Ruth and George, who was married to Tamar Neesham
and living with his cousin Anthony and Tamar's sister Margaret
at Modesty.

But there was no Sarah, John, Thomas, or Moses, and no
William and Mary. Word had come that the mines of Wharfedale
were experiencing a relative boom and sometime between 1858
and 1861 the two little families made the decision to leave Gunnerside, and head south: a woman in her sixties, with her son

and daughter-in-law with their four children all under ten; her younger teenage sons and her grandchild, a tot of three or four. Over Crackpot and Satron Moors they went, through Askrigg and over the highlands that separate Wensleydale from the valley of the Wharfe and the gentle, saucer-shaped country past Starbotton and into the beautiful village of Kettlewell. There they were when the census was taken in 1861. William and Mary had set up house near West Seale Park and their children were all in school except the youngest, Dorothy, who was only four. Nearby, beside the Blue Bell Inn, lived Sarah, 63, head of her family of three boys: John, 20, and Thomas, 18, lead miners, and Moses, 6, a scholar.

It was a great time for Methodism in the dales. Among the Methodist ministers there in the early sixties was the grandfather of Rudyard Kipling, who preached at Skipton, whose father before him had preached at Lythe near Whitby. It will be remembered that there were families of Kipling in Swaledale in the far-off days of seventeenth-century Grinton. As Kettlewell is part of Skipton district it is highly probable that the Pratts were acquainted with Mr. Kipling. Like the relationship with Charlotte Brontë, however, that with the Kiplings will remain a guessing game forever.

The democratic influences of Methodism were nowhere better revealed than in the restless, and what might have been termed in our time "angry," verse of Ebenezer Elliott. In Methodist churches today the hymn he wrote, importuning a deaf heaven on behalf of the victims of the nineteenth century, is still sung, but probably with a great deal less of the fervour and urgency with which the words were uttered then:

When wilt thou save the people?
O God of mercy, when?
The people, Lord, the people,
Not thrones and crowns, but men.

There existed in Wharfedale an academy run by Joseph Lawrence, a wealthy man who had the interests of the faith at heart. Lawrence must have seen the great reserves of zeal and intelligence among the poor of Yorkshire and longed to harness it into the service of the Methodist church. In his academy, which was probably heavily subsidized, he set out to train young men for the cost of the time they could spare from their work, and it was his task to recruit from the college probationers for Newfoundland and Nova Scotia. Along with the mining boom in the area, Lawrence's academy may have been a contributing factor in the decision of the Pratts to emigrate to Kettlewell. For among the young men of the mining community who had seen a bright shining in the distance were William, John, and Thomas Pratt. After their long days in the lead mines they would gather around the table in the evenings in the peace of their Kettlewell cottage by the Blue Bell Inn while the evening light of the green valley grew dim around them, and then by lamplight they would spend the night hours, sometimes until dawn, studying, discussing, and pondering the words of the Bible.

All the places where my grandfather preached in England I do not know. Certainly he preached at Gunnerside. And during these exhilarating sixties he must have met many who worked in the Methodist vineyard. One of his friends, we know, was Charles Spurgeon the evangelist, whose congregation was the Metropolitan Church in London, for on his visit to England in the early 1890s Spurgeon invited him to preach there and introduced him as his great friend from Newfoundland. He also preached at London's City Temple, and my father spoke many times of it, and the sound of his voice as he told of it created a glow that shone around my vision of the temple like the light emanating from the tabernacles raised by the people of Israel in the wilderness of Sinai.

For the next few years John Pratt worked and preached, and along with William and Thomas took care of his mother and of Moses whom they loved deeply. In 1866 Thomas's eye caught sight of a woman, six years his senior and with a small daughter, coming out of church in Eston. He had, said his granddaughter, Mrs. Ball, never seen anything so beautiful. She was Mrs. Stoddard and, as luck would have it, a widow and he made haste to acquire her and her child Maria. They seem to have moved away, for his three daughters were born in the Midlands. It is possible that Thomas may have attended the academy, but his marriage made it necessary for him to continue to work in the mines, and it is unlikely he had time for much lay preaching. As soon as Moses was old enough to leave school he also went into the mines. By 2 April 1871 John and Moses had left Kettlewell, probably for Burnley, where Moses continued to work in the coal mines and John became a preacher on the Rochdale-Burnley circuit. Their mother Sarah had moved into the house of William and Mary, whose two oldest daughters, Sarah Ann* and Bella, had by this time moved away. James at sixteen is listed in the census returns as a lead miner. Dorothy at fourteen, a "miner's daughter," had left school and was helping her mother at home. Elizabeth does not appear in the census at all, and, as she would have been but eleven and probably living at home, one can only suppose that she had died. Mary Jane, born in 1863 after the move to Kettlewell, was the youngest of the family and still in school. Sarah, the widowed mother, listed as an annuitant, may have been receiving a small pension. Within the next two or three years this family, too, had made the move out of the sweet air of Wharfedale into the dirty, noxious smoke of the industrial town of Burnley.

It was not in the stars of John Pratt, however, that he should live out his days in Burnley, nor in those of Thomas that he should stay in the Midlands. The last quarter of the nineteenth century saw an unprecedented change.

At home in Gunnerside there still lived the families of Thomas and Ann. Their nine children were all married, and, as the mines were playing out, making the transition to farm life. Thomas was on the committee for the new Gunnerside Chapel built in 1867. Ann died the following year after all but one of her children had married, and was followed by Thomas in 1875. Agnes, their first child, born in 1824, married George Buxton in 1841; William, born in 1826, married Martha Neesham, daughter of Charles, the shoemaker in Gunnerside, in 1861. After five years of marriage William died, and Martha married John Harker, who also had a store in Gunnerside. Mary, born in 1830, married John Buxton in 1847; and Ann, born in 1833, married John Mathers in 1850. Jane, born in 1843, married George Milner in 1867; and Hannah, born in 1837, married Thomas Urwin in 1867, the year the Chapel was built. Until that time Hannah had been a servant in the household of George Calvert.

Thomas's fourth son was John, born in 1835, four years before his cousin John who was to go to Newfoundland four decades

*That Bella is remembered by the grandchildren and Sarah Ann is not would indicate that the latter may not have lived for very long.

later. In 1859 John married Mary Sunter of the Sunter family who were butchers in Gunnerside at that time. Elizabeth married Thomas Waggett in 1859; and Thomas, Jane Raw in 1877.

Anthony and James, too, the two sons of George and Ruth Pratt, continued to live in Gunnerside. Anthony, who was also on the committee for the new Chapel, had married Tamar Neesham in 1858 and was living at Modesty. James, after his mother married Anthony Milner, went to live with his Uncle Thomas and Aunt Ann until his marriage in 1866 to Ann Rutter. In 1875 the two brothers had a shop in Gunnerside near the Methodist school that burned down in 1963, on the left side of the road as one approaches the village from the east.

It is difficult to know of the fortunes of Ruth after she married Anthony Milner. We do not know the date that he was drowned in the Swale, nor whether Ruth outlived him. Their son Ralph moved to Reeth where he became wealthy in due course and presented a large piece of ground for the enlargement of the Methodist cemetery in Gunnerside, but whether Ruth lived to see this is not known. Joseph and Ann Buxton and William and Ruth Pratt seem to have remained in Gunnerside.

Robert had gone early to Bradford and was in the construction business with his mother's people, the Metcalfes. Christopher's business, under the name of Pratt and Prince, was flourishing, and his sons William, Benjamin, Thomas, and Job, as they became old enough, entered into partnership. In 1860, with the death of Thomas Prince, the firm of Pratt and Prince became Christopher Pratt & Sons.

The winds of change indicated at once a withering away of family solidarity and an explosion into new areas of life, catapulted by economic need and lubricated by Methodism. In 1873 John was to exchange the Burnley circuit for a wider pastorate, and Gunnerside, Kettlewell, and Starbotton in the beautiful and familiar Yorkshire dales for Western Bay, Bonavista, Cupids, Fortune, and Grand Bank at the far end of the inhospitable sea. In 1878 Thomas was to leave dark-heathered Cleveland, Normanby, Eston, and Shildon and England's smoke-filled chimneys to lengthen his life among New Zealand's mountains with deep draughts of air constantly washed by the clean winds of the South Pacific and of the Tasman Sea. Here he would eventually take a Baptist charge. James, son of William and Annas, had al-

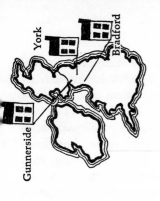

Gunnerside, York, Bradford

Gunnerside: Thomas and Ann
George and Ruth

Bradford: Christopher and Jane

York: James and Sarah (temporarily)

Iowa: James and Hannah

Iowa
Dubuque

The Pratts in 1840

ready gone to America where he founded the town of Dubuque, Iowa, and established Methodism there. By 1867 his sister Mrs. Eliza Bradbury, and his two nephews, Adam and William Thwaites, were also in the United States. And Metcalf Pratt was there, and perhaps James and Anthony. In 1852 two simple entries appear on the passenger list of the "City of Glasgow" from England into the port of Philadelphia: "A. Pratt, travelling with James Pratt." Benjamin, second son of Christopher, had no sooner become established with the family firm than he too heard the call of the gospel and took off for Hyderabad where he became a famous and much-loved missionary. Newfoundland, New Zealand, America, India in one decade were among the targets of the centrifugal forces that had been unleashed by the developments of the nineteenth century.

The Tea Fortune

Among the lore of most families there is buried treasure of some kind – lost, stolen, or purely in the imagination. That is where we might expect the Pratt treasure to be. And surely it might as well have been there for all the Pratts saw of it.

In the 1840s and 50s an old tea merchant called, so some remember, "Old Warland," used to trudge up and down the dales selling tea to the dalesfolk. Tea, which had been introduced into England in the middle of the seventeenth century, was at first very expensive and for a hundred years or so drunk chiefly by the rich. It came very late into the dales, and was still an unfamiliar drink when John Wesley used to visit Low Row in the 1760s and 70s and the Pratt brothers lived at Feetham.

One of the early tea stories was told of John Wesley on one of these visits. Among the neighbours of the Pratts and Spensleys at Blades was John Wiseman. John had a sister in London who was acquainted with Wesley and was eager to have him meet her brother and preach to the neighbours. As a treat she sent up with him a packet of that rare commodity, tea, which he asked his hostess to have prepared for him. The good lady was nonplussed but took the packet to the kitchen and returned sometime later with a dish of boiled leaves, having pitched away the useless liquid in which they had been brewed.[1]

By the middle of the nineteenth century, when Jimmie Pratt of Gunnerside was host to the tea man, the drink was more common, but still expensive enough. The first I heard of the fortune was in a letter from Ada Ball in New Zealand which I received while in England in 1967. The letter reads in part:

"Did you ever hear of the ¼ million in Chancery, left to the Pratts by an old tea merchant who used to peddle the tea from door to door, at the rate of £1 for 1 lb? I guess it would be 'ounces.' Anyway some relation sent a newspaper clipping to Grandad Pratt when we lived in Seddonville on the west coast, 50 years ago, and they said they had kept it for a year or two before sending it on. I believe it was advertising for Thomas Pratt, son of James Pratt of Yorkshire (I could not give further particulars now, not even the tea merchant's name) or any relatives. Aunt Lib & Aunt Ruth searched countless papers in London in 1909, spent hours and days, I believe, also at Somerset House and never found a trace. I do not know where the clipping has gone to."

In a letter to her daughters while they were on that trip in England, dated June 6 of that year, Sarah Pratt wrote from New Zealand: "We have had no word about the big money yet. They have had plenty of time to answer." Once in chancery always in chancery, but one wonders if the relative who delayed a year or two before sending on the clipping was a lawyer there himself.

The tea fortune provided excellent conversation. Sympathy lay, not only with James and Sally and their children, although if anybody could have used it they could, but also with "Old Warland" who had undoubtedly been befriended by the Pratts and thought he would be doing something nice for them in return by leaving them a quarter of a million pounds.*

"Oh, yes," said Laura Legge, "that was the estate my great uncle was murdered over – the one whose butler did him in."

*Other sources have placed the figure at a half a million pounds.

"There was a murder over the fortune," I said to Jean Milner.
"That doesn't sound like the family at all," she answered.
"He was murdered," I said, "not the murderer."
"The Pratts don't get murdered," said she.

Laura said she'd look up the case. But in the meantime the name of it, which she thought she had, had disappeared and has never turned up.

The search for clues that might solve the mystery of the tea fortune led me further into an acquaintance with the family who seemed convinced that the two fortunes were the same.

In 1968 I called on a descendant of the family and we spent an interesting and pleasant weekend investigating our pasts, which seemed not to be so common after all but diverged more and more widely as we worked backwards. The home was that of John and Amy Hatton, whose mother Mrs. Fallon lived with them. Mrs. Fallon is the daughter of Albert Pratt, brother of James Edward, the grandfather of Laura Legge. Albert and James Edward were sons of James Pratt, son of "Gentleman John" whose father was Colonel Pratt of Banbury. The sobriquet "Gentleman John" is important as it may provide one tenuous link that might possibly connect the families.

"My father never talked," said Mrs. Fallon. "There had been some hard feeling, and he wanted nothing of the estate. 'There is my fortune,' he would say, slapping his pocket vigorously, 'and very coppery it is.' Another of his favourite sayings was 'Three generations up, three generations down!' and by that he meant that the palmy days were over for the Pratts." They had reached their apex with Gentleman John who loved to ride around the estate distributing coins to all and sundry, a quality strong in the Pratts as I know them. If this family came out of Swaledale, however, it must have been not later than the 1780s, if it was Colonel Pratt who was the one to leave, and earlier if it was not. Much depends on the first name of Colonel Pratt, and this nobody seems to know.

All of which is a far cry from the tea merchant, whose good deed turned to dust and ashes in the iniquitous and mercifully obsolete legal system known as "chancery."

On my visit to New Zealand in 1969, however, I found among the papers loaned me to read a letter concerning the fortune which yielded some treasure of another kind. It was written by one James Heslop to his Uncle Thomas on 13 July 1908, and read:

Dear Uncle Thomas:

I write a few lines to you to see if you could give me information concerning an old friend of Grandfather's whose name was Warland. He used to travel round Swaledale with tea, I think, when you were a little boy. Do you remember him? When I was living at Grandfather's he called when I was ill in bed. He used to pay visits to Grandfather about sixty or seventy years ago. He had no relatives and was very wealthy. I saw his name in Lloyd's paper about ten years ago. He must have gone to London for he died there leaving a fortune to James Pratt of half a million sterling.

The news was in Lloyd's paper about ten years ago, which I saw in the paper concerning Legacy left to James Pratt formally deceased.

Warland died in the place called Battersea, St. George Road, London.

The money was left in Chancery Office, London.

Warland was known by the older members of the family, by Uncle James, Elizabeth, my mother, and Uncle William.

Can you give me any light on this subject or can you remember anything about him, or do you know if he was a native of Reeth? Do you remember him being in that part of the country?

James Heslop

This letter seems to have been copied from the original, for in the same hand follows this note:

"This James Heslop is Grandson of James Pratt and nephew of Thomas Pratt of Seddonville who is the only surviving son of James Pratt.

"There being a large family & James Heslop descending from the older end of the family, making him the same age as his Uncle Thomas Pratt, he being the youngest son."

From this letter several points of interest were gleaned.

First, James Heslop must have been very much a part of the family when the younger Pratt boys were growing up, staying there to be looked after by his Grandma while he was ill. He was there sometime during the 1840s and 50s and must have been, not only the nephew of John and Thomas Pratt but their play-mate of the same age as well.

Second, in order to have been a grandson of James Pratt, James Heslop must have been the son of one of James Pratt's daughters. Since only two daughters are recorded and since Sar'an's family have all been accounted for, he must be the son of Dorothy for whom no information but her christening is on record. This would indicate that a Mr. Heslop had put in an appearance, probably at Barnard Castle, and that Dorothy and he had been married.

Third, "Warland was known by the older members of the family, by Uncle James, Elizabeth, my mother & Uncle William." Uncle James will have been the son born in 1824, Uncle William that in 1828. "My mother" in all probability refers to Dorothy. But "Elizabeth," pure and simple? It was not in the way of this generation to refer to their aunts and uncles without their titles, yet who could she have been? It is logical to suppose that, as one of the "older members of the family," she was sister of James, Dorothy, and William. And it will be remembered that Mrs. McFarlane, cousin to James Heslop, in her entry on Mrs. Whit-field refers to "Aunts Sarah Ann and Bessie."* Moreover, lurk-ing in the hollows of my memory is a thirteenth child. Between 1828 and 1935 there is a large hiatus and it is more than likely a child may have been born during that time and named Eliza-beth after her grandmother.

As one continues a search, fitting clue to clue, some mysteries are cleared up but following hard upon them new mysteries emerge. After the revelation in New Zealand I turned again to Somerset House for a possible marriage between Dorothy Pratt and a Mr. Heslop around 1840 in which year Dorothy would have been eighteen. A search was made and a reply came. A marriage had taken place, it said, on 20 May 1840 between Wil-liam *Bellis*, full age, bachelor, a dealer in China, his father Ed-ward Bellis, a paper maker, and Dorothy Pratt, full age (barely!) whose father was listed as James Pratt (rising excitement), a *tea dealer*. To mystify things even further the marriage took place in the town of *York*. I wrote back asking for a further search. The name of Bellis has a place in the family (see page

*See page 64.

134), but these facts were just too eccentric to fit the case. The family were in Barnard Castle, not York; James was a miner, not a dealer in tea; and James Heslop had referred to Elizabeth and his mother (Dorothy), not Dorothy and his mother (Elizabeth). His mother could be none other than Dorothy, unless by chance there may have been yet another daughter. Dorothy might have been married twice but if James Heslop was the same age as Thomas Pratt (born 1843) it must have been a very hasty second marriage and not a likely one.

Then one night in the wee small hours the flotsam of the past began to drift into a tenuous but recognizable pattern. It will be remembered that the 1841 census returns showed no sign of the family in either Barnard Castle or Gunnerside. They may have missed the census but they may not have, especially if for some reason they had gone to the town of York. And what business may they have had in York? Tea? Old Warland was a tea merchant and evidently a close friend of James Pratt. Times were bad and James had varied his occupation with each child that had been born in Barnard Castle (see page 85). What more probable than that his friend should have persuaded him to try the lucrative tea trade? It began to seem more than possible that old James, setting a precedent for his grandson, Edwin John, should go with high hopes into business – and fail dismally.

Microfilms of the York Census for 1841 did not reveal the family but since many pages had not reproduced, I felt that nothing had been proved. I wrote in haste and excitement to Cousin Sallie in New Zealand who had said she'd make it her last business to find out where in the Pratt family her stepmother Elizabeth Ann Bellis fitted in. She replied: "You have found it at last. It was Dorothy Pratt who would have been her grandmother!"

The move to York makes it quite probable that Elizabeth Pratt may have been born there in 1840 or 1841 rather than in the earlier hiatus between Gunnerside and Barnard Castle.* But the mystery remains of the identity of James Heslop. And a further confusion of names was to occur as my search continued. Mrs. Colechin supplied me with the address of her stepmother's sister, the only surviving Bellis. Although she was by that time in a nursing home and unable to write or remember anything, I had

*The case against this is found in James Heslop's letter in which he refers to Elizabeth as being one of the older members of the family.

her age and was able to secure her birth certificate and learned that she was the daughter of Edwin Bellis and Ellen Gill, of Batley, near Birstal. Census returns of Birstal had the family recorded: William Bellis, *Mary* Bellis (birthplace Swaledale), and Edwin Bellis. Here was another circular argument. Since Mary Bellis was the only inhabitant of Birstal to have come from Swaledale, it looks as though she may have been of the Pratt household. Might Dorothy have changed her name? She might have died and been succeeded by Mary, but then where would the Heslops fit in? All explanations are unlikely, but it looks as though the unlikeliest may have been true: that there had been a divorce in the Victorian household of Swaledale Pratts.

A Parcel of Wild People

Of the many branches on our family tree there are only a few that I have been able to bring to the living present. Except for the descendants of James and Sally, and of Christopher and Jane, they are families confined to the area around the dales, for I have not been successful in finding many of the emigrants.

The Greek and Latin Teacher of Michigan
It will be seen on Chart C that the families of Anthony's sons William and Thomas are not extended beyond the second or third generations. From Anthony and Phillis issues a line which, crossing with that of William and Annas, reaches down to the present. As mentioned earlier Anthony and James, who were the sons of George and Ruth, had a shop in Gunnerside. Of Anthony's five surviving children there are no records of marriages or of children. It is possible that they all left the dale. Mrs. Batty quotes a letter from one John Bell of an old form mate of the 1860s at Gunnerside School. Mr. Bell's recollections concerned "Anthony Pratt who lived in Cardy Garth near the school. 'The family

emigrated to America [he wrote] and he became a Professor of Greek and Latin in Michigan,' but [Mrs. Batty goes on to say] it has not been possible to trace this particular family."[1]

In correspondence with Pratt families in Los Angeles, I received a letter from the widow of one Anthony Pratt. The letter reads in part:

"My husband was born March 2, 1874, in Gunnerside, Yorkshire. His father worked in the mines and his death resulted from an accident. Anthony's mother brought 5 children, I believe, to Michigan when Anthony was about 10 years of age. I did not know any of the family except a sister Mary Ann and her husband James Smith who came to California.

"Anthony attended the University at Ann Arbor and taught Latin and Greek a short time. He became interested in Civic Affairs and came to Los Angeles."

There can be no doubt that this is Mrs. Batty's Anthony Pratt, even though John Bell's date would need to be inaccurate. And although there is a discrepancy of a few months in the date of his birth, it is a temptation to identify him with the grandson of George (grandson of Anthony and Phillis) and of Ruth (daughter of William and Annas) who was one of five surviving children of James Pratt and Ann Rutter (see genealogy 100-13, p. 210).

Thomas and Ann

Of the families issuing from William Pratt and Annas Metcalfe, other than that of Christopher, I have established contact with one and managed, with the help of charts, to trace another to the present generation. The latter of these two is the family of Robert, believed to be Pratt's Petrol, until recently a flourishing business in England and Scotland.* The other comprises the descendants of Thomas, through John Pratt and Mary Sunter, who are to be found dotted around England, and who pay yearly visits to the ancestral dales. The sons of John and Mary, as a granddaughter remembers them, "were all a very good and lovable family and lived as they preached." Of the six sons, three were farmers, one of whom carried on the Sunter family tradition of butcher as well; one was a school officer, and another a school-

*See p. 26.

master and the family historian.* Five of the six were local preachers in addition to their salaried work. Of the nine of them, John, Elizabeth, and Christopher did not marry, and Thomas, who married twice, left no children. The oldest daughter, Dorothy, married John Thomas Wiseman, a farmer bearing a name familiar in Swaledale from the beginning of its recorded history, and whose children are still living in and around Richmond. The second daughter Ann also married a farmer, Matthew Bell.† The descendants of George, William, and James are still in the north country and have close ties with the dale.

This family was known to Mrs. McFarlane and Mrs. Hall who visited them on that famous trip in 1925. On Good Friday of that year Sister Bessie took the children's service at Keld. Many spoke to her afterwards and she wrote of "a party of four who came in about half through, a man of 50 and another of about 60, with two ladies. At the close of the service Mr. Taylor brought them to be introduced, & after careful study of the family tree found they were Dad's cousins. It was a delight to meet them. . . . Mr. Tom Pratt, Mr. Willie the schoolmaster & his wife sat opposite Ru & me, & Mrs. Bell who was a Pratt opposite her brother." In Sister Bessie's album are autographs from Mr. Tom, "For a memorable & happy meeting with Sister Bessie T. Pratt," and from Mr. Willie, "With kindly memories of the blessings received at our meeting at Keld, Swaledale, & with best wishes for your happiness while here and a safe return to God's Own Country.** William Pratt (a Swaledale boy)." A week later the two New Zealand sisters "had tea with our other detachment of cousins, Mrs. Wiseman" in Low Row.†† "As it was raining very heavy we rigged up in clogs, cape, etc., clattered our way over the moor. When we reached their flagged pathway there was no doubt as to our being there. A right good tea it was all home made or produced & what a welcome." On Sunday Sister Bessie was again to preach, this time in Gunnerside.

*This was William who did not live long enough to write up his findings. It was he who was referred to in Christopher Pratt's letter (see p. 26).
†References are made to these Bells in Mrs. McFarlane's diary, p. 156.
**Rhapsodic impressions over the beauties of the motherland must not have dulled their pride in the land of their adoption, one notes with pleasure.
††The Hillcrest Pratts.

"I felt dead scared till I gave out the first hymn. Then I was quite
at home. After the service one after another told us they were
related and how and as one of the old standards remarked we
were akin to half the church. Tea with Mr. and Mrs. Wagget
after which we went to see a Mrs. Milner, a cousin of Dad's. She
was pretty deaf but pleased to see us. Her daughter Maggie
is a fine young woman with a good voice & who is in the Choir.
Good time at night & the centre body of the Chapel was full
for the after-meeting. It was a red-letter day all through. After
service we had to go in to see another cousin who was too
unwell to go to Chapel that day. Then back to supper. The motor
came about ten, picking up the preachers, & we reached the
cottage at 11.
"Monday. Rested all day.
"Tuesday. Walked to Gunnerside, spent the day there, & after
seeing Miss Coates & others walked back, Maggie going with
us a couple of miles on our way."*

In 1925 there were, still to be shared, memories in Gunnerside.

James of Dubuque
Of the Gunnerside Pratts the first inheritor of the wind-filled
freedom of the Yorkshire landscape was James, oldest son of
William and Annas and brother of Christopher. The pioneer
spirit was strong in James. Having arrived in Ohio,† he spent
two years clearing fifty acres of heavily timbered land, earning
his living by hiring himself out in seed-time to his neighbours
for fifty cents a day. By the time he had established a livable
farm in which to leave Hannah, his feet had begun to itch once
more and off he went to explore the lead district of Galena in
northern Iowa. For seventeen and a half days he tramped the
five hundred miles to the site of the present-day town of Dubuque. "I swam rivers," he said, "and waded creeks, slept on the
ground o'nights, ate in houses when I could, and killed game

*Maggie Milner is still resident in Gunnerside but no longer remembers the
the Pratt connection.
†Among the passengers of the "Washington" into New York on 15 June
1833 are listed James Pratt, farmer, and his wife, Hannah.

109

when I was hungry elsewhere. Sometimes I followed roads, some-times paths through the woods and over the prairie and some-times made my own paths. I was a great walker in those days!"

Having arrived in the Galena lead district, the veteran miner worked there for some months and then returned to his wife and farm, this time steaming along the Ohio and Mississippi Rivers that he had swum on his way out, and paying his passage by working as a deck hand. Two years later, in 1836, he sold his farm and set out again with his wife for northern Iowa where, with two others he bought a mill, known by the name of Cat-fish, to crack corn for farmers within a radius of several hundred miles. So successful was this enterprise that larger and larger mills had to be built until around 1865 the earlier structures were replaced by Rockdale Mills, around which the community of Dubuque developed.

In keeping with the Pratt tradition of old, James took an active part in the affairs of the community which he helped to found. He was a Methodist Class Leader holding meetings at Catfish Mill until a Methodist Chapel was built. From the mill went out many an anonymous sack of flour to the miners during the period be-tween 1842 and 1857 when times were hard. In 1858 a local branch of the State of Iowa Bank was opened, with James Pratt as one of the stockholders, and it was he to whom the cash capital of $10,000 was entrusted until the Bank was opened. By the time James died in 1867 this bank was one of three of which he was director, the others being the National State Bank and the First National.

James and Hannah had no children. When he died his estate was left to his widow and those of his family who had followed him to America. These consisted of his sister, Eliza Bradbury, next in age to himself, and the two sons of James and Mary Thwaites, Adam and William. The spirit of the West of those early days was expressed in the Dubuque *Times* of 30 December 1867, which carried the obituary of James Pratt:

"One by one the old settlers of Dubuque are passing away. They who came here and erected huts and toiled for the support of their families either at the windlass or in the bowels of the earth when this present metropolis of Iowa was an almost unknown hamlet in the territory of Michigan, will soon every one be num-

110

bered among the residents of God's Acre. They did pioneer work in the upbuilding of this portion of the Northwest. One of the oldest of these 'old settlers' – one of the noblest of them all – James Pratt, died yesterday at three o'clock."[2]

Christopher Pratt & Sons of Bradford

The family for which the most complete records exist is that of James's brother Christopher Pratt and his wife Jane Cheesborough. The firm of Pratt & Prince, which at the death of Thomas Prince in 1880 became Christopher Pratt & Sons, continued to flourish and has a high reputation for quality furnishings. It remains a successful testimony to the business acumen of the family which, although in other branches the spirit may have indeed been willing, and the flesh also for that matter, remained in the realm of dreams or turned in the direction of less tangible wealth. Christopher and Jane, with their family empire around them, lived in good health to enjoy their Golden Wedding in 1892. "It was a matter for special thankfulness," it was written in the Bradford paper, "that one of the sons, the Rev. Benjamin Pratt, and his family were able to be present, he having been for the last twelve years engaged in Mission work in India, and having arrived at home on the previous day."[*] An almost complete gathering it lacked only the grandson Edward, across the world in Australia. The following year the celebrants returned to Bedale, the valley of Jane's childhood, to live out their retirement years at Holly Hill, a rambling old country house, in Well. Five years later Jane was to die there, and five years after her, Christopher himself. Their four sons – William, Benjamin, Thomas, and Job – all entered the firm. William, after his father's retirement in 1894, resigned and went into business for himself.[3] He died on 14 June 1914. Benjamin, after some years, decided his calling was not with business and left to study for the Wesleyan Methodist ministry. Job, the youngest, combined to a remarkable degree the artistic and business elements so much at play within the family. His death at thirty-seven was a severe blow, especially to Thomas who became the only surviving son in the business.[4]

It was Thomas who was destined to lead the firm and this he

*From a clipping in the possession of Ewart Pratt, St. John's, which must have been sent to John Pratt by Christopher with whom he was in correspondence.

did despite ill health which caused so much concern that at one point it was thought that Thomas would have to be the "gentleman of the family."[5] But his interest in the firm was very great. In 1880, at the time of the retirement of Thomas Prince, trade was booming. Christopher was not growing any younger and it was evident that Thomas had made himself indispensable and had absorbed the business body and soul. The offices he held in the business world are too numerous to mention and in 1919 he accepted the highest position modern distributive trade organization could then offer: the presidency of the National Chamber of Trade.[6]

True to Pratt tradition, Thomas was an active Methodist and was many times a member of the Wesleyan Annual Conference. In 1884 he married Elizabeth Annie Webster and in 1911 took her to Canada when he went as a delegate to the Oecumenical Conference in Toronto. On this trip they visited all the relatives they could who were living in the United States and Canada, and probably went west to see Harold. This was the year my father graduated from the University of Toronto and was in the process of becoming a Methodist minister himself. Had they known of one another they could easily have met. They might have done so in any case, and in view of their common religious preoccupations at that time it is a wonder they did not. Similarly, Elizabeth McFarlane in her diary for 1909 writes that Mr. and Mrs. Pratt (of Bradford) had just returned from the Lincoln Conference, at which she herself had been present. And both unknown to each other.

After a lifetime of incredible activity for anyone in good health, let alone a man with a weak heart, on 14 August 1923 the illness that had beset him from his youth caught up with Thomas and finally conquered him. *The Bradford Chamber of Trade Journal* carried the announcement of his death and funeral. The Rev. C. Gilbert Muir, who took the service, "described Mr. Pratt," the *Journal* went on to say,

"as a big man of amazing versatility, by no means ignorant of books upon abstruse subjects and a great reader of newspapers. He was emphatically a man of his own time. He had, at any rate from his own standpoint, a clear vision of what the country needed and did not hesitate to offer his ungrudging services

1/The village of Gunnerside, taken from the vicinity of Spring End across the Swale. The ghyll can be seen rippling along the road, the chapel and cemetery on the left.

1

2/William Pratt, third son of James and Sally, with his
grandchildren, Sarah (Mrs. Colechin) and Herbert Driver.

3/The family in New Zealand of Thomas Pratt, youngest son of James and Sally. Left to right: Elizabeth McFarlane, Maria Rigg, Thomas's wife Sarah, Ruth Hall, Hanna McCaffrey, Thomas.

4/The Newfoundland family of John Pratt, fifth son of James and Sally. Left to right: John, Lottie Harris with Floss on her knee, Edwin John behind, Will, Jim, Art, John's wife Fanny. Cal reclines on the floor.

5

6   7

5/The family of Christopher and Jane Pratt. Left to right: Ruth, Job, Thomas, Mary, Benjamin, Agnes, William, Elizabeth. Christopher and Jane are seated on the couch.

6/James Pratt, who founded Dubuque, Iowa, near the Galena lead mines to which many Swaledale folk emigrated.

7/John and Fanny Pratt dressed for the dinner given the Duke and Duchess of York (later King George and Queen Mary) in St. John's, Newfoundland.

8

9

10

8/The home of Sally Pratt, John, Thomas, and Moses near the Blue Bell Inn at Kettlewell.

9/Elizabeth McFarlane and the chair upon which John Wesley stood to preach at Harker's farm in Swaledale.

10/The new chapel, built in 1867, by the Gunnerside Ghyll, looking westward toward the head of the Swale valley.

11

12

13

11/"Winter Moon." Woodcut by Claire Pratt, Toronto.

12/"Bird." Fabric collage by Rosemary Murray, Essex, England.

13/"The Lynx." Serigraph by Christopher Pratt, Newfoundland.

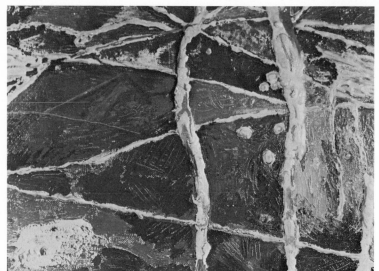

14

15

14/"Cornwall." Oil by Penelope Skeet, Essex, England.

15/"Seawreck." Oil by James C. Pratt, Newfoundland.

for the attainment of his ideals. He was the head of a great business, held many directorates, was President of the National Chamber of Trade for two successive years, and a councillor in his own city – a post which he greatly valued. The whole energy of his mind and heart went out in every direction. He was a man of real, hard granite rock, and the man or the cause securing his support knew that he would never let him or it down. . . . Of those earnest laymen who were keen for the spiritual welfare of the city Mr. Pratt was one of the greatest stalwarts."

Eulogies from friends and colleagues followed.

Mr. Fred Pickering spoke of him in tribute as one whose "whole desire was to be helpful to traders in times of difficulties. . . . His wise counsel and rare judgment settled many disputes between members of this organization, or between members and others, in a manner which sent both parties away reconciled in the belief that each one had won their case." And S. T. Nicholson of Hull, the Honorary Secretary of the National Chamber of Trade, described him as able under the most difficult circumstances to "laugh quietly," and the thought of whom in time of catastrophe was "so restful in the storm." "I certainly have known," he wrote, "no one to whom Shakespeare's eulogy was more appropriate – 'His life was gentle, and the elements so mix'd in him that Nature might stand up and say to all the world 'This was a Man.' "

Assisting Thomas since 1896 was his nephew William Goodhugh Dawson, son of Agnes who had married the Rev. W. G. Dawson, a Methodist minister from Barnard Castle. When Thomas died in 1922, William became Chairman of the Board of Directors. He died in August 1937 at the age of fifty-eight.

Thomas Pratt and Elizabeth Annie Webster were the parents of nine sons and two daughters. At the outbreak of the Great War in 1914 the boys were either of an age to join or nearly so. Five of them saw active service and four were wounded. With the wealth of so many sons, the family interest in the firm was assured, and the professions of law, medicine, and engineering were well represented. Leonard Webster, born 1886, was to become the family historian. In Leonard, the literary and artistic bent fought an almost even battle with business aptitude, but practical considerations won and Leonard entered the family business in the curtain and upholstery departments, which gave him an outlet for the artistic leanings he indulged by taking courses in art, first at the Technical College and then at the Bradford City School of Art. In 1908 and 1909 he was in London with the firm of Charles Hammond at which time he joined the Thirteenth City of London Regiment. He transferred to the Sixth West Yorkshire Regiment when he returned to Bradford. In 1913 he was appointed a director of the company, but with the outbreak of war he entered the fray as a private, was sent to France in 1915, was wounded in 1916, and returned to England. In 1917 he rejoined the firm. Deaf now, from his war experiences, he spent much of his spare time in literary pursuits preparing many typewritten manuscripts. Of these, *Yesterday Our Ancestry* has been printed to preserve the research he had done and has been a help in the writing of the present document. In 1925 he wrote to his uncle Benjamin in British Columbia asking for material for his record. In 1922 he wrote *The Light on the Cliff* on the centenary of the Undercliffe Wesleyan Sunday School. On 1 January 1934, at the unripe age of forty-seven, Leonard died of cancer of the lung caused, it is said, from the poison gas of the war. His secretarial duties devolved upon William Dawson who had succeeded his uncle as head of the firm.

The second son was Christopher, the same who was to be the penfriend of Arthur Pratt. He also attended the Bradford School of Art where he received his diploma before entering the firm in 1903. In 1913 the business became a limited liability company and Christopher was made a director. During the war when the firm was asked to manufacture wooden parts for aeroplanes, it was done under Christopher's management and supervision. He was an amateur photographer and used this hobby in his study of bird and insect life. His sons, Barry and David, both entered the firm, one to become a director and the other head of the radio and television departments. Their sister Ruth is married to the Rev. Harold Evans who was given the task of editing Leonard's manuscript, "Yesterday Our Ancestry," and preparing it for publication.

Christopher Pratt used to visit Gunnerside regularly and cut a bit of an awe-inspiring figure among its reserved and retiring inhabitants. He it was who martialled the material left by Leonard and prepared the pamphlet "Christopher Pratt & Sons," so frequently referred to here. He had also preserved two letters written long ago to his grandfather and namesake from my grandfather in Newfoundland and handed them safely over to our family upon his chance contact with it, letters only to be lost along with all the other atoms of information that alone can put flesh and character on the wraiths of the past. And the year 1964 saw the death of Christopher Pratt.

Next to Christopher is Geoffrey Cheesborough who, with his wife Jean, lives in Well, not far from their grandfather's home at Holly Hill. In her separate quarters called "Dolsend," at the end of Geoffrey's house, lives the seventh child and first daughter of Thomas Pratt. Agnes Dorothea (Dol), now retired, was a nurse in a Manchester hospital, and is a favourite aunt and godmother to many, both Protestant and Catholic. She is one of the few members of the family not involved in Methodism, having joined the Roman Catholic faith, and has published several small books of verse. Below Geoffrey and Dol lives Christopher's widow Mary, in a bungalow.

The fourth son was Wilfred Ellington who, along with his brothers, had some part in the family firm. Married in 1926 to Sarah Smith, he has one daughter, Joan Mary.

Thomas Dawson, known familiarly as "T.D.", was born in 1893 and the first of the family to enter the medical profession. His studies were interrupted by the war and he went as a member of the Duke of Wellington's Regiment with the British Expeditionary Force to France in 1915. He was severely wounded in 1916 and on his recovery completed his studies, qualifying as a doctor in 1918. He acted as unqualified houseman – both physician and surgeon – at the General Infirmary of Leeds and was later resident medical officer there. One of his colleagues wrote that despite his ability "he cared nothing for the limelight of specializing, his object being to become the ideal G. P. In this he was singularly successful."[7] In 1957 he became ill with heart disease and retired to Thirsk where he died on 18 January 1960. His son Thomas Leonard Cheesborough, living in Darlington, County Durham, has followed in his father's footsteps and become a consultant radiologist.

Next there were Basil and Redvers, born in 1898 and 1900. Basil became a lawyer and was a local government solicitor on the local council at Birkenhead. Now retired from his law practice, he lives in Ripon with his artist wife, Winifred Buzzard. Alfred Stuart Redvers, although only fourteen at the outbreak of the First World War, was nevertheless a member of the Royal Air Force in 1918. After the war he attended Leeds University where he obtained a diploma in electrical engineering and then joined the firm where he took over the management of the electrical department. He became a director in 1935 and was a part-time lecturer in electrical installation at the Bradford Technical College. In 1925 he married Kathleen Bedford and chose Gunnerside for his honeymoon where he ran into the sisters from New Zealand. Redvers Pratt transformed the family tree into printed circles with the ancestry showing as a legend in the lower right-hand corner (see p. 27). In October 1966 he died suddenly of a heart attack at the age of sixty-six.

The "black sheep" of the Christopher Pratts, so-called because of his decision to leave the family firm, was Benjamin, born in 1854. Having joined the Wesleyan Methodist ministry, he went in 1880 out to Hyderabad to join the Rev. William Burgess who had a mission there.[8] He, like his father Christopher, was in close touch with their cousin John in Newfoundland, and the name of the "cousin who had gone to India" was known to some of John's sons there. The years of Benjamin's outstanding mission have been written by V. S. Sackett in *Vision and Venture*. It would be interesting to make a study of the parallel careers of Benjamin and John Pratt, one in the warmth and lassitude of a great Oriental country, the other in a tiny fog-bound, storm-tossed island at the other end of the world. Echoing the plaque in Grand Bank in memory of John Pratt, stands another in the church Benjamin built himself in Secunderabad and in which he preached until forced by illness to leave India:

In memory
of
Rev. Benjamin Pratt
1853-1931

He was the first itinerant Wesleyan Missionary in the villages of Hyderabad, and laid the foundation of widespread Evangelism among the outcastes of the land. For many years he was the

124

Chairman of the District and spent his last years in retirement, broken in health by his incessant toil.

By his friendliness and faith, his preaching and personal piety, he won the love of all who knew him.

Benjamin married Mary Newsholme and to them was born in India, Henry Newsholme Pratt. Soon after his birth his mother died and, as India was a difficult country in which to bring up a child, Henry was taken home to England to be brought up by his mother's people who adopted him. To please his uncle, Sir Arthur Newsholme, he reversed his name so that he became Henry Pratt Newsholme. He entered the medical profession and became medical officer of health for Birmingham.

A few years after Mary's death, Benjamin married Edith Ball, a nurse whose profession made her of invaluable help in her husband's work. As a nurse she often had to take the role of a doctor and, among other operations, she was called upon to remove cataracts. Four children were born to Benjamin and Edith. The first was Constance, followed the next year by Harold. These children lived their early years in India where Harold remembers the tomtoms throbbing through the night and the "yu-hu-hu, yu-hu-hu" chanting of the runners as they padded along beside the litter in which they travelled. When it came time to go to school the children went home to England for their education, so that recollections of India, though vivid, are spotty in the manner of childhood memories. Constance had diphtheria on the boat en route home, which she survived despite the conditions of travel, never, even at their best, conducive to proper medical care.

Back to the old home at Holly Hill they went to be brought up by their father's sister, Aunt Ruth. To this day memories are warm of Aunt Ruth who loved them, took them for long walks, and saved the childish drawings and letters and the later notebooks and nature-study sketches so carefully and skilfully compiled by them.

Harold Pratt spent a large part of his boyhood in and around Gunnerside where his grandfather had been born. Tramping the hills in summer he had absorbed much of the beauty of Swaledale by the time he set off, in 1906, with the family's blessing, for Canada (see page 28). The family had a friend in Okotoks

125

and Harold worked for a time on a farm there until he made enough money to buy his own property upon which he built a house and took to farming his own land.

About 1914 Constance, now a registered nurse, joined him, and became a very useful member of the community, nursing all the neighbours through their illnesses and childbirths. In 1916 at St. Peter's Church she married Henry Harper, commonly known as Hal.

The year after his sister's wedding Harold married Margaret Bridge, and the next brother, Hugh, came out from England and lived for a time with them on the farm. Later, the last brother, Geoffrey, arrived and went to work in the city. And in 1919 came the Rev. Benjamin and Mrs. Pratt, having retired after thirty-five years on the mission fields of India, to live on the farm, and with their advent the entire family, with the exception of Henry Newsholme, were gathered into Canada. The grandparents lived with Harold and his family until they died – Benjamin in 1931 and Mrs. Benjamin in 1946.

By 1925 Harold's and Margaret's two children – Jean and Christopher – had arrived and Margaret's health began to fail. The family had no choice, now, but to leave the farm they loved and go to Victoria where Harold went to work in a real estate office. Holidays were spent in the country and the children grew up with it in their blood, and Jean with a passion for horses. She was to graduate from the University of British Columbia in Biochemistry and marry into a family that long ago had lived among her ancestors at Gunnerside. In 1945 she married James Bryce Milner, a six-generation Canadian and a member of the Law Department of the University of Toronto. Christopher joined the Royal Canadian Navy, and after the war stayed with the sea, becoming captain of one of the Navy's ships. He married Mary Warlow and they live in Halifax with their four children. Both Jean and Christopher are rooted, not only in the ranches and mountains of Canada, but also in the tiny settlements that straggle over Melbecks Moor. Until Jim Milner died in 1969, he and Jean went on pilgrimage there every three years. Harold, around 1964, had an eye operation after which his sight was badly impaired. In spite of this he managed to care for his wife until her death in May of 1968.

The Children of James and Sally

Among the records of James and Sarah Pratt there is evidence that there had been at least twelve children, and now from the New Zealand papers, a thirteenth. Of these the first four died in infancy or early childhood. Of the remaining nine there are three who, if they married and left families, have disappeared from sight. These are James, Elizabeth, and Anthony. None of them are listed in any of the census returns of 1841, 51, or 61 for Gunnerside or Kettlewell.

For these nothing but scraps of memory and the odd notation exists to restore their names to the family. A member in Burnley speaks of James and Anthony as among the brothers who lived together there at one time. James, he recalls, probing with his memory into the haze of distance, left for America where he played the violin for the Indians, then returned as a member of the Salvation Army.* The reference to "Uncle James" in James Heslop's letter substantiates his continuation into adulthood. This same letter and Mrs. McFarlane's diary have perpetuated Elizabeth (see p. 64). Anthony's name is familiar to several but there are no specific memories of him other than his name.

Of Dorothy, the oldest, there is the record of her baptism and her probable marriage to William Bellis. On the New Zealand copy of *Methodism in Swaledale* there is a notation in the hand of one of the daughters of Thomas Pratt which reads: "Birthplace of my Father Thomas Pratt who was Born at Spring End Gunnerside. W. His Brother is mentioned in this Book James and Anty Pratt Dorothy his Sister." On page 89, however, there is another notation opposite the name of Dorothy Pratt, m. (married), indicating that it is the writer's great grandmother, Dorothy Chapman, and not Miss Pratt, the sister of Thomas. This is, furthermore, the only Dorothy Pratt mentioned in the book, and she belonged to the Methodist class in 1796, twenty-eight years prior to the birth of sister Dorothy. That Thomas Pratt had a sister known to his children as Aunt Dorothy,† we may infer from the

---

*It is suspected that two or three Jameses may have become one here.
†Three daughters, with the names of Dorothy (after her paternal grandmother), Elizabeth (after her paternal great grandmother), and Sarah Ann (after her mother and maternal grandmother) illustrates neatly the probability that these three were sisters.

notation in the book, even though she could not possibly be the one mentioned in it. The marriage record of William Bellis and Dorothy Pratt has placed her more firmly yet on the genealogical map. She seems to have been the grandmother of that trio of Birstal – Eva, Elizabeth Ann, and Amy. Their father had been Edwin Bellis, a son perhaps of that Dorothy and William who had been married in York in 1840 (see p. 107). There is moreover, a tenuous hope that the clue to the Charlotte Brontë mystery may lie with Dorothy Bellis. Charlotte's best friend was Ellen Nussey who lived at Birstal and would have been a contemporary of Dorothy Pratt. The photograph in the possession of my grandfather may have been a parting gift from his sister before he left for Newfoundland. A letter to Amy, the youngest, was sent to the nursing home where, at ninety, she now lives, but once again it was too late for, according to the kind friend who answered the letter, her memory has gone.

Sallie Colechin remembers a Horace Bellis but nobody seems to know what relation he bears to the family, although he was probably a brother of the three sisters. He is said to have emigrated to Canada and letters were sent to the eight Bellises resident in Toronto, with no positive results. It is still hoped that a direct line to the present-day descendants of Dorothy Pratt, born in Swaledale in 1822, may yet be traced.

With regard to Metcalf, a valuable piece of information had come to light in the Newfoundland *Methodist Monthly Greeting*, vol. IV, no. 8, p. 124. In this issue a letter reads:

Brigus, Feb. 9th, 1892
Dear Editors, – This last American mail brought me very sad news of the death of a brother of mine. I enclose a short obituary, which I cut out from an American paper, which I will be obliged if you will insert in the *Greeting*. It would be difficult for there to be a kinder son and brother than he was. I may state one act, which will show the nature of the man. Some few years after he went out, he desired a sister of mine to go out there, and sent £70 stg. to pay her passage; but, in case she did not go, the money was to be given to his father and mother, which was done. I have not seen him since he was a husband and father, but I have no doubt he was the same to them. He was of a most lively, happy disposition. May God

comfort his poor widow and children!
J. Pratt

The letter is followed by the obituary:

"The sad death of Metcalf Pratt, of Palisade, Nevada, on December 26th, deserves more than a passing notice. While crossing a bridge near Gerald he was struck by a Central Pacific train, and instantly killed. He was born in Yorkshire, England. His parents were members of the Methodist Wesleyan Church, in which faith and belief he was raised. He was married to Miss Hannah Wardle in 1850, and came to California* the same year, and to Mineral Hill, this county, in 1870, where he was generally beloved by all who knew him. Besides the grief-striken widow, he leaves three sons and two daughters to mourn his untimely death. On Monday, December 28, his relatives and many friends assembled to pay their last respects to the departed. Capt. J. C. Palmer, an old friend, made a feeling address from Psalm 37, 37: 'Mark the perfect man, behold the upright, for the end of that man is peace.' "

The 1880 census for Nevada was consulted. At that time the state, still not populous, was very much frontier country and to the small villages had congregated mining communities mainly composed of English, American, Chinese and Indians. These were the neighbours of Metcalf and Hannah Pratt in the village of Mineral Hill† where I found them with little difficulty among the sparse listings. Of their five children, four, all born in California, were living at home. Charles W., 21, was also a miner, and at school were Elizabeth, 15; Margaret, 11; and John, 8. Discovery of the grandsons of Metcalf Pratt was made while this book was in proof.

The five children of James and Sally Pratt whose descendants have been traced to the present day are Metcalf, William, Sarah Ann, John, and Thomas.

Metcalf and Hannah
Triggered by the story of the strange Jack Pratt on the San Francisco street, I set out with a fine-toothed comb to discover the

---

*Investigation revealed that they lived in Grass Valley, where two infants of theirs were buried in 1858 and 1859.
†Now a ghost town.

descendants of Metcalf and Hannah Pratt. All the Pratts in and around Los Angeles and San Francisco (over two hundred of them) received letters from me, and many of them replied with courteous and informative letters regarding their forebears. With the exception of the Greek and Latin teacher of Michigan, however, none of them had emerged from Swaledale.

I wrote numerous letters to offices and historical societies in both California and Nevada, and received replies of a disappointing unanimity. Finally, after I had given up in despair and typesetting had already commenced on this book, two letters, with Pratt names in the left-hand corners of both, arrived in the deluge of Christmas mail. They came from the broad ranches beneath the high sierras of Nevada, and were from Oliver and John, the only two grandsons of the Metcalf I had been so assiduously and vainly trying to locate. Each wrote a charming and surprised letter and were almost, I think, as excited as I, for they did not know they had a Pratt relative in the entire world. They sent pictures of themselves, and somewhere in the high foreheads or the thin and sensitive lips lurked a definite Pratt physiognomy.

Oliver, born in 1903, and John, in 1907, are sons of Oliver Metcalf, youngest child of Metcalf and Hannah. This son did not appear in the 1880 Nevada census and his name, like that of the youngest daughter of Thomas Pratt in New Zealand, was quite new to me. Old Metcalf had died long before Oliver and John were born and they and their sister Annie, orphaned at a very early age, were brought up by their maternal grandmother in the Roman Catholic faith. They did not know of the traditional Methodism of the Swaledale Pratts and thought vaguely that the early Pratts might have been Mormons.

Both Palisade and Mineral Hill, where Metcalf worked in the mines until his death, are ghost towns now. "Palisade," wrote John Pratt, "is about all gone – a brush fire burned most of it and people have torn a lot of it down, including Grandma Pratt's house which was still standing until a few years ago." There is nothing now left but the cemetery in Palisade where Metcalf and some of his family are buried and where once a year Oliver and John meet to decorate the graves.

Another outcome of my laborious search was that I received concrete evidence regarding the Metcalf Pratts. They had had at least eight children, two of whom died in infancy and were buried in Grass Valley. Two daughters, Lizzie and Maggie, each married a man named Doolittle. The sons of Oliver Metcalf have both mentioned their cousin Genevieve West, daughter of Maggie Doolittle who, in 1944, lived in Denver, Colorado. A letter addressed to her there was returned. Charles and John were bachelors. Charles was a miner all his life and lived to be ninety-one. John was a master mechanic on the narrow-gauge railroad that ran the eighty-four miles from Palisade to Eureka.

As in the case of the New Zealand family, the Pratt line has flourished through one child only – Oliver Metcalf, who married Annie McBride and who was a railroad engineer on the same railway as his brother John.

During the Christmas holidays a second letter from Oliver added a few more leaves for the family tree. Oliver has been with the United States Government and was honoured at a testimonial dinner upon his retirement in 1969 from the position of Chief Clerk of the United States District Court for the State of Nevada. He retired with his wife, Edna Walker, to their two-acre estate and an assortment of animals: a jackass, some ponies, calves, and sheep. His son, Oliver junior, is a full Colonel in the Nevada National Guard. Married to Rose Marie Satti, he has two children, Linda and Joseph. On their five-acre ranch they are able to indulge their hobby of raising Arabian horses. A second son, Gordon, is an accountant with the county school district and has two stepdaughters. His daughter, Shirley, divorced from Ryland Cunningham, is employed at the Capitol Convalescent Center. She has three children: Elaine, Larry, and Coleen.

The second brother, John, in 1969 was honoured at a presentation dinner for his thirty years' service on the maintenance division of the Nevada State Highway Department, of which he was superintendent. He is married to Agnes Billett and they have a daughter, Pauline, and two sons, Dale and James. At the time of writing no further information on John's family is available.

William and Mary
Between 1871 and 1878 William and Mary left Kettlewell for Burnley, where they settled down at 12 Russell Street. Sarah, in her old age, continued to live with them and it was there at the

age of seventy-nine that she died of "bronchitis" on 25 April 1876.

In that house on Russell Street William and Mary watched their youngest children grow to adulthood. These were James, Dorothy, and Mary Jane whom they called Polly.

The spirit of Reform was to be extended yet again in this branch of the Pratts. In lineal descent of the mighty spiritual awakening engendered by John Wesley was General Booth of the Salvation Army.[9] He was an ordained Methodist minister who by 1878 had formed a militant organization founded on Christian brotherhood and, armed with the sword of the spirit, was prepared to march to the gates of hell itself to free the loneliest outcast.

In 1878 James Pratt, son of William, was twenty-four, and an active worker in Fulledge Wesleyan Church in Burnley. He seems to have been something of a traveller as well, for a grandson remembers that he lived for a short spell in South Africa. Sometime, during the next ten years, James Pratt saw in a public house a beautiful young lass in the uniform of the Salvation Army and selling *The War Cry*. This was Miss Ashworth, whose charms and powers were great enough to steer him out of the staunch Wesleyanism of the Pratts and into the Army of General Booth. Soon they were married and James became an Envoy and played the E-flat trumpet in the Band.

On 18 November 1889 their first child, William Ashworth, was born and was followed by Alice Emma, Dora, and Adelaide. It was apparently William who went to Cornwall and was possibly the relative who made the journey home to see his Uncle John on his visit from Newfoundland in 1902. In 1910 William entered the Army Training Centre in London and was commissioned an officer later that year. In the early years of the First World War William met and married Sergeant-Major Nellie Jago. Their four children are Wycliffe, Alicia, Bramwell, and William, all bearing the second name of Ashworth and all now officers in the Salvation Army. On 13 November 1940 William was sheltering in the doorway of the citadel in Dover when he became the first Salvation Army officer killed as the long-range guns were fired from Calais.

James's sister, Dorothy Pratt, went to work as a winder in a cotton mill and there it was that she met John Driver, a weaver in the same mill, and married him around 1882. It was at the Driver home where William and Mary lived out their latter years, and William died there about 1898. Four children were born to John and Dorothy Driver: Mary, the oldest, died of tuberculosis in the unwholesome air of Burnley, at the age of nineteen. William, a local preacher for fifty years, married Mary Ibbotson in 1913 and had one son, Harry, now married and living in Burnley. The two youngest were James Herbert, born in 1889, and Sarah, born in 1891.

In 1914 Herbert married Emily Hitchen, two years his junior, also from Burnley. Emily had been familiar with Gunnerside before her marriage, however, as Burnley was filled with emigrés from Swaledale. In 1910 one of the young ladies with whom Emily worked became engaged to one of the Woodwards in Gunnerside, and Emily and a friend were invited to spend a week there among the Sunters, Reynoldsons, Calverts and Rutters, relatives of many of Emily's friends who attended Brooklands Road Chapel in Burnley where the Hitchens worshipped. "A Mr. Pratt from Durham," she wrote, "always went there for the sports. He was a very strong man and took three first prizes." There was also a Mr. Driver at that time spending a holiday over the moor at Askrigg with a pal of his. To see the girls they trudged the six miles, following the path the folks of old had taken to attend services at Gunnerside in the early days of Methodism. They never forgot it, Herbert said, "not just for the company, but for the long dreary walk there and back. It took a couple of days to get over it." The incentive was strong, but even stronger must have been the pull that brought the hardworking folk who were not on holiday over those dreary miles each Sunday to the services by the Swale.

Herbert and Emily Driver named their only child for her grandmother, Dorothy Pratt, and in her the artistic side of the Pratts, as well as her mother's penchant for dress designing, became evident in her choice of career. She attended the art school for design and became a designer-cutter for a clothing firm. Married in 1940 to William Boardman, manager of the Cooperative Stores, she now has three grandchildren of their only child, Jean, who married Brian Doidge in 1962.

In 1913 Ruth Hall of New Zealand made a trip to England to visit her cousin Dorothy Driver, of whom she was very fond.

While Ruth was yet on the sea, Dorothy died of cancer at the age of fifty-six, and upon her arrival Ruth found a sorrowing household, one that had lost not only its mother, but its older sister as well, and the younger one, Sarah, was very ill from grief and the bad air that had caused her sister's death. Accompanied by Ruth, Sarah visited her mother's childhood home at Kettlewell, went to Gunnerside for a week, and then to Birstal where there lived Elizabeth Ann, Eva, and Amy – three sisters who bore the name of Bellis. Elizabeth Ann Bellis was later to marry her cousin's widower, John Driver. When final farewells had been said, Sarah left with Ruth for the clean fresh air of New Zealand and never returned to her native land. Upon her arrival the New Zealand relatives, in their distaste of too much formalism, insisted she be called henceforth "Sallie." There she married Charles Colechin, and in 1925 they adopted a three-year-old child whose parents had both died. This was Fae, now the mother of eight boys, and a grandmother. In 1930, the Colechins had a daughter of their own, named Ruth for the dear cousin who had brought Sallie to New Zealand and who lived her latter years with them. During the Second World War her nephew Harry put in at New Zealand when his ship was hit off the Solomon Islands, and Sallie was able to welcome the only relative she had seen since leaving England.

The youngest child of William and Mary was Mary Jane (Polly) who is well remembered, although no trace of her family, if any, has been discovered. Auntie Polly married John William Roberts and they lived in Blackpool where Herbert Driver remembers visiting them in the holidays of his boyhood. They were the leaders of the Spiritualist sect in town and later moved to Canada where they were ardent missionaries of Spiritualism and where Mr. Roberts became the mayor of one of the cities. Investigations have failed to reveal which one, and no medium has been found to put us in touch with them.

Sarah Ann

On 7 July 1857 Sar'an married Anthony Alderson in Gunnerside, and her first daughter, Jane, was born in Richmond or Soltaire, Yorkshire, the following year. It seems likely that the Aldersons may have remained in Swaledale after Sally Pratt had gone with her boys to Kettlewell, at least for awhile. Grandchildren, far removed in time and space, recall that Jane married in Gunnerside and left with her husband for Lancashire, probably Burnley, shortly thereafter. If this is the case, it is reasonable to suppose that all the Alderson sisters were born in or around Gunnerside, and that the family moved to Burnley around the 1870s, where their father died and where their mother married again. In the 1880s they were living at Park Gate, in the shadow of a large church.

"They all seemed to lead," wrote Joyce Hall, "a most bohemian existence. Sarah Ann was the same, too – no money, very hard times in fact – but free and easy around the house, not much of a homemaker and yet this tremendous religious zeal for holding church meetings, reading the Bible, and making music." In women's preaching, Jane's mother had already established a precedent. Standing tall and erect on a lorry in the market place, her black eyes flashing, she would hold forth to a crowd of boisterous men on the evils of excessive drinking. Sar'an was loved, admired, and feared, in equal measure, by the members of her family. Her grandson, Edgar Calvert, remembers her delight at the news of his admission into the Wesleyan ministry, in preparation for which he had suffered incredible hardship, of how she leapt across the room, all six feet of her, to clasp him in her ecstatic arms. Another cousin recalls with distaste Aunt Sarah Ann's visits, as she tended to dominate a gentler woman in the bringing up of her children. Sarah Ann was not, in any case, a negative character, having absorbed the strength and stubbornness of the Yorkshire moors that had been passed along to her through the Pratts or the Bells or both.

Particularly close to the heart of John Pratt was his nephew Moses, and it was not until the latter was nineteen that he left him reluctantly behind when he went to Newfoundland. Jane, also, was close to her Uncle John, and her daughter remembers her devotion to him until this day. If John Pratt wanted to take Moses along with him to Newfoundland, Jane wanted to go with him herself and become a preacher there too. "He was my best-loved uncle," she wrote to her cousin Maud, and she described how he spoke often to her of his wife Fanny in Newfoundland. There must have been many letters for, as far as we know, his visits home were only two.

Moses, having achieved the age when a lad could no longer expect to be classed as "A scholar," went into the mines along with his uncles, and at some point he made the transition from lead to coal.

135

Wesley may have succeeded in bringing a measure of spiritual welfare to the vast number of workers in England, but the indirect effects of his teaching on social legislation were slow. Two years younger than Moses Pratt was Keir Hardie, a coal miner in Scotland at the same time that Moses was a coal miner in the Lancashire pits. He worked in the mines from the age of ten until his conversion at twenty-two, brought on by the influence of Ruskin and a study of the Gospels, in much the same way that the Pratt brothers and numerous others must have applied themselves to study in the smoky lamplight of the midnight hours. In 1878, Keir Hardie became an evangelist of extraordinary humanitarian dimensions. It was a time when the British Trade Union movement was putting up a valiant struggle against the forces of reaction. We don't know whether Moses was active in the movement or whether he had a chance to be, but we do know he was working hard to better the lot of his fellow workers. For his efforts he was punished by being forced to work standing up to his waist in water.

During the seventies, when the call of new worlds was threatening to complete the great rifts begun two decades earlier, Moses must have been tempted more than once to leave England, and might have followed his uncle John who was keen to have him go to Newfoundland. All the reasons for his staying are not clear, but he did, in 1878, empty his pockets and clean out his savings, meagre as they were, in order to help send Thomas to New Zealand. The money may have been a loan but Thomas, with his wife and four daughters, was never in any position to repay it, and in return left Moses his inscribed copy of *Pilgrim's Progress*, now in the possession of Joyce Hall.

And so Moses stayed and in 1882 married Maria Heys, and their five children were all born in Burnley. The fourth, John, was born in 1894 and was named for the uncle to whom Moses was so attached. Herbert, two years older than John, was the only one of the family who, having caught Gunnerside fever, would take his family year after year to the Midsummer Festival at the little grey village on Melbecks Moor. His daughter Joyce writes of her childhood spent there:

". . . I remember the beds – one a great four-poster, and another hung with heavy red curtains which drew across the bed and

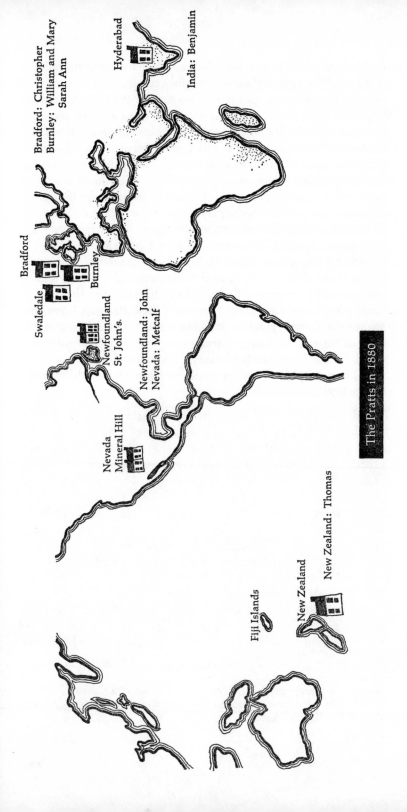

The Pratts in 1880

Bradford: Christopher
Burnley: William and Mary
Sarah Ann

India: Benjamin

Bradford

Swaledale

Burnley

Newfoundland
St. John's.

Newfoundland: John
Nevada: Metcalf

Nevada
Mineral Hill

Fiji Islands

New Zealand

New Zealand: Thomas

in front of the face. We were looked after by someone called Annie and the whole place was terribly run down. Every year we threatened to go somewhere else for the annual holiday but every June found us in Gunnerside. The owner of the house, a formidable old lady and a notable cook in her time, sat on a chair in the kitchen. She was I think very old and ill – we certainly never saw her out of the chair. We made our own fun; down by the beck decorating our mud pies with the wild rose petals, watching the men fishing for trout in the Swale – walking through the woods, playing with the village children in the schoolyard and competing with them in the races at the midsummer festival. There used to be a sweet shop by the school, kept by a Mrs. Percival. It was straight out of a Beatrix Potter story. A little bell tinkled as you opened the door and you had to be very careful you didn't fall down the three stone steps into the dark, cool depths of the little shop. I remember trips to Calvert Houses, drinking warm milk straight after milking time at the Cherry farm – watching the blacksmith at work. I think he was called Calvert.* Even going up year after year I remember the thrill as we drove from Muker and over the bridge into Gunnerside."

The dalesman's love of drama now and again becomes a dominant characteristic in individual Pratts. One of these is Joyce, who early displayed a histrionic ability she was able to put into practice, unhampered by the religious scruples of an earlier generation. Before her marriage to Gordon Hall, she was an actress in a Burnley Theatre group. Dark-haired and pretty, she forsook her vocation to marry. When their first child, Guy, was but a year old, the Halls went to Canada where they lived for ten years. Here Joyce resumed her dramatic career, acting with the Domino Theatre in Kingston, Ontario. Here Jonathan, an extremely gifted and sensitive child, was born. Peter Lyndon, the third son, was born after the family returned to Surrey.

Around 1884 Jane Alderson married James Calvert† of Gunnerside and they came to live in Burnley, where James pursued his occupation of mining. Their son Edgar remembers his father,

---

*Blacksmiths in Gunnerside seem to have been called Calvert since time immemorial.

†Named, his son recalls, for the Rev. James Calvert who played a considerable role in the conversion of the great and enigmatic cannibal chief of Fiji, King Thakabau.

138

short of stature like himself, gently instilling, amid the grinding poverty in which they lived, the values of honesty, piety and integrity, that were to be their guide lines throughout their lives. They were poor, nearly destitute. There were times when the larder was so empty that there was one potato for their daily fare. In 1897 James's labour was cut short by an accident in the mine, and for the next twenty-two years he was unable to support his family at all. They were grim days, but the strength of Sarah Ann had been passed to her daughter Jane who, along with her children, as they one by one became old enough, went to work and learned the art of self-reliance. In spite of great hardship, Edgar was able to receive an education to fit him for the ministry. Sar'an gave up her room to him and there he was able to study in the damp chill of an unheated Burnley house until he was ready to do his family proud. He married his childhood sweetheart, Lizzie Holgate, a few months after his grandmother's death. His two daughters, Penelope, married to Derek Skeet, and her sister Rosemary, wife of Brian Murray and mother of Paul Calvert, are both artists and teachers of art and have developed the technique of fabric collage. The Skeets, with whom the Rev. Edgar Calvert now lives in comfortable quarters of his own, and the Murrays live in Leigh-on-Sea, on the attractive coast of Essex.

After the death of Anthony Alderson, Sarah Ann married Mr. Wharton, and two sons were born to them: James and George. Jim Wharton served in the war and then became a plainclothes-detective and Mounted Policeman with the Bolton Police Force. Sarah Ann Alderson, Jr., who was born around 1860, had married Frank Brunt, the owner of a hair-styling establishment in Burnley, and it may have been through his brother-in-law that young George Wharton became interested in this profession also.

The first quarter of the twentieth century saw the breaking up of Sarah Ann's family. In 1913 Moses died, two years before his mother who, living with her daughter Jane, died on 12 March 1915. Edgar had already left for his preaching mission in the West Indies. After the death of James Calvert in 1919 Jane stayed on in Burnley for a few years and then, her sons and daughters grown up and married, she decided in 1925 to take her youngest child Doris and emigrate to Canada where she took a position with an emigrant from Manchester whom Doris was later to marry. For a few days before her departure they stayed with Arthur and Maud Pratt in Wallasey, and a correspondence between Maud and Jane was kept up until the latter's death in 1939.

Of the Brunts' two sons, the elder, Thomas, became his father's apprentice until he was ready to operate his own establishment. Married to Jane Beatty, he had one son Tom who died of consumption – the ubiquitous disease of industrial England. The second son, Francis, had married and become father to one daughter Lily before the First World War in which he lost his life. The two youngest of the Alderson daughters were Lily and Rosamond, both of whom remained unmarried and died in their youth.

The name Rosamond is an unusual one among the Pratts and is, in our branch, limited to the family of Sarah Ann. It is worth noting, therefore, that a Rosamond Pratt lived long ago in the hamlet of Ivelet, just west of Gunnerside. She and her brother William, born in 1835 and 1837 respectively, were the children of William and Susan Pratt, and seemed to be orphans for, in the 1841 census, they were being raised by one Susannah Coates.

Rosamond would probably have remained nothing more than a card in a growing file of Pratts had it not been for a letter received from Mrs. Mabel Farnell of Chorley, Lancashire, who was searching out a Rosamond Pratt, born around 1836, the author of a sampler worked in 1843 at Mrs. Cope's school in Thwaites. That Rosamond and Sarah Ann were approximately the same age would lead to speculation that they may have been friends and probably cousins and that Sarah Ann's youngest daughter may have been the namesake of the elusive Rosamond of Swaledale. It is another of those delightfully exasperating mysteries that bounce around like bubbles on the genealogical sea.

The Winds of Newfoundland

In 1873 John Pratt bade farewell to his family and to his mother forever. It is difficult for us to imagine the leave-takings of those days. We remember the pain of parting from Gunnerside a generation earlier, and the hatred of the great sea that stretched out as a frightful barrier. The lonely missioner had need of the light that shone in the distance beyond the storm. He wanted to take Moses with him, but Sar'an would not part with her first-born. Some think that James and Anthony accompanied their brother to the New World, but there is nothing to substantiate this. Whatever the facts, the ties remained close and many was the visiting Methodist to Newfoundland who preached in Parson Pratt's church and was entertained in his hospitable home.

On 1 February 1876 John Pratt wrote a letter to a Newfoundland seaman, Captain William Knight, the son of Michael and Rachael. The Knights had been in Newfoundland for nearly two centuries, and Michael was born on the island in 1776. In 1722 one William Knight took his ten-year-old daughter Catherine to Poole, Dorset, for her baptism, where the event is duly recorded among the parish records of Poole folk born abroad. A fifty-year hiatus between William and Michael would suggest that the former may have been the grandfather of the latter and great grandfather of his namesake, the sea captain.

Of Captain Knight many tales were told and he seems to have been something of a yarner himself, having had a "large experience" in the "adventurous business of seals and sealing."[10] In 1859 a book was published entitled *After Icebergs with a Painter: Summer Voyage to Labrador and Around Newfoundland.* Its author was the Reverend Louis L. Noble and the artist was Frederick Edwin Church, both of New England. These two set off in a ship called "Integrity" under the command of Captain Knight, "a respected citizen of St. John's, and an accomplished sailor" in whom lay "the sheet anchor and mainstay . . . of our hopes for a pleasant and successful trip, humanly speaking,"[11] to write about and paint the majestic bergs off the Labrador coast.

Painting and writing, in between bouts of sea-sickness for these two landlubbers on the rolling northern seas, took up most of their time but they had "a pleasant custom of coming up, after dinner, and eating nuts and fruits on deck" and before betaking themselves to "reading, the pencil, and the brush," would engage in conversation and listen to some of the tales of Captain Knight. It was during one of these sessions they listened to the reason the captain had been available to take command of their expedition. He had recently

"lost a fine brig with a costly outfit for a sealing voyage, under the following circumstances: Immersed in the densest fog,

and driven by the gale, he was running down a narrow lane or
opening in the ice, when the shout of breakers ahead, and the
crash of bows upon a reef, came in the same moment. Instantly,
overboard they sprang, forty men of them, and saw their
strong and beautiful vessel almost immediately buried in the
ocean. There they stood, on the heaving field of ice, gazing
in mournful silence upon the great black billows as they rolled
on, one after another, bursting in thunder on the sunken
cliffs, a tremendous display of surf where the trembling spars
of the brig had disappeared forever. To the west of them
were the precipitous shores of Cape Bonavista, lashed by the
surge, and the dizzy roost of wild sea birds. For this, the
nearest land, in single file, with Captain Knight at their head,
they commenced at sunset their dreadful, and almost hopeless march. All night, without refreshment or rest, they went
stumbling and plunging on their perilous way, now and then
sinking into the slush between the pans or ice-cakes, and having
to be drawn out by their companions. But for their leader
and a few bold spirits, the party would have sunk down by
fatigue and despair, and perished. At daybreak, they were
still on the rolling icefields, beclouded with fog, and with nothing
in prospect but the terrible Cape and its solitary chance of
escape. Thirsty, famished, and worn down, they toiled on, all
the morning, all the forenoon, all the afternoon, more and
more slowly, and with increasing silence, bewildered and lost
in the dreadful cloud travelling along parallel with the coast,
and passing the Cape, but without knowing it at the time. But
for some remarkable interposition of Divine Providence, the
approaching sunset would be their last. Only the most determined
would continue the march into the next night. The worn out
and hopeless ones would drop down singly, or gather into little
groups on the cold ice, and die. As the Captain looked back
on them, a drawn-out line of suffering men, now in the hollow
of the waves, and then crossing the ridge, the last of them
scarcely seen in the mist, he prayed that God would interpose,
and save them. A man who prays in fair weather, may trust
God in the storm. So thought Captain Knight, when he thought
of home, and wife and children, and the wives and children
of his men, and made his supplication. They had shouted until
they were hoarse, and looked into the endless, gray cloud
until they had no heart for looking any longer. Wonderful to

tell! Just before sundown they came to a vessel. A few rods
to the right or to the left, and they must have missed it, and
been lost."[12]

Some time later Captain Knight received from Mr. Church
some colours and equipment to paint the land and sea scapes of
Newfoundland himself. How much he did no one knows but that
he successfully tried his hand at crafts is suggested in a citation
in the *Evening Telegram* of 7 February 1864, of a medal awarded
Mr. Wm. Knight for "a very ingenious model of a Sealing Vessel
in the ice."

On 7 January 1841 Captain Knight married Charlotte, born in
1820, the daughter of John Pitts (1783-1825) and Elizabeth Picco
and the granddaughter of one James Pitts (1735-1805) who had
come as a farmer-fisherman from the green and gentle village
of Kennford, Devon, to Lance Cove on the shores of Bell Island
in Conception Bay as a boy of fourteen.

The letter of John Pratt to Captain Knight ran:

My dear Mr. Knight,
I hope you will excuse me for the liberty I am taking in
sending you this note. You will have perceived before this time
by my conduct that I have been & am still paying special
attention to your daughter Fanny for whom I have special respect
& love.

I should like to be treading on sure & honourable ground &
to set my mind free & at rest I desire to have the consent of
her father & mother to the engagement. If you can so oblige me
I will promise you if ever the day come when your daughter
will be under my care & protection that she shall have every
comfort & attention that a Wesleyan Minister can bestow.

Can you please give me an answer to this note this evening
or tonight as I expect to go to the Cove tomorrow.
I am dear Sir
Yours faithfully,
John Pratt

Fanny became the wife of the Itinerant preacher from Yorkshire in 1877 and embarked with him on his pastoral career on
the island of Newfoundland. Until 1880 they were in St. John's
where William Knight, named for his grandfather the sea captain,
and James Charles Spurgeon, for his grandfather Pratt and the

143

famed Baptist evangelist, were born in 1878 and 1880.* Then began the biennial moves and in each of the windswept coastal villages from then on a new child was born to them. In 1882, in the great bleak arc of Western Bay, came Edwin John, named for his father and for his mother's brother; in 1884 at Bonavista, Charlotte Pitts, for her mother's mother; in 1886 at Cupids, Arthur Milligan, named for his mother's brother and his father's friend; in 1888 Calvert Coates in Blackhead; in 1892 at St. John's, Florence Sophia for her mother's sister; and in 1896 at Fortune, Nellie Beatrice.

Will, the oldest, a brilliant sensitive scholar, moved away to New York where he married and worked as an editor on an encyclopedia. In December of 1924, unable to endure the stresses of his life, he brought it to an end.

Jim Pratt, like his cousin Job in Bradford, combined the ability of the businessman with an artistic flair. He was a fine musician on the piano and after his retirement began painting the Newfoundland landscape – the gentle coves, icy harbour, the naked starrigans, and the fearful sea. In 1906 he married Marion Kerr (Minnie) of Scotland and they lived in St. John's where their five children were born. Gwenyth, born in 1907, married Hal Puddester, a magistrate and son of Sir John Puddester, a member of the commission of government before the island's entrance into confederation with Canada in 1949. The Puddesters' only child, James, born in 1946 is married to Margaret Hudson, a nurse, and their son Leigh was born in 1967.

Jack was born in 1909 and entered his father's business. In 1934 he married Christine Dawe and they have two sons. Christopher, an artist and poet of international repute, was born in 1935 and married to Mary West in 1957. Their children are John, born in 1958 when Christopher was on an art scholarship in England; Anne, in 1960; Barbara, in 1963; and Edwyn James (Ned), in 1964 and named for his great grandfather's brother, Edwin John.† This little family lives back of beyond in a cottage

*It is a mark of the chivalry of John Pratt that their first-born was named not traditionally for his paternal grandfather but for his mother's parent.
†Since there was already a John in the family, the name became James, a more suitable choice for, while retaining the initial J, it also perpetuates the ancient name of James within the family.

144

on the untamed shore of the Salmonier River in Newfoundland where Christopher may work out his salvation undisturbed by the clutter of man. The second son of Jack and Christine Pratt is Philip, born in 1946. He also possesses artistic longings which have been diverted into the more practical field of architecture, and which have won for him an international scholarship.

Max, born in 1911, went into business for himself and became manager of the Royal Trust Company in St. John's. In 1939 he married Jean Stirling, a teacher in the English Department of Memorial University. They have no children, and in 1967 moved to Halifax where their advent has been noticed by Christopher and Mary Pratt of the Bradford line who have been confused with Christopher and Mary of Newfoundland.*

Daphne, born in 1916, graduated from Mount Allison University and became, first the organizer of the Junior Red Cross in Newfoundland and later Director of Health Education for the island. Like her father, she also paints, interpreting her beloved Newfoundland in oil. In 1952 she married William House but their brief marriage was cut short by his untimely death in 1963.

Arthur, born in 1922, was the fifth and last child of Jim and Minnie Pratt. Although he tried his hand at business for a while, his chief love was journalism in which he conveyed deep feeling for his native country; the characters he created became known and loved throughout Newfoundland. In 1947 he married Minnie Parsons and their two sons are Douglas and Gerald. Both boys are endowed with artistic talent. Arthur was another not destined to live out his full life. He died after a trip to the Labrador he loved in 1968, a year after his mother and twelve years after his father.

Edwin John, known in his youth as Ed but in maturity as Ned, left school while very young to become apprenticed to a draper. Three years of it happily cured him of business and back to school he went, completing his high school with honours, after which he taught and preached in Newfoundland and, what must have pleased his father greatly, turned his face toward the Methodist ministry. He attended Victoria College at the University of Toronto, where he graduated and after a year or so in the ministry decided his vocation was teaching. He ultimately joined the staff

*The fact that both Marys are artists serves in no way to solve the confusion.

145

of the English Department of Victoria College where he settled into a happy career that gave him the opportunity of becoming the major poet he was. In 1918 he married Viola Whitney, and their only child, Claire, was born in 1921. E. J. Pratt died in 1964.

Lottie, living in Grand Bank – her father's last charge and place of his death – taught music. She was married to George Harris and they had no children. They had many trips, one of which was to England where they saw the ancestral valley. George and Lottie both died in 1954.

Arthur Milligan served in the First World War, earning for himself the reputation of being the most courageous soldier in a platoon noted for its reckless daring. After the war he remained in England and in 1924 married Maud Legg, of Scottish origin, who belongs to the same family as Robert Burns. Although his Methodist background was strong in him and would not permit him to attend the theatre, Art Pratt's love of the dramatic dominated his life. He was in business, but as in many of the Pratts his interest was elsewhere and he took his chief outlet in the writing of comic verse, publishing one volume entitled *Bally Rot*. Art and Maud lived in Wallasey until his death in 1961, after which the family moved to Cheltenham in the beautiful Cotswold area of Gloucestershire. Five children were born to this family. The first was Eleanor in 1925. She graduated with a teaching diploma in music and taught school, for some years in Canterbury and then in Cheltenham. Nearly two years later was born the first son Gerald who lived only six months and died in May 1927. In 1928 came John who is an architect, married to Diana Middleton. They have two daughters – Jennifer, born in 1963 and Catherine, in 1968. After living the first few years of their married life in Cheltenham they went to Edinburgh and live now at Penicuik in the heart of Midlothian. Margaret was born in 1931. She became an occupational therapist and spent two years in Toronto early in her career. On 6 August 1966, on the groom's birthday, Margaret married Roy Putnam, an engineer lately having entered the Methodist ministry. They immediately proceeded to Roy's first charge at Romily, near Birmingham, and their first child, Christopher, was born there just in time for the Christmas of 1967. The youngest of the children of Art and Maud is Florence Gertrude, born in 1934 and named for a sister of her father and a sister of her mother. Florence was in handcrafts before her marriage in 1958 to Alan Bland, an architect and an ardent naturalist, particularly fond of fish of the generic name of *lebistes*. They live in Hoylake, Cheshire, in the second of two houses designed by Alan, beside a pond abounding in wild life. Their two children are William, born in 1962, and Christine, born in 1964.

Calvert Coates was the business genius of the family, and started a dynasty similar to that of Christopher Pratt in Bradford. Premier Smallwood described him as "the ablest man Newfoundland has ever produced." Perhaps the York tea party of 1840 had in it a stronger brew than history has shown. Calvert's field, like that of his cousin Thomas, encompassed politics, philanthropy, and human relations. His business activities were multifaceted, and as President of Steers Limited he introduced them into all areas of Newfoundland commerce. An editorial in the *Daily News* at the time of his death in 1963 ran: "Senator Calvert Pratt was among the last of that outstanding and distinctive category of Newfoundland businessmen whose enterprise, courage and dynamic, gave to the economic life of the country a special vitality through the difficult century that preceded the era of Confederation."

As a member of the Canadian Senate after Confederation in 1949, Calvert Pratt never missed an opportunity to speak forcefully on all issues concerning Newfoundland. From the profits of a war contract for the building of six minesweepers he set up a scholarship for the education of the children of Newfoundland ex-servicemen. The conception and financing of the Agnes Pratt Home in St. John's for elderly citizens was his lasting memorial to his wife.

Finally, as a husband, father, brother, uncle, and friend, he was unparalleled. In the midst of his overly active life, he never appeared to have anything but endless time to make an extra trip if anyone needed him, or just for the sake of friendship. He never omitted the writing of a letter, and that by hand, on occasions of congratulation, bereavement, or acknowledgement. His correspondence, like that of his father and all his brothers, was voluminous. At the risk of repetition, and because of the strong similarity to Thomas Pratt, I can do nothing better than quote again Mark Antony's eulogy:

His life was gentle, and the elements
So mix'd in him that Nature might stand up
And say to all the world "This was a Man."

Calvert Coates was married in 1917 to Agnes Horwood, and their two sons – Ewart, born in 1919, and Calvert Coates, Jr., born in 1921, inherited the business which they now run with great zeal and success. Ewart served in the Navy in the Second World War, and married Yvonne Rorke in 1943. They have one daughter, Kathleen, born in 1948, and one son, James, born in 1949. In 1947 Calvert married Yvonne's cousin, Mary Rorke, and their three boys are Calvert Coates III, born in 1948; Robert, born in 1950; and Douglas, born in 1959.

The two youngest daughters, Floss and Nellie, remained unmarried. After her mother's death in 1926, Floss lived partly in St. John's with her brother Jim, partly in Toronto with her brother Ned, until in 1944 she made a great friend in Toronto with whom she made her permanent home.* Nellie trained as a nurse in Brooklyn, New York, where she worked and lived until arthritis forced her to leave the United States and return to Newfoundland. There she died in the spring of 1966.

The Antipodes
The mines were taking their toll of the daughters of Thomas Pratt, of his wife, and of himself. After his marriage to Mrs. Stoddard, Thomas seems to have moved several times, and the names Shildon, Eston, Cleveland, and Normanby figure large among the places remembered by his New Zealand grandchildren. Like his father's long ago in Gunnerside, his lungs were beginning to give way under the constant exposure to the lead. Nor could he meet the increasingly heavy cost of living nor adequately provide for Sarah and their four daughters. Maria Stoddard, a little girl in her early teens, was out in service with a "most tedious woman" who kept "little Ri on the go from 6 a.m. till 11 p.m. for £8 a year." In a letter to her brother Joshua in New Zealand, Sarah Pratt exclaimed that she "could not bear to think of the future for my four lovely girls." They would come to New Zealand, she wrote, if there was any carpentry work for Thomas, whose health was in grave jeopardy.

The invitation was issued and accepted, and in 1878, with the help of Moses, the little family set sail. That year Maria was in

*This was Margaret Violet (Peggy) Ray, who became the Librarian of Victoria University.

her middle teens; Lib was thirteen; Ruth, eleven; and Hannah, nine. The crossing and the early days of the emigrants have been described by their granddaughter, Mrs. Ada Ball:

". . . in 1878 Grandad was ordered a sea trip for his health. Lead, I expect, from the mine. He was the life of the ship, and even the captain sent for 'Mr. Pratt' to go and talk to a sailor in irons, or run the social side with games, and also the church services, etc. They came to Wellington to Grandma's brother Joshua Bell, six feet six, and he built them a house, just a shell near the Chinaman's gardens. Mum said the flies were terrible. They used to swish down the walls at night with wet cloths. Work was hard to get, and Grandad got a job milking and delivering same. Then they went to the coast and Grandad went into the mountains prospecting for gold and lived in one-roomed wharies, or batched. Grandma lived with the four girls as best she could, making hats, etc. There was a three-mile walk steadily uphill to Deniston perched on the rocks and terraces above, and when anyone saw a weary family group breasting the hill top, she would call to the girls to put the gurdle on the fire (open grate) and call them in for a rest, and tea and hot scones. I don't know what they lived on. Except for a time Grandad worked in the coal mines, or got a contract to paint the school or odd jobs. I never remember him in regular work. They bought an Island thirty miles from Westport and Grandma kept chooks and a cow or two, and kept the family in hats. She was a rare one, was Grandma, and highly respected and loved wherever she went. So was Grandad but, as was usual then, Grandad had very set ideas, and pushed them on to all the visitors when mum asked them round to tea on Sunday. My father was a strong, stocky, silent Scot, and used to get a little uncomfortable at some of Grandad's aired views, but would sit and wag his foot and say now't."

A few years after their arrival when they had moved to the mining area on the west coast, the daughters began to marry. Maria Stoddard became Mrs. Rigg. In 1886, at nineteen, Elizabeth married Hugh McFarlane, a blacksmith from Ireland and twelve years her senior. Some years after the marriage, Mr. Mc-Farlane was badly kicked by a horse he was shoeing and sent to the hospital for six weeks, after which he was sent home to die.

149

He was, however, a big strong man so that he lingered for years and died around 1905. Lib cared for him faithfully and earned their living by keeping a shop and doing tailoring and dressmaking. In 1896 Ruth married David Hall, the widowed father of a friend and thirty-three years older than herself. Thomas said at this ratio if he'd had any more daughters they'd have begun to marry centenarians. Mr. Hall, a city missioner for Wellington, was a man of property and comfortably off. After his death Ruth, who was an excellent manager, divided the estate equally into three parts, for her husband's daughter, his son, and herself. Hannah had married James McCaffrey in 1891, the silent Scot born in Glasgow in 1853, who had come to Dunedin in 1871, seven years before the Pratts.

For the first thirty years life was not easy. It was impossible to find jobs in the economic slump of the 1880s, and Thomas never had steady work. Sarah did not complain but in a letter to her daughters while they were visiting England she said: "When we got your letters I realize you had already been to Eston,* and oh how I longed to be there! It takes your letters so long and ships are so slow. I will wait for the flying machine to make the trip." Thomas's facility with his hands was a godsend during these years, and each time the family moved he built the house in which they were to live. After working at carpentry and catch as catch can for nearly thirty years, however, the time finally came when Grandad Thomas moved into his rightful sphere and took command of a Baptist Church at Lincoln when nearly seventy years old. Like his brother John in Newfoundland, he was a forceful and moving speaker, and the Lincoln days must have been the happiest of his life. Mrs. Colechin remembers that everyone for miles around always turned out when Mr. Pratt was slated to speak for the brilliant colour of his language and his original turn of phrase. Like his brother John he lived on a plane quite above the local cant of the times which showed the two of them distinctly not "hep." This sometimes led to merriment at their expense and a mild bewilderment would pass over their faces. A nephew of Fanny Pratt in Newfoundland remembers Parson John preaching on Hannah in the temple, her lips

*Mrs. Ball believes this may have been her grandmother's home town and the place in which she was married. We know from Elizabeth McFarlane's obituary that she was born there.

moving and no sound coming forth. "Why," asked the people, watching Hannah talking to herself, "what's the matter with Hannah?" John Pratt, quite unaware as the quotation passed his lips that it was a catch phrase at the time for the contrariness of things was astonished at the giggling of the congregation.[13] Similarly, Parson Thomas preaching on the Jeremiah, rolling phrases off his tongue, brought his point to a conclusion by exclaiming "Oh, for more Jeremiahs!" not knowing that "Jeremiah" was the current term for chamber pot.[14]

Lib, now widowed, moved with her parents to the new pastorate and, on her bicycle, helped with the church visiting, which must have been greatly appreciated by her father whose general health had been permanently damaged in his youth and who suffered much from shortness of breath. Weekends at the manse and Christmas parties and concerts are still remembered with joy. Elizabeth was a witty speaker and a fine singer as well.

It was during these years that Elizabeth McFarlane and Ruth Hall, also widowed by this time, took their trips to England and established the valuable connections that ultimately led to my rediscovery of the family in New Zealand. It was on one of these trips, Mrs. Ball thinks, that they acquired the black-bordered copy of John Pratt's letter to his congregation, and must have learned all kinds of details. Mrs. McFarlane's diaries of the 1909 and 1925 trips still exist and have provided much useful information.* The entries made while in the north of England are particularly interesting and are worth quoting in full.

"Thurs. June 12. Suddenly we took it into our heads to go and see our Birstal cousins. John Bell went with us and they were delighted to see us. Amy is married and has a baby 3 months old. Elizabeth Ann† and Eva live with Horace. They have a very pretty home & are very fine girls & well respected. They insisted on us going to stay with them.

"Sat. June 14. [at Haworth]. Halfway up was an uncompromising looking Wesleyan Chapel built 100 years ago & like the character of the people round about it looked as if it defied the world and sin.

*Ruth Hall also kept diaries but these have, unfortunately, been destroyed.
†She later became the second wife of John Driver.

"Mond. June 16. Went to see C. Pratt who is *the* furnisher of Bradford. C. was dead, but Thomas his son reigned in his stead. We found him to be very nice indeed & promised to go & see them at Highcliffe.

"Tues. June 17. John saw us off in the 1:30 train to Burnley. We had to wait half an hour at Halifax but did not see much of the town & arrived at Burnley at 3:30. Dorothy & her son Herbert met us at Manchester Rd Station. Herbert with his friend carried our things & we were soon at 82 Dall St. . . . John Driver gave us a very warm welcome, he is a most lovable character. William the eldest is a local preacher & like Dad as can be.* Sarah is 17, a very sweet girl with a good voice. Herbert is a fine young man in the drapery at the Co'op. Mary the eldest girl is dead. After tea Dorothy took us down to Jane's to see Aunt Sarah Ann who was delighted to see us, as indeed they all were. Edgar, Jane's son is the pride of his grandmother. He is in the Wesleyan ministry. James Anty is a good musician. Cissie is a lovely singer. Rose recites well & sings alto with little Doris. On the way up called to see Pollie & Jim† for a few minutes then to see Moses & his family. They are a handsome intelligent family, 4 boys & a girl. Moses, Maria, & Dorothy took us to Lowerby Park, . . . Had tea with Moses, then went over Healy Heights with John & Dorothy.

"Friday, June 17. Aunt came up for the day yesterday where she put in a good talk. To-day she went with us to see Sarah Ann.** . . . John came home & said that he was told at the mill that Ru was an M.P. in N.Z. & that I was a leading suffragette. Not bad, eh!

"Monday. . . . James†† brought his family in this morning to see us. His son is going into the Army*** work immediately. Had a long talk before we went to Jane's††† to tea.

"Tuesday. Went for a chat with Aunt this morning. She is very

*Whether this refers to William's Dad or Mrs. McFarlane's Dad is uncertain.
†Probably Sar'an's son, James Wharton, though Polly was George's wife.
**Her daughter, Mrs. Brunt.
††Dorothy Driver's older brother, James Pratt.
***The Salvation Army.
†††Probably Jane Calvert.

unwell but pleased to see us. She gave us some very interesting facts about Gunnerside & I spent some time reading letters from Spurgie & Willie in their young days.* . . . Herbert is not very well & is in bed for a few days.

"Friday. On Wed. we went to George & Polly's† for dinner & tea. James Anty & Cissie came in & we had some music. Next day went to see Aunt who loves a talk. Came back to dinner & as it was very wet had a good read.

"Saturday. Had dinner with Aunt who had come to Dorothy's . . . Went to the cemetery where we looked for Grandma's grave** but could not find it. Saw Uncle & Aunt's†† also Mary Driver's."

This is the last Burnley entry and the sisters seem to have left.

It was the day of elaborate autograph albums and Elizabeth McFarlane's was no exception. Mid flowers and scrolls the Burnley family wrote their farewell messages, pious, loving, and humorous. Among the several verses contributed by James Herbert Driver was the following original stanza written especially for Elizabeth and Ruth:

I write these few lines with gladness
And just with a touch of sadness
As we part from Elizabeth & Ruth
But though the Ocean may part us
The memory will *ne'er* depart us
Of Cousins *Elizabeth & Ruth.*

And Aunt Sarah Ann optimistically wrote:

it is
all is well that ends well
and has a good beginning.

The diary continues:

*It is intriguing who these two may have been. The only "Spurgie" of whom I have heard was James Charles Spurgeon of Newfoundland. Is it possible that the two oldest sons of John Pratt had sent letters to their Aunt Sarah Ann?
†The Wharton's, son and daughter-in-law of Sarah Ann.
**Sarah Pratt who died in 1876.
††William and Mary Driver.

"Wednesday. Went to Highcliffe House today, a lovely big place & a fine family of 9 boys & 1 girl. They showed us their conservatory & collection of butterflies & altogether gave us a good time. There is to be a garden party of the Eastbrook Brotherhood there on Wed. Mr. & Mrs. Pratt had just returned from the conference at Lincoln.

"Thurs, 15 July. Spent the morning in 'Spurgeon's Tabernacle' where every kindness was shown to us. It is a wonderful place for hearing & is a very fine property."

This last entry must have been made in London when they visited Metropolitan Church. Gunnerside itself does not appear in the 1909 diary, although it seems strange that they would not have visited there.

In 1912 Ruth Hall went alone to England to visit the Drivers, as has been mentioned above. In 1925, however, the sisters took a long journey and were in England for several months. They were in the Dales by Easter, and Mrs. McFarlane's diary has this entry for Wednesday the 9th (of April presumably):

"The bus came to the back door at nine & into it was trundled Blankets, easy chair, broom, buckets, boxes of eats, & Amy, Ru, & I. Enjoyed the ride [to Richmond]. The dale opened out on both sides, lovely fields enclosed by grey stone walls & all looking as if they were done up for the weekend – woods with lacy looking trees, primrose-dotted hedgerows & banks, smooth winding roads made a picture which will live as long as the kindness which prompted such a treat. Through Grinton with its old church, past Reeth, a town of considerable importance as the head of the Circuit, having a Superintendent Minister: to Helaugh where we were met by a stalwart gentle-spoken dalesman who said he thought we should be here soon. We here transferred our cargo to the little cart pulled by a shaggy horse, & ourselves onto the road, our liers [?] returned to Darlington & we went up the lane, where fresh beauties or fresh views of the same met us. Primroses or palms were picked for table decorations after rising in the world. We struck off to the left where we squeezed through small gaps in stone walls, & we were content to fill a little space, for a short time even Amy the slim one, filled the gap. Heather Cottage was soon

154

reached & we were once more at home. We all had an empty
feeling so dinner was once more on the table, & nearly as soon
off. It was an excellent distributing area. An egg and bacon
pie which came out of a wonder box of eats soon looked the worse
for wear, and we so much the better. It was an Adamless Eden,
& we put in a busy time till eight o'clock including another meal,
when, enter Adam. A talk & supper followed by bed did much
to make life worth living.

"Good Friday. Mr. Bearpark called at ten to make plans for our
convoy to Keld. We were to meet the motor at three for Keld.
It was a glorious ride up the Dale. We saw a winding road in the
distance beside a snowy bit of hillside which we were told
was Keld. Though raining most of the time we managed to see
banks of primroses. On arriving at the Chapel we found a
stove in the centre giving out a good heat, & we sat round till the
children came, as I was to take the Children's Service. They
came trouping in together with several who were not children.
The minister, a lad of 22, who looked 18, came in. Talking
to him I found he was a Medcar boy, & had preached several
times in Lingdale Chapel. We had a good sing and a good
service. . . . [See page 108.] After a little local sightseeing we
went back to the Chapel at 6:15 & found it rapidly filling up
for the meeting at 7. By 6:45 it was packed so off we went into
'When I survey' to 'Job.' The magnificent old tune seemed to
shake the Chapel. Speech after speech followed. 'Jesus shall
reign' to 'Rennington,' after my talk, was sung & then an
appeal was made to which four responded. We motored home
after a great supper in a big garage owned by the Lord of the
Manor, reached Heather Cottage, Mr. Taylor coming with us. It
was funny springing from tussock to heather clump. We
reached home at 12:15 & bed half an hour later.

"Saturday. Showery and sunny. In the afternoon we went to see
Mrs. Whitfield who is almost a relation, a lovely old dear who
knew Aunts Sarah Ann & Bessie. Her daughter Agnes is a local
preacher & a woman of wide reading & much culture. They
made us very welcome & Mrs. W. lived her young life over
again. Our cousins are her cousins so we are almost akin. I
had been asked to preach at Helaugh Chapel Anniversary on
Easter Sunday. Ru was not well, so after Ch, in the afternoon

she rested, but did not feel up to the long walk to Helaugh so Jack, Amy & I set off at 5:40 & found a splendid congregation. We all had a fine time, at least they said so & I knew it. Our new cousins had walked the two miles to be there.

"Monday. Lovely, fresh moorland air, combined with a smell of bacon frying, sent us flying downstairs to begin another day. After dinner we went to Mrs. Bell's where we had a proper Yorkshire tea. Mr. Mattaha [sic] Bell is a local preacher with a forty years record & we had a time. Home after a 40-minute walk, supper & bed.

"Tues. Jack took me for a ride to Arkengarthdale, through Reeth. Amy & Ru walked the four miles over the top. After visiting the Church & Chapel he ran Amy and me a mile up the moor, where we walked over, passing on our way the Surrender Mine, now abandoned & sat on the Bridge eating an orange, he going back for Ru, & taking her the long way round – a long, happy tiring day. The Ch. is partly a 13 Cent. the other part restored 1890. The Chapel, compactly built in 1840, seats 350. . . .

"Thurs. Amy left us to-day, very wet. Fine in the afternoon when we went to Mrs. Bell's, then to Harker's Farm their old home, now the home of their daughter Mary. Ru took a snap of me standing by the chair used by Wesley as an open air pulpit. Then I took one of Ru & Mary.

"Friday we spent in walking to Gunnerside over the tops. In passing Blades Ru took a snap of me standing in the doorway of the house where John Wesley frequently stayed when in the dale & from the doorsteps preached to the lead miners who have done so much to make the Methodism of the Dales the sturdy plant that it now is. I took one of Ru, with his porridge bowl & spoon in her hand, but somehow it vanished off the film. At least it has never been seen since. Reached Gunnerside after a four-hour walk where we got a cup of tea. Saw Mr. Redvers Pratt who with his bride were enjoying their honeymoon. Heard from Mrs. Shaw (a character of W. Riley's in Rachel Bland) that Uncle John's son had been there a year ago, enquiring for any of the Pratt family, but who left no address.*
Caught the three o'clock mail & off to Low Row.

*Had he known what a shrine Gunnerside was to become and with whom he should leave an address he most certainly would have done so.

156

"Sat. [See p. 108 for description of tea with Mrs. Wiseman.] . . .
As the clocks were put back an hour, we shifted ours when
we went to bed, & Sunday was the first day of Summer time.

"Sunday. At 1:30 we met the Circuit car, which must be made
of elastic. It takes the preachers to their appointments. It had
dropped three and there were three when we got in. Reached
the Chapel five minutes late & found half the Congregation waiting for us. I was taken to the vestry & Ru in at the door. After
arranging hymns, etc., we went into the Chapel. [For the re-
mainder of the stay in Gunnerside, see p. 108.]"

On Saturday 26 April they left Swaledale, and on Sunday a
simple entry reads: "Met Mr. W. Heslop," with no clue as to
what, if any, relation he was to James Heslop.

On Thursday 14 May they came to Kettlewell where their
father had lived out his boyhood years. On the day of their
arrival it was

"wet in the morning but lovely in the afternoon. Libby, Ru & I
came by train, Agnes, Sydney, Grace, & the baby later.
Langcliff looked lovely. After the beds were made we all got in,
glad of the rest. There is a wonderful little church here, the
old part dating from 1100. There is a list on the church porch of
the Vicars of Kettlewell from 1348 to 1888. . . . The weather
is simply glorious & Ru & I took a walk to Starbotton yesterday
. . . houses all over the village bear the date of 1635 & 1655
& look it."

On this trip Sister Bessie preached many times on a circuit
plan.

"Skeeby. Tuesday [19th or 26th]. The chairlady introduced me
and I was off. The interest was most flattering. . . . What a
sing! Yorkshire Methodism is a lovely thing.* [For the meeting
with Mr. James Bell, see p. 89.]

"May 30. Left for Burnley . . . longest 70 miles I ever travelled. I
drank a cup of tea which Mary† got for me & tumbled into
bed. Harry is a fine little chap, the apple of his Mother's eye.
Willie is good company very, & Mary was very good to us.

*How John Pratt would have rejoiced in this niece.
†Mrs. William Driver.

"Sunday, May 31. Went with Mary to School where I gave greetings from N. Z. I told them I had been a scholar there as a little girl,* also mentioned Sallie who was remembered by the teachers, several of them sending messages to her."

From Burnley they travelled to other parts of England, and in July were back in the dales once more.

"Sat. July 4. Ru went to Gunnerside today to the Feast there. I am sure she will have a good time.

"Wed. July 8. Cousin came in to the kitchen where I was making a shirt for her & said Mr. Freeman had come in to say that he was taking Rev. Henry Howard to Gunnerside and would I like to go, if so would I be ready in half an hour. I was, and we went to corner of Stanhope Rd to meet the car. Rev. Henry was a tall gentlemanly man, I should think in the early sixties. He had missed his connection at Skipton where he had gone to have a talk with Rev. Wiseman in reference to a case at Blackpool. . . . We were soon off. The leafy Blackwell woods were at their very best . . . & on through Skeeby where we had such a success with the W. A. till Richmond was reached, that strong-hold of ancient times with its date of 1067. . . . Then came the snake like road up the Dale crossing & recrossing the Swale as its brown waters are fed by many a peaty stream from the moors. The whole road is marked by notice boards giving caution to drivers, & late as we were we had to slack down & go 6 miles an hour when 60 would have put us there in good time. . . . Did the pace as fast as we could but still we were an hour & 15 min. late. As we came within sight of Low Row we got a glimpse of the worried looking face of our energetic friend Mr. Taylor who said 'Sister what have you been doing to keep Mr. Howard all this time?' . . . To see Ru's face as she looked up at the close of the prayer & saw me sitting there with Mr. Howard nearly sent me off into fits. After tea at the Matthew Bells back to Chapel. . . . Ru had a great time, particulars of which are in her diary.

"Sat. . . . we changed into bus for Lingdale where, since our childhood Days, Mountains had shrunk to hills, rushing

*Thomas and Sarah Pratt must have lived in Burnley also for a little while, unless Elizabeth had been sent to relatives for her schooling.

158

streams to tiny rills . . . went around . . . to the schools where we
went as Children, to the Chapel which to us were peopled
by those who had 'Crossed the Flood.' . . . We met a few who
remembered Dad & Mother."

Thomas's family was perpetuated through his youngest daughter
only. The McCaffreys had nine children, five of whom lived to
adulthood. The oldest is Ada who has supplied so much information for this story. Born in 1892, she married John William Goss
Ball, a descendant of John Ball who led the Peasant's Revolt in
the fourteenth century, was executed for it in 1381, and was later
interred in Westminster Abbey. In his name survives also another of his forebears, the composer, John William Goss. Ada and
John have three children: Frank, born in 1925, is an electrician
and married to Patricia Cottee who is an opera singer and soloist.
Nancy, born in 1927, inherited the missionary zeal of her ancestors and was for nine years a teacher-missionary in the Solomon Islands and then infant supervisor in a local school. Winton,
born in 1929, is a building contractor and married to Glenys
Bullard, who is a music teacher, organist, and noted pianist.

John was born in 1894. A merchant ships officer in the First
World War, he was rescued by the British Navy when his ship
was torpedoed off the African Coast. In 1949 he was killed in an
accident on board ship just off Chile. Hugh, born in 1898, is the
owner of an orchestra and a furniture factory and is interested
in antiques. In 1923 he married Violet Bruce and they have taken
two world trips. Their daughter Maureen, born in 1932, is married to Trevor Garing, an electronic designer, in charge of the
New Zealand Broadcasting Corporation's TV studio development
section in their engineering department. Before her marriage and
the birth of their two children, Maureen also worked for NZBC
and still does some free-lance broadcasting. Their daughters
Andrea and Gillian, born in 1959 and 1963, are nearly responsible
for a chapter on Pratt pets, so keen was Gillian that her dog
Koko, a Japanese Pug, be represented.

Thomas, born in 1899, became a farmer in Canterbury, New
Zealand. He was in the Second World War and was three years
in Greece and Egypt. In 1955 on the way to a tennis match
Thomas and his daughter Patricia were killed in an accident.
Arthur, born in 1903, is an organist and music teacher, married

to Esther Hopwood. Their five children are Rae Esther, married to Bruce Scammell, a Methodist minister; Rex Arthur, researcher; Dulcie, a violinist and schoolteacher before her marriage to Ernest Powell in 1960; Vera, a flutist and piano teacher; and Gwenyth, studying for a commercial career.

By the end of the First World War the Lincoln years were drawing to their close. Among the millions who fell prey to the world flu epidemic in 1918 was Thomas Pratt and he died on 25 November, a few days after the Armistice, the last child of James and Sarah Pratt. Sarah, his wife, survived him by two and a half years. Aunt Lib died in 1933 and Aunt Ruth, in her old age, went to live with the cousin she had brought out to New Zealand so many years before, and stayed on with her until her death in 1940. The little sister Hannah, through whom the family survived and flourished, died in 1949, thirteen years after her husband.

By These Fruits

For the amount of time, effort, cost and research that has gone into this project, the results are comparatively disappointing. Two things, however, must be kept in mind. First, the obscure origins of the Pratt family who, as recently as three and even two generations back, were illiterate. So nothing prior to that time can have been preserved in writing. Second, emigrants usually did not, or could not, keep in touch with their families, once they had taken the painful step of parting. With their faces turned towards the New World and a new life, they passed few backward glimpses along to their children who, beyond the knowledge that their fathers came out from the Old Country, showed little interest in their past. Thus, people bearing the name of Pratt, who are now legion as there is a strong male gene running through the family, with whom I have had contact, either cannot locate their ancestral home or lack the incentive to try. The Pratt family in America, in existence since the sixteenth century, has expanded into a thousand fragments, and many branches have been traced back to the time of arrival, having come from all parts of England, with a heavy concentration on the

Midlands. Many also came from Yorkshire, but never yet have I discovered anyone, other than those written of here, whose roots were in Swaledale.

In assessing the qualities of a family, especially one of whom only a small part is known, one runs into many difficulties. In the long run, many-faceted man exists in all our families, so that one cannot point and say "See, there goes my tribe." Like most families, this one has its share of fools, and its share of wise men, and of those who, foolish in some respects, are wise in others; it shares with humanity the lazy and the ambitious, the weak and the strong, the open and the closed. I have lived for several years now in close proximity to a thousand or so members of my clan, both living and dead, and a few qualities and characteristics have, however, emerged.

As has been mentioned above, the Pratts, along with countless other families in England and throughout the world, were born, suffered, and died in an ambience of poverty and religion, and these two forces cannot be overestimated in the influence they have had on the family, both ancient and modern. Poverty was the great foe; religion the great ally. Nor, when poverty abated, did religion necessarily diminish, though it may have taken new forms. Poverty is fought in different ways. Until the mines began to slow down in the early part of the nineteenth century, the Pratts relied on religion and their own humour and resilience. They also loved their village and their valley. But no village or valley, indeed no religion, can suffice when it comes to feeding hungry children. Christopher Pratt, as the grandson of his Grandfather Metcalfe, took advantage of the move out of Swaledale to release himself and his family for all time to come from the limitations of poverty. It is suspected that the business ability may have been due to the Metcalfes rather than the Pratts, although they indeed could not be responsible for Calvert Coates.

In looking at the qualities, laid out as on a wide and airy panorama stretching backwards and forwards in time, one is struck by the lack of roughness, toughness, and coarseness that might be expected among the members of a mining community, and their descendants. The overriding quality, as far as I have been able to see, is that of gentleness. Sometimes it is the fearless gentleness of the prophet or saint which forsakes itself at the sight of unrighteousness, but which saves the zealot from fanaticism; sometimes the gentleness of the weak who buckle under

161

the strokes of fortune. Most times it is the gentleness of the humorous and loving man, vulnerable to hurt, and not always resilient.

To gentleness and sensitivity is added a strong element of conservatism and its sister caution – an unwillingness to stick out one's neck for fear of losing one's head. This may account for the fact that the Pratt family as a whole is not a talkative one. Among the lot of them I don't believe I have encountered that very common phenomenon, the compulsive talker. Conversationalists, yes, but quietly keeping to themselves their own private world. Dealings with Swaledale folk have confirmed this. "Do you know," said Mrs. Margaret Batty of Reeth, "that the Pratts have a reputation for two things: one, being close, and two, being leaders in the community? 'Close' in Swaledale means that they do not discuss their affairs, particularly regarding money." And, closer to home, Daphne House earned for herself the sobriquet of "Clam Daphne" for whom the weather was the most favoured topic.

Courage is also there, of the kind that must outwit the enemy of the day, but the windmills at which one is tempted to tilt are confined to the realm of the mind and the artistic spirit, in which the gentle meadows have remained to smile and flower in the sun and rain. To outwit the enemy of the day – or to live by one's wits, as did Lefwinus Prat in the ancient days of Hereward the Wake. Perhaps the demon who presides over man's wits travelled along with the Pratts over the centuries during their passage through and out of the lead mines of the dale. We've seen evidence of it in the business enterprises of Christopher and of Calvert Pratt. Perhaps it was this demon that spurred Edgar Calvert into the making of a most elaborate booby trap during the Second World War, designed to polish off the first of the enemy who made for the privy under which it was hung. Perhaps the demon of wits in cahoots with the demon of pratfalls worked through tricks, fun and games toward the survival of the clan. The clowning of Arthur Pratt, down on his knees reciting a prayer to Venus to his sister-in-law while she was struggling to get past him in order to serve dinner to eighty guests; the humorous enterprises of my father who attempted to make his fortune by selling a brilliantly concocted mixture entitled "Universal Lung Healer" may be attributed to these demons, while the demon of pratfalls was strong in Floss Pratt who could never resist an opportunity to make a pun or slip into a comic role if the situation showed her any loophole.

This essay has tried to show how the battle was fought by each member of the family. It is doubtful that the Swaledale folk took an active part in politics, isolated as they were, or that they even had any. Wesleyans, however, were espoused not to socialism, as one might expect, but to the rising forces of liberalism. They were patriots and religious zealots and although the ideals of Wesley were those of socialism, socialism itself was too new, too foreign, too anti-religious to be accepted. The Pratts, as they began to be more sophisticated, were capital L Liberals. Gladstone was one of the heroes of my grandfather, and it is appropriate that his grandson Ewart should have received the name of the great Liberal statesman. But the Pratts as a family took little part in politics, with the exception of Thomas of Bradford, who was elected unanimously to the Bradford City Council in a by-election in 1919 and was re-elected in 1920 by an overwhelming majority over the Socialist opponent, and, a generation later, Calvert Coates of Newfoundland who was appointed, as a Liberal Independent, to the Canadian Senate.

As both Liberals and Methodists became respectable, so did the Pratts become conservative with a small c, though adhering loyally to the Liberal Party. But for most of them, politics was a bore. The visionaries among them could not clutter themselves with it. John in Newfoundland kept his mystic eye on the next world, so did Thomas of New Zealand, and my father kept his on the riches of the mind. Some of his greatest joys were in the realm of the imagination where all things are possible and the hungry fed. His vision of the apocalyptic feast to which he must have invited, among all the underprivileged of the world, the folk of the ancestral mines of Swaledale, reflects, in "The Depression Ends," the sky as the limit of his hospitality.

If I could take within my hand
The rod of Prospero for an hour,
With space and speed at my command,
And astro-physics in my power,
Having no reason for my scheme
Beyond the logic of a dream
To change a world predestinate

From the eternal loom of fate,
I'd realize my mad chimera
By smashing distaff and the spinner,
And usher in the golden era
With an apocalyptic dinner.
I'd place a table in the skies
No earthly mind could visualize:
No instruments of earth could bound it –
'Twould take the light-years to go round it.
And to this feast I would invite
Only the faithful, the elect –
The shabby ones of earth's despite,
The victims of her rude neglect,
The most unkempt and motley throng
Ever described in tale or song.
All the good lads I've ever known
From the twelve winds of sea and land
Should hear my shattering bugle tone
And feel its summoning command.
No one should come who never knew
A famine day of rationed gruel,
Nor heard his stomach like a flue
Roaring with wind instead of fuel:
No self-made men who proudly claim
To be the architects of fame;
No profiteers whose double chins
Are battened on the Corn-Exchange,
While continental breadlines range
Before the dust of flour-bins.
These shall not enter, nor shall those
Who soured with the sun complain
Of all their manufactured woes,
Yet never had an honest pain:
Not these – the well-groomed and the sleeked,
But all the gaunt, the cavern-cheeked,
The waifs whose tightened belts declare
The thinness of their daily fare;
The ill starred from their natal days,
The gaffers and the stowaways,
The road tramps and the alley-bred
Who leap to scraps that others fling,

With luck less than the Tishbite's fed
On manna from the raven's wing.

This dinner, now years overdue,
Shall centre in a barbecue.
Orion's club – no longer fable –
Shall fall upon the Taurus head.
No less than Centaurs shall be led
In roaring pairs forth from their stable
And harnessed to the Wain to pull
The mighty carcass of the bull
Across the tundras to the table,
Where he shall stretch from head to stern,
Roasted and basted to a turn.
I'd have the Pleiades prepare
Jugged Lepus (to the vulgar *hare*),
Galactic venison just done
From the corona of the sun,
Hoof jellies from Monoceros,
Planked tuna, shad, stewed terrapin,
And red-gut salmon captured in
The deltas of the Southern Cross.
Devilled shrimps, and scalloped clams,
Flamingoes, capons, luscious yams
And cherries from Hesperides;
And every man and every beast,
Known to the stars' directories
For speed of foot and strength of back,
Would be the couriers to this feast –
Mercury, Atlas, Hercules,
Each bearing a capacious pack.
I would conscript the Gemini,
Persuading Castor to compete
With Pollux on a heavy wager,
Buckboard against the sled, that he,
With Capricornus could not beat
His brother mushing Canis Major.
And on the journey there I'd hail
Aquarius with his nets and pail,
And Neptune with his prong to meet us
At some point on the shores of Cetus,

And bid them superintend a cargo
Of fresh sea food upon the Argo –
Sturgeon and shell fish that might serve
To fill the side boards with *hors d'oeuvres.*

And worthy of the banquet spread
Within this royal court of night,
A curving canopy of light
Shall roof it myriad-diamonded.
For high above the table head
Shall sway a candelabrum where,
According to the legend, dwelt a
Lady seated in a chair
With Alpha, Beta, Gamma, Delta,
Busy braiding up her hair.
Sirius, the dog star, shall be put
Immediately above the foot,
And central from the cupola
Shall hang the cluster – Auriga,
With that deep sapphire-hearted stella,
The loveliest of the lamps, Capella.

For all old men whose pilgrim feet
Were calloused with life's dust and heat,
Whose throats were arid with its thirst,
I'd smite Jove's taverns till they burst,
And punch the spigots of his vats,
Till flagons, kegs and barrels all
Were drained of their ambrosial
As dry as the Sahara flats,
For toothless, winded ladies who,
Timid and hesitating, fear
They might not stand the barbecue
(Being so near their obsequies),
I'd serve purees fresh from the ear
Of Spica with a mild ragout –
To satisfy the calories –
Of breast of Cygnus stiffened by
The hind left leg of Aries,
As a last wind-up before they die.
And I would have no wardens there,

Searching the platters for a reason
To seize Diana and declare
That venison is out of season.
For all those children hunger-worn
From drought or flood and harvest failing,
Whether from Nile or Danube hailing,
Or Yangtze or the Volga born,
I'd communize the total yields
Of summer in the Elysian fields,
Gather the berries from the shrubs
To crown soufflés and syllabubs.
Dumplings and trifles and *éclairs*
And rolypolies shall be theirs;
Search as you may, you will not find
One dash of oil, one dish of prunes
To spoil the taste of the macaroons,
And I would have you bear in mind
No dietetic aunt-in-law,
With hook nose and prognathic jaw,
Will try her vain reducing fads
Upon these wenches and these lads.
Now that these grand festivities
Might start with holy auspices,
I would select with Christian care,
To offer up the vesper prayer,
A padre of high blood – no white
Self-pinched, self-punished anchorite,
Who credits up against his dying
His boasted hours of mortifying,
Who thinks he hears a funeral bell
In dinner gongs on principle.
He shall be left to mourn this night,
Walled in his dim religious light:
Unto this feast he shall not come
To breathe his gloom. No! rather some
Sagacious and expansive friar,
Who beams good will, who loves a briar,
Who, when he has his fellows with him
Around a board, can make a grace
Sonorous, full of liquid rhythm,
Boom from his lungs' majestic bass;

Who, when requested by his host
To do the honours to a toast,
Calls on the clan to rise and hold
Their glasses to the light a minute,
Just to observe the mellow gold
And the rare glint of autumn in it.

Now even at this hour he stands,
The benison upon his face,
In his white hair and moulded hands,
No less than in his spoken grace.
"We thank thee for this table spread
In such a hall, on such a night,
With such unusual stores of bread,
O Lord of love! O Lord of light!
We magnify thy name in praise
At what thy messengers have brought,
For not since Galilean days
Has such a miracle been wrought.
The guests whom thou hast bidden come,
The starved, the maimed, the deaf, and dumb,
Were misfits in a world of evil,
And ridden hard by man and devil.
The seven years they have passed through
Were leaner than what Israel knew.
Dear Lord, forgive my liberty,
In telling what thou mayst not know,
For it must seem so queer to thee,
What happens on our earth below:
The sheep graze on a thousand hills,
The cattle roam upon the plains,
The cotton waits upon the mills,
The stores are bursting with their grains,
And yet these ragged ones that kneel
To take thy grace before their meal
Are said to be thy chosen ones,
Lord of the Planets and the suns!
Therefore let thy favours fall
In rich abundance on them all.
May not one stomach here tonight
Turn traitor on its appetite.

Take under thy peculiar care
The infants and the aged. Bestow
Upon all invalids a rare
Release of their digestive flow,
That they, with health returned, may know
A hunger equal to the fare,
And for these mercies, Lord, we'll praise
Thee to the limit of our days."

He ended. The salubrious feast
Began: with inundating mirth
It drowned all memories of earth:
It quenched the midnight chimes: nor ceased
It till the wand of Prospero,
Turning its magic on the east,
Broke on a master charm, when lo!
Answering the summons of her name,
Fresh from the surf of Neptune came
Aurora to the Portico.

   Perhaps this spacious feast in all its extravaganza may be
theirs, who knows? In any case it may please them to whom
some of the secrets of the universe may now be shared to know
that such a shindig has been prepared for them by one of their
own issue. It is hoped that they will enjoy it, and that it will
make amends for the inconvenience of the resurrection this story
has brought upon them.

The Poetry of E. J. Pratt

The will she made contained no room for strife,
For twisted words concerning gold or lands,
For all the wealth that she had saved from life
Was such as lay within her folded hands.

She would have been less rich with other store,
And we the poorer if she had not willed
Only her heart, and then gone out the door,
Leaving that cupboard on the latch and filled.
"A Legacy"

In looking at my father from the perspective reached by six years of genealogical study, I am impressed by many likenesses to his ancestry on his father's side. Much has been written of him and of his work and in most of the biographical and critical material he is viewed against his background as a Newfoundlander in whose blood flows the same salt as that of the sea. This is, of course, true, but back of that is an entire area, harking back to a time long out of memory in which forces are inevitably at work forming and composing the sinews of thought and habit that ran as inevitably through his life and writing as did those of the sea.

Out on the remote hills of Yorkshire is a quality of expanse, of hugeness, in which man, like the incidental characters in a Japanese mountain landscape, is in his place, of nature as well as in it. He belongs there as much as do the leaves on the trees, making rustles in the wind as it passes through them, or as do the curlew and the lapwing who scream their way through the airways above the hills or the larks eternally singing on their way to the sun.

The Yorkshire-born singer, Janet Baker, hinted at this when she spoke of the broad vocal ranges that develop among the folk of Yorkshire in response to the sweep of their environment.

A music which the earth has only known
In the drab hours of its emptiness.[1]

Indeed, the very term "broad Yorkshire" indicates something of what is meant. There is an element of hugeness, and in writing of its influence on my father I see it as humanity whose vehicle is language. It can be broken down into two main categories: the struggle, from which emerges the hero; and the wind, giving rise to the mystic. In discussing the various aspects of my father's work, these two elements will be seen to run like interweaving threads. The rhythm of the sea replaces the rhythm of the eternal hills, but the faithfulness of God in his seasons remains the same. Seedtime and harvest, ebb and flow; the wind that lashes the waves against the rock is the same wind that hurls the snow against the moor, and the fisherman's hut with its "dreams that survive the night" and "doors held ajar in storms" is but another version of the miner's cottage with its lantern shining in the dark to welcome and guide the weary feet returning through sleet and blizzard from the dusky mines.

In the previous chapter I mentioned gentleness and sensitivity as two of the predominant qualities among the Pratts as I have discovered them. I shall again begin with them here for without this backdrop it is difficult to understand properly the heroic narratives and the love of a fight that were characteristic of E. J. Pratt.

These two qualities come first to my mind, as his daughter, and I feel compelled to try to explain a little of the quality of this gentleness. By the time my first memories of him had become clear he was past forty and had settled already into a quieter routine of living than in the days of the Universal Lung Healer, mountain climbing, and peddling the Standard Dictionary of Facts through the prairies on a bicycle. Evenings and weekends, when he was not playing golf, saw him in his den in a huge chair beside the fire, filling black notebooks with a tiny stub of pencil which he would sharpen from time to time with a pen-knife into the fire. In the summer the setting would change to our cottage at Bobcaygeon in what was then deep country stillness where he would settle comfortably, feet up, into a chair on the screened-in verandah, or in the green den he had built for himself fifty yards from the cottage and nearer the lake where there was nothing to disturb him but the occasional odious crow. I don't remember him ever using a pencil more than two inches long. His writing was equally tiny and would fill every available millimeter of the page. And although it became shortly afterwards illegible even to himself, it gave him pleasure to see an overpopulated sheet of paper, giving itself utterly to the purpose for which it was made.*

Disciplining his daughter was a very subtle art. For along with his gentleness went iron-clad rules. There was very little in the way of punishment, which he scarcely ever had the heart to inflict, and yet by some osmosis that many of us would give our

---

*It is interesting to note that the Brontës, living in the vast reaches of the Yorkshire moors, filled tiny notebooks with even tinier writing. It may be argued that they worked at a time when paper was scarce.
When my father wrote, not only was paper not scarce, but he was the last one to have been bothered saving it, if it had been.

eye-teeth to understand, the message came unmistakenly through that there was to be *no noise* nor disturbing commotion. Not only did the tiny writing require it but so did his sensitively strung brain require a maximum of rest and this he was able to command without so much as lifting a finger. "Early to bed and late to rise" was his maxim. One of my uncles remembers me at the age of three sitting patiently at the top of the stairs from five to eight o'clock on Christmas morning, not daring to stir until he had had his sleep out. And, later, I remember a small niece, also at the age of three, sitting quietly on the sofa, large-eyed and hands folded for longer than one would think possible for fear "Uncle Ned will give me the deuce" though he had said nothing more than "Go and sit on the sofa" and that not at all harshly.

Nor did the adult world escape. After he had gone to bed no one spoke above a whisper. Two floors away he was able to hear (or sense) me erasing pencil marks with india rubber. Guests at a dinner party, if they did not know when to go home, were often minus a host by a certain hour, and no hard feelings. In fact people took it for granted. This discipline is difficult to describe without making him seem like a martinet rather than the gentlest of men, except by the fact of osmosis. But this ability was one of his greatest assets and his most valuable protection, and it was fortunate for him and for his work that he possessed it.

Similarly he loathed the harsh and discourteous. A loud voice was not to be borne. The hardships endured by the Jesuit missionaries in Huronia reflected his own feelings on this score. ". . . the rasp of speech maintained/All day by men who never learned to talk/In quiet tones" and "squaws and reeking children" who "violated/The hours of rest, were penances unnamed/Within the iron code of good Ignatius." While mosquitoes, another of his anathemas, plagued them during the hours when ". . . whatever sleep was possible/To snatch from the occasional lull of cries/Was broken by uncovenanted fleas/That fastened on the priestly flesh like hornets."

The sources of the mystics were drawn from the same well as those of the Stoics and these were much admired by Pratt. They were the "oaks and beeches of our species" and in his poem "The Stoics" he conjures them for their formula against the "ferments rattling underneath our skin" and "along the quivering labyrinth of nerves."

Not so far back and just as close as Newfoundland stick the influences of Methodism, brought to the New World from its cradle in England. These have been discussed in earlier chapters and it has been noted that John Pratt's children were born to an age in which the old practices had lost their charm. They did not, however, rebel completely, and it is interesting to note that all eight of them, or at least seven (for little is known of William in his adult years), remained within the Methodist Church until the union of 1925 when it became the United Church of Canada, and remained not ardent but loyal supporters of it.

What remained in my father, and perhaps in him alone, is what I can only refer to as pentecost, and I use the term in what may be called its aesthetic sense – the sense in which we speak of the Descent of the Dove or of the Holy Wind that "bloweth where it listeth." The early revival meetings in Newfoundland left their mark upon my father, and to the end of his life he was stirred by great religious rallies. That he did not bother to try to square them intellectually with what he knew of the world is expressed in his poem "The Mystic."

The *proof*, that slays the reason, has no power
To stem your will, corrode your soul – though lime
Conspire with earth and water to devour
The finest cultures from the lust of slime;

Although he had strong scientific predilections, as is evidenced in so much of his poetry, he did, like so many scientists, concede that to some things there just is no rational answer and took the view of William James in his pronouncement that if one ponders a problem long enough it ceases to be a problem simply because one no longer is concerned.

The poem in which the mysticism of the Methodist may perhaps be most clearly seen is, strangely, the Catholic narrative *Brébeuf and His Brethren*. Here the raptures of Swaledale have been transmuted into the religious zeal of the Holy Fathers. If I may make a personal comment here, I shall say that this has always been my favourite of the longer poems. There are many reasons for this, I am sure. There is a deep commitment, an identification that to me seems stronger than in many of the

173

others, although one of the noteworthy things about his poetry is his strong sense of identification with his subjects. He would come home late at night after many hours in his office writing this poem, aglow with a light not seen on land or sea. To his frail and sensitive body had been given a strength to withstand the tortures of the martyrs who had stood behind him as he wrote, for he could not bear to hear of pain. He knew they were there. He travelled with them when

On many a night in lonely intervals,
The priest would wander to the pines and build
His oratory where celestial visions
Sustained his soul.

Was their sustenance of the same order as that of John Pratt as he lay dying in his ecstasy?

... [When] the welts
Hung on their shoulders, then the Fathers sought
The balm that never failed. Under the stars,
Along an incandescent avenue
The visions trembled, tender, placid, pure,
More beautiful than the doorway of Rheims
And sweeter than the Galilean fields.
For what was hunger and burn of wounds
In those assuaging, healing moments when
The clearing mists revealed the face of Mary
And the lips of Jesus breathing benedictions?

The poem is filled with suffering beyond the realm of mortal imaginings, but it is the suffering of the martyrs about which the psychiatrists have much to say. It is masochistic suffering at its most intense level. But beyond this there is a grace above the explanations of the psychiatrists, and I think it is this that gives the poem its melody. The pentecostal wind blows through it from first to last, the wind that blew the missionaries to the far corners of the world and that carried with it the song so familiar to those whose lives have been conditioned to the broad sweeps of nature such as are found among the moors of Yorkshire.

The air was charged with song beyond the range
Of larks, with wings beyond the stretch of eagles.
Skylines unknown to maps broke from the mists
And there was laughter on the seas.

As a singer dwells upon the full and pear-shaped sounds of his song, so Pratt savoured the sound of the spoken and written word. He had his favourite words, or rather his favourite sounds, for his vocabulary was immense. He hated clichés and obvious words and his spoken conversation was almost as rich as his poetry. His use of the Latin polysyllables has been frequently commented on. These words were part of the opulence of his language and reflect his taste for variety of sound. Space-measuring words such as meridians, parallels, latitudes, and longitudes, occur frequently in his poems. He was, however, pre-disposed to the open vowel sounds and labials often in short stumpy words, upon which the tongue could linger over a more extended duration than over short vowels and explosive consonants. The loneliness and power of the *oo* sound would come out in his use of *typhoons* and *dunes*, *broods*, even *festoons* – a word he used often in everyday conversation to describe Christmas decorations, cobwebs in the murky woods, wool tangled over chairs.

Examples of these wide sounds may be found in all his poetry, particularly in his earlier work. In *Newfoundland Verse*, writing of the ubiquitous winds,

They blow with the rising octaves of dawn,
They die with the largo of dusk.

Largo, harbour, yards, bar, barm. From *The Great Feud*, he writes of "a hundred yards of bar." Again, from the *Cachalot*, "a thick festoon of lichen crawled from crag to crag." With words such as *solar*, *polar*, and *aurora* he unites sound and symbol, words resident in vastness, the empyrean. From *The Roosevelt and the Antinoe:*

As if a god might thus salute the deed,
And ratify the venture with the screed
Of an aurora milled in solar flame.

Or, from *The Iron Door:*

And I was left alone, aware
Of blindness falling with terrestrial day
On sight enfeebled by the solar glare.

The use of words as symbols leads at once to other favourites and here again is the open moor with its passion for freedom, power, and flight, and it is here also where Pratt's heroic world is moulded. His heroic symbols are eagles, whales, leviathan, dinosaurs, icebergs, storms. This fact has often led to a confusion among his critics, as has been intimated by John Sutherland who said:

"He has been called robust, energetic, masculine, genial, muscular, vital, exuberant, hearty, high-spirited, and a thousand other things redolent of good beef and whiskey."[2]

Of all these adjectives I would pluck out as totally applicable (as far as any adjective ever is totally applicable) the word *genial*; slightly less so, *exuberant*; and the others quite misleading in a description of the outward man. They cling to him like so many burrs gathered at stag parties where his outward exuberance was always at its height, and in doing so they crowd out many other of his qualities not evident at playful gatherings.

I say these qualities are misleading in description of the outward man and in saying this I do not deny that they are present in his poetry. But one need not look far to find parallels of artists whose work does not give an accurate picture of the outward man. I think of César Franck, living his life in the ivory tower of the organ loft with little outward evidence of the adventurous strains of the D Minor Symphony; or of my father's favourite composer, Mozart, whose assured and jubilant melodies reflect in small part the tragedy of his life; or of Charles Dickens, whose life belied his identification with the poor of England; or of John Milton and countless others living in a world created by the fertility of their genius. E. J. Pratt was all the qualities attributed to him, in more or less degree, in his poetry; that is, in his intellect and in his thoughts and yearnings. But by no stretch of the imagination could he have been called *muscular*, for example, at any time of his life, except in his creation of strength and his admiration of it.

All those things, *redolent of good beef and whiskey*. Gargantua he was not, but temperate in his habits by the standards of Pantagruel, and he was certainly not the beefy Englishman. That he loved the sight of a well-appointed table was true: crisp brown bits of beef or pork ready to melt off the roast to be savoured with concentration and chased with amber liquid from a crystal decanter that caught light from the cheerful lamps and threw its diffracted rays back to the gourmet's eyes. It was an aesthetic experience to be enjoyed doubly in the presence of good fellowship, attested to in many of his poems wherein are catalogued his favourite dishes.

To return to the heroic symbols and the world created by Pratt. This heroic world is the medium wherein his character with all its contradictions, seeming or real, is resolved. John Sutherland again refers to "an emotional duality, an interfusion of exaltation and terror" that forms the basis of a paradox in which "the spectacle of wholesale destruction actually seems to intensify rather than to diminish the poet's characteristic exaltation."[3]

"*The Titanic*, as I have remarked, begins and ends with an image of terror and with a view of the 'paleolithic face'; yet, although the terror is real enough in the conclusion, the final pages are dominated by a sense of great exaltation. In the conclusions of the *Feud* and *The Cachalot* we encounter the same paradox of an exaltation that rides above but does not cancel out a persistent image of terror. Somewhat the same effect would be achieved if the head of the Sphinx itself were to be found adorning a cathedral or a scrawl from the Dragon's claw were to appear on the lower corner of a page of scripture."[4]

To face squarely up to the unanswerable tribulations and agonies of the world, two qualities may well serve as armour: laughter and pentecost.

Laughter is here defined as the expression of sheer exuberance. It results from a gamut of experience that runs from the joy of recognition of a beloved friend to an acceptance of things as they are. Laughter in its two parts: delight and humour, often, but not inevitably, intertwined. The exuberance mentioned above had, for my father, its most characteristic outlet in the laughter of delight. His eager face shone with a laughter that might be termed naïveté at the visit of a friend, or over the solution of a problem. Similarly was his delight expressed over all good things and small mercies, such as the sale of books however few, over all things that touched his life and pleased him.

He was fond of jokes and anecdotes and could get more yardage out of a story than anyone I ever knew. People sat enthralled listening to a tale which from the tongues of many people would have bored them to tears. His appreciation of the suchness of things accounted, I think, largely for this ability. Less laughter-producing but equally salutary is the kind of humour that accepts what is, with crossed t's and dotted i's. That what is may be that which is seen by the physical eye or by the eye of the imagination does not much matter.

The Gargantuan myth, however, may well be explained by the existence of a high state of euphoria in my father's poetry. Poetry he once defined as one gigantic binge, and this is nowhere more in evidence than in the extravaganzas. It is not without interest that the two wildest of his poems, *The Witches' Brew* and *The Great Feud*, should deal with one of the juxtapositions of nature that fascinated him most: the existence of and differences between the cold-blooded aquatic world and the mammals. It is first seen in "The Shark":

That strange fish,
Tubular, tapered, smoke-blue,
Part vulture, part wolf,
Part neither – for his blood was cold.

There is mystery in the silent, the stealthy, as is clearly evident in the poem "Silences" which will be considered later. But in the two longer poems fish and mammals are given special treatment. Both poems were written in sheer exuberance with their deeper layers of meaning well in the conscious background. *The Witches' Brew*, written on the occasion of my parents' fifth wedding anniversary in 1923, bore the dedication "For my Wife"; *The Great Feud*, "To the boys of the stag parties." That the deeper layers exist there is no doubt, especially in *The Great Feud*, but there is equally no doubt that the poems were written primarily for pure joy. That they are both concerned with vast destruction and intense suffering seems to involve us in the paradox to which John Sutherland has drawn our attention in the paragraph quoted above.

Henry W. Wells sees the paradox as a dualism in the life of the author himself:

"In so far as he is a Newfoundlander he is a cold-blooded water animal, whose soul is a battleground of stark natural forces and who is in all respects oceanic, epic and austere; in so far

178

as he is a Canadian or professor of English in Toronto, he is a warm-blooded, civilized, land animal, blessed with accumulative sophistication, knowledge, humanism and culture."[5]

Be that as it may, Pratt in *The Witches' Brew* set the stage with relish:

Perched on a dead volcanic pile,
Now charted as a submerged peak,
Near to a moon-washed coral isle,
A hundred leagues from Mozambique,
Three water-witches of the East,
Under the stimulus of rum,
Decided that the hour had come
To hold a Saturnalian feast,
In course of which they hoped to find
For their black art, once and for all,
The true effect of alcohol
Upon the cold, aquatic mind.

There follows the greatest bash one can imagine, not a struggle between the warm-blooded and the cold, as in *The Great Feud*, but a great prank played upon the cold, for the joy of seeing them soused. Not only alcohol went into the brew. Things terrestrial and aquatic, as well as "Cold blooded things yet not marine/ And not of earth, but half-between." A sputtering mixture of animal, vegetable, and mineral is contributed in the "bull-moose that had died from gas/while eating toadstools near Ungava/ One bitter-cold November day." Gone are the liquid labials and pear-shaped vowels in favour of explosives in the most ludicrous of combinations, and yet one sympathizes with this moose trying to get his bit of sustenance on a chilly day at the ends of the earth.

In *The Great Feud*, it is significant that the peril awaiting creation in the forthcoming struggle should be outlined by the warm-blooded simian, the nearly human she-ape. She describes the danger thus:

For years reports have been received
From distant countries occupied
By furs, feathers and hairs allied
By blood, how they have been bereaved

179

And plunged in blackest misery
By that insane, consuming hate
Of ignorant, inarticulate
Cold-blooded barbarians of the sea.

There is no doubt upon whose side the poet is. The oratory of the ape summons the courage and enthusiasm in "ye thirsty carnivores" to forgo the taste of blood and meat in order to shore up the tides of appetite the better to "charge on the aquatics here/And trap them in the great Lagoons." At the end of her speech

... every throat and lung
Of herbivore and carnivore,
In volleying symphonic roar,
Rang with persuasion of her tongue.

There follows a description of the bloodiest and most ludicrous carnage ever staged. Bengal tigers, full of caraway and rice; caracul, their stomachs full of rhododendrons; leopards full of okra pods; and farinaceous lions ready themselves to take on the "dolphins hot and blubberous," "phantoms blue and ashen pale," swordfish, "their long blades flashing in the sun"; "thornbacks with their poisoned spikes/Torpedo rays with scorpion stings." This Pleiocene Armageddon is described with the greatest relish in all its detail. In the era of Freud it could be said to represent an outpouring of all the pent-up aggression of the human race.

It was written by a man who could not endure violence in his life, of any kind whatsoever. From an argument in which he might possibly become involved himself he would withdraw, either physically, if possible, or escape into a quiet world of his own behind a newspaper or, with eyes closed on the scene, lie back in his large armchair and enter who knows what airy spaces of complete and utter peace.

If there were no question about his own involvement, there was no one who loved a fight or struggle better than he, provided he were only an onlooker. The quarrelling of others not only did not bother him, but intrigued him and he delighted in the spectacle of the weaker combatant putting it over the stronger. Wrestling and boxing matches were part of his weekly diet for years and he would go off on Thursday nights with a neighbour of as mild habits as himself and become refreshed by the evening's round of legitimate struggle between strength and strength.

Sheer brute strength enthralled him and is featured in all its attributes throughout the major and minor poems. "The Brawler in *Who's Who*" is a brief biography of the destruction caused by might ungoverned by reason or intellect. The "brawler" represents a certain type well-known in most circles, if here a little exaggerated.

The doctors claimed they never had
A case to handle quite so bad
A record weight, abnormal girth,
And such disturbance at a birth.
The infant murdered his twin brother
And shortly after that his mother,
To celebrate his debut on the earth.

The infant proceeds to school where in diabolical high spirits he commits so much destruction that his school fellows and teachers are themselves destroyed. The war, as might be expected, is the highlight of his life and the one event in which he is a success by accepted standards. He outlives three wives and then dies by a stab in the back (fouled by a technical knockout) while heading a riot on roaches. But even death cannot quell him, as the undertaker tries in vain to straighten out his knotted fists and, on the very night of his burial, with "his left hook and lethal right" he was unable to refrain from putting a dozen shades to rout.

There are echoes here of the great innocent, the Moby Dick, or better still *tyrannosaurus rex* from *The Great Feud*. The brawler was made as he was made, but misses becoming a great character as he does not suffer from his actions, but keeps the upper hand even in death. One cannot be convinced of his destruction. The poem is, of course, a minor one, its significance stemming from the fact that it shows the poet's admiration for human strength falls to pieces when that strength is unaccompanied by the greater quality of magnanimity.

It is this quality that has given "The Big Fellow" greater depth, although I think this may be, in part, owing to its greater seriousness, in the same way that *The Cachalot*, being a serious treatment of its subject, has been taken more seriously, except by John Sutherland, than *The Great Feud*. It is beneath the dignity of the strong man, if he is endowed with the grace of magnanimity, to strike back at the small vicious efforts of the weak in character as well as in physical frame. It is not worth the time of day.

And I thought of the big Newfoundland
I saw, asleep by a rock
The day before,
That was galvanized by a challenge.
But eyeing a cur,
He turned,
Yawned,
Closed one eye,
Then the other,
And slept.

It is important to consider the type of combatants who appealed to Pratt. Although the strong man fascinated him he had nothing but contempt for the bully. He was an out-and-out hero-worshipper and had most definite likes and dislikes. The personality that fascinated him, perhaps more than any other, was Napoleon Bonaparte. He read every book about him he could get his hands on and in his declining years he would have my mother reread these books to him by the hour. He knew Napoleon better than Napoleon knew himself. Oddly enough he never wrote about him. Perhaps he felt he knew him too well, or perhaps the sheer quantity of material already on the general put him off.

It was the same with Shakespeare, who was his special field. Come to think of it, he did not write about any of his favourite people, who also included Mozart, Robert Burns, and Abraham Lincoln. But it was the character of Napoleon, in whom he saw, I believe, a hero of the Shakespearean type destroyed in the end by his tragic flaw – that same particular flaw that so often accounts for the downfall of the successful man, the demigod, no matter how pure his original motives may be. He could see that great lover of freedom, Beethoven, tear up his dedication to the Eroica Symphony, as he watched the tragic drama on the battlefield of Napoleon's soul. It was then he would try to link up Napoleon's genius with the heart of Lincoln. What might have happened then?

No, it was not the heroes of his life that he wrote about. He was faithful in his devotion to the Irish people whom he loved beyond any others. Although he had not a drop of Irish blood in him, it was commonly thought he was pure Eire, and I think sometimes he thought so himself. That the myth took shape in part from the Newfoundland accent which never left him is true, but he cultivated it and was not abashed to ask for Irish music on all occasions, even at parties and weddings where the principals were Scottish, Russian, or Portuguese. "Kathleen Mavourneen" and "The Harp that once through Tara's Halls" played themselves out of their grooves on our Victrola. He was not immune to the Celtic twilight and loved the poetry of Yeats, Synge, and the Irish dramatists.

And yet, only once does an Irishman figure in his poetry. In *Behind the Log*, among the convoy of unsung heroes, appears O'Leary "in a stupor."

"Yeoman, you dropped no markers with that pattern.
That's standing orders now – smoke-floats to mark
Areas attacked. Ever heard it? Don't you know
Your drill? You'll be in my report in the morning."
O'Leary gagged upon his chewing quid,
Hiccupped, sending a spurt of nicotine
And hydrochloric acid on the sea.
"He said to me, said he, 'O'Leary, don't
You know your drill?' – Say, how the hell would I know?
Nobody tells me nothing in this Navy."

A very dusky Celtic twilight this!
In contrast the Scot emerges in *Towards the Last Spike*, from a mess of oatmeal, like a rock.

The food released its fearsome racial products:—
The power to strike a bargain like a foe,
To win an argument upon a burr,
Invest the language with a Bannockburn,
Culloden or the warnings of Lochiel,
Weave loyalties and rivalries in tartans,
Present for the amazement of the world
Kilts and the civilized barbaric Fling,
And pipes which, when they acted on the mash,
Fermented lullabies to *Scots wha hae.*

Out of Scotland came another of his heroes, Robert Burns. He loved to talk on Burns Night, of the Immortal Memory, and if he would not eat *haggis* he loved to talk about it, for the word has a rugged sound and can be piped in in ceremony to the skirl of the bagpipes and the flinging kilt.

If he did not write about his heroes *per se*, their qualities appear again and again in such poems as "The Dying Eagle" or "Putting Winter to Bed." It is the great one put down, finally, by forces beyond his control. It is in these where the need for humour is most urgent, the need for accepting life as it is, on a plane where humour becomes one with compassion. Life is what life is.

In the above-mentioned poems a fine line is drawn between a serious and a humorous treatment. In both cases there exists a compassion for the fallen hero, for nobility beaten. In "The Dying Eagle" there is nothing recognizable as humour, only infinite pity at the sight of ultimate acceptance, simply because there is nothing else to be done when faced with a power beyond our comprehension.

He was old, yet it was not his age
Which made him roost on the crags
Like a rain-drenched raven
On the branch of an oak in November.
Nor was it the night, for there was an hour
To go before sunset.

The eagle had met the challenge with all his skill, technique, and courage – of which he had an ample supply. "The eagle never yet had known/A rival that he would not grapple" and this flying dragon, with its "two whirling eyes/That took unshuttered /The full blaze of the meridian," its glistening shoulders, thunder in its throat, and speed double his own, would be no exception.

But what disturbed him most, angered
And disgraced him was the unconcern
With which this supercilious bird
Cut through the aquiline dominion,
Snubbing the ancient suzerain
With extra-territorial insolence,
And disappeared.

The total unconcern. For what do we exist if we are not notice-

able, if we are not visible? The ultimate horror of all is to have
nothing against which even to pit our courage.

So evening found him on the crags again,
This time with sloven shoulders
And nerveless claws.
Dusk had outridden the sunset by an hour
To haunt his unhorizoned eyes.
And soon his flock flushed with the chase
Would be returning, threading their glorious curves
Up through the crimson archipelagoes
Only to find him there –
Deaf to the mighty symphony of wings,
And brooding
Over the lost empire of the peaks.

Here is acceptance through total defeat, not only of himself, but
of the proud flock he had fed and nourished, and a heart-breaking
thing it is.

"Putting Winter to Bed," one of his favourite poems for reading aloud, is a fantasy, a light treatment of the fallen hero, full
of gentleness, humour, and, yes, fight, because fight there must
be and we must come to terms with it. It begins with a rollicking
joust between March, the stripling, and the majestic lord of ice
and snow. The latter puts up a noble struggle, but is doomed to
defeat by the inevitable progression of events.

And yet before the week was passed,
Neuralgic headaches thick and fast
Were blinding him with tears;
Despite the boast, he needed rest
To stop the panting in his breast,
That buzzing in his ears.

He wanders to a frozen brook
Beneath dank willows where he took
His usual noon-day nap;
He heard dull subterranean calls,
Narcotic sounds from crystal falls,
The climbing of the sap.
He laid his head against a stump,
One arm reclined upon a clump

Of glaciated boulders;
The other held his side – he had
Pleuritic pains and very bad
Rheumatic hips and shoulders.

Here the pitiful royal figure blinded with tears causes a gentle mirth. He wanders to a frozen brook where he is accustomed to have a short nap at noon but is plagued by the bucolic sound of rising sap. A stump serves as a regal pillow and he clutches, almost vaudeville-like, at a clump of boulders. But nature is kind. After he has suffered the tortures of the damned, an infinitely gentle April comes:

She spent the morning in the search
For twigs of alder and of birch
And shoots of pussy willow;
She wove these through a maze of fern,
Added some moss on her return,
And made the downiest pillow.

What uneasy crown-bearing head would not rejoice at the prospect of such delightful rest?

So with her first aid rendered, she
Began her ancient sorcery,
Quietly to restore
His over-burdened mind to sleep,
Dreamless and passionless and deep,
Out of her wild-wood lore.

But before the king may sink into a well-deserved rest, she exacts a pledge from him by which, kept for eight months, he will be rewarded by his grand return on Christmas Day. How lovely it would be were all the fallen heroes to enjoy such a compromise.

Compare this version of the myth of Persephone, in which the good and evil of nature are in proper balance, with the one-sided perversion of human nature, repeated a thousand times during wars and persecutions, to be found in *Brébeuf and His Brethren* when the allegedly peace-loving Hurons make an example of an Iroquois brave:

His body smeared with pitch and bound with belts
Of bark, the Iroquois was forced to run

The fires, stopped at each end by the young braves,
And swiftly driven back, and when he swooned,
They carried him outside to the night air,
Laid him on fresh damp moss, poured cooling water
Into his mouth, and to his burns applied
The soothing balsams. With resuscitation
They lavished on him all the courtesies
Of speech and gesture, gave him food and drink.
Compassionately spoke of his wounds and pain.
The ordeal every hour was resumed
And halted, but, with each recurrence, blows
Were added to the burns and gibes gave place
To yells until the sacrificial dawn,
Lighting the scaffold, dimming the red glow
Of the hatchet collar, closed the festival.

Religious men have always tended to dwell with relish on the
prospects of hell. It was a favourite topic of Non-Conformist
sermons and provided drama in what might otherwise have been
a boring sermon. This perversion, as it may well be in some cases,
is but another expression of the "interfusion of exaltation and
terror" of which John Sutherland speaks. It is a distorted image
of Aristotle's theory of tragedy as a catharsis through pity and
terror. That it may work to the degradation of man rather than
to his salvation may be because of the paucity of artistic genius
and, on the other side of the coin, the inability of the audience
to receive and understand the message. Art, however, serves to
transform the bestial element into the service of man's psyche so
that instead of dying in fear and trembling as so many victims
of religious exhortations have had to do, man is purged and forti-
fied into a transcendental acceptance. Where laughter is the
shield, pentecost is the buckler of our armour. Where the poet
may burst his sides over the "inventory of Hades" in *The Witches'
Brew*, he may be transported upon the singing wind by the cat-
alogue of suffering in Brébeuf's tablet and the consolation that
far outweighs the burdens.

It was not only to the symbol that my father transferred his
hero worship in his poetry, but also to the group hero, the anonymous man (he would refuse to call him "little") whose unsung deeds permeate his verse. Rescues at sea dominate these

deeds for reasons already known. In *The Iron Door*, which I believe contains some of his most lyrical poetry and, along with *The Truant*, the core of his philosophy, is full of the courage of man against the fury of the elements, his dignity as it was taught him by Wesley in his view of the common man. There is the master mariner,

... old and travel-stained,
And his face grained
With rebel questionings
Urged with unsurrendered dignity;
For he had lost three sons at sea,
In a work of rescue known
To the high Atlantic records of that year.

and the young man who

... struck against the door
Demanding with his sanguine prime,
If the eternal steward registered
The unrecorded acts of time;
Not for himself insisting, but for one –
A stranger at his side –
For whom he had staked his life,
And on the daring odds had died.
No one had seen this young man go,
Or watched his plunge,
To save another whom he did not know.
. . . .

Do courage and honour receive
On the wastes of your realm, their fair name and title?
As they do at our sea grey altars, – by your leave.

In *The Titanic* the metal of man is tapped while cad and hero move as in a game of chess. There were those who donned women's clothes to qualify for the boats and others who, safe in half-empty boats, pushed away. One of the most deeply moving incidents was that of a man, struggling in the water, who "clutched at the rim/Of a gunwale, and a woman's jewelled fist/Struck at his face." Simply, in pain and rejection, "he released his hold." The account recalls the pathos and simplicity

188

of the record at Grinton of the Milner brothers killed in the mine: "These was two brothers –" But against these scenes where order failed were others, such as the two who redressed the balance by seizing the drowning man's wrist "and gathering him/Over the side, they staunched the cut from the ring," Ida Straus who would not leave her husband's side, and a ten-year-old boy who added inches to his stature by giving up his place to a woman and her child.

It was in *The Roosevelt and the Antinoe*, however, where, all stops out, the rescue operations take on a purely Homeric movement. In this poem of sea wind and snow, roaring and blindness, it would seem that out on the Atlantic Ocean the quality known as humanity is engaged in the attempt to rescue the entire universe from the fury of the gods.

The *Antinoe's* resources had completely run out in the hurricane and snow of the north Atlantic. Her signals in the end had been going out unheeded and unheard by human ear. "Magnetic messengers" were hurling at light-speed

Past day and night and the terrestrial air,
To add their wasted sum to a plethora
Of speed and power in those void spaces where
Light-years go drifting by Andromeda.

She was lost, not only to sight, but in the grip of a gale that made controlled movement impossible. Much has been written of the mob instinct in its pursuit of the helpless, of the hysteria that builds a monolith out of individuals. But what balances the score is a kindred instinct that will risk life, limb, and reason to save as well as to destroy.

The ship with unremitting search despite
The chances stacked against her, steamed on far
Into the night, past midnight and the slow
Hours, blindly heading into snow;
Not a sextant reading off a star;
No radio now with subtle fingering
Untied the snarl of the freighter's wayward course.
Nothing but log and the dead reckoning,
And the *Roosevelt's* instruments stating the force
Of wind, direction and the tidal stress,

189

Nothing but these and the wheel's luck to trail her, –
Unless there might be added to the sum
Of them an unexplored residuum –
The bone-and-marrow judgment of a sailor.

"The bone-and-marrow judgment of a sailor." This in the end
is the real stuff of the universe.

E. J. Pratt was concerned with the place of silence in all its complex manifestations. It may be remembered in Chapter 9 that the
Swaledale Pratts were noted for being close-mouthed. This was
generally true also of my father. He loved to talk in company.
He was fond of companionship but often said he preferred more
than one companion at a time. Conversation with one person
would often become stuck. He seldom discussed his private affairs
with anyone. It went completely against the grain to talk of
money, of which he never had any. However, he liked to talk
about any small cheque from the sale of books, and he liked to
hand "a bit o' jink" out to all and sundry. "Gentleman John" was
a kindred spirit in this regard. One of the favourite games he and
my mother would play at Bobcaygeon was how they would
spend their money if they were required to live for a year on
10 cents a day. It was a wonderful game to sharpen one's in-
genuity and provided an endless source of amusement. He liked
to "go into business" and enjoyed believing he would make
some money but he had no more aptitude for it than his grandfather Pratt in his tea enterprise. However, he would never admit
to being short of money, nor give away any secrets on that
score.

He was brought up in the middle days of Queen Victoria and
in many ways remained a Victorian throughout his life. Emotions
deeply felt were silent. The mysteries of birth, love, and death
were not fit topics for conversation at a serious level. Other things
were simply private. His letters were frequently full of nonsense,
for he had a horror of saying anything that might be read by
others that was no business of theirs. His telegrams, which of
necessity had to be public, were even more foolish and one he
tried to send up north when worried about his family was so
ludicrous that the telegraph agent, without saying a word to him,
refused to send it, causing him a very anxious weekend.

"Ned, you never write love poems," remarked one of his
friends. "No," he answered, "they would burn up the paper."

They were also, to put it another way, slightly indecent and much too private. As a narrative poet, he was in his element, for here he could reveal his emotions to the utmost in identification with his subject. As Northrop Frye put it: "He has tried to cut away two things: the intrusion of the poet on his reader, and the detachment of the poet from his surroundings."[6]

The subject of silence was for him a complex one. Physical silence was a necessity and he wrapped it around him like a benediction. Emotional silence was a natural concomitant and arose from his background. But both these silences are dangerous and this he knew right well, as is evident in his poem – one of his favourites – "Silences." I would like to quote it in full, not only for its relevance to his own life and to those of his ancestors, but to the civilized need for ordered, meaningful sound.

There is no silence upon the earth or under the earth like the
    silence under the sea;
No cries announcing birth,
No sounds declaring death.
There is silence when the milt is laid on the spawn in the weeds
    and fungus of the rock-clefts;
And silence in the growth and struggle for life.
The bonitoes pounce upon the mackerel,
And are themselves caught by the barracudas,
The sharks kill the barracudas
And the great molluscs rend the sharks,
And all noiselessly –
Though swift be the action and final the conflict,
The drama is silent.

There is no fury upon the earth like the fury under the sea.
For growl and cough and snarl are the tokens of spendthrifts who
    know not the ultimate economy of rage.
Moreover, the pace of the blood is too fast.
But under the waves the blood is sluggard and has the same
    temperature as that of the sea.

There is something pre-reptilian about a silent kill.

Two men may end their hostilities just with their battle-cries.
"The devil take you," says one.
"I'll see you in hell first," says the other.

And these introductory salutes followed by a hail of gutturals
    and sibilants are often the beginning of friendship, for who
    would not prefer to be lustily damned than to be half-heartedly
    blessed?
No one need fear oaths that are properly enunciated, for they
    belong to the inheritance of just men made perfect, and,
    for all we know, of such may be the Kingdom of Heaven.
But let silent hate be put away for it feeds upon the heart of the
    hater.
Today I watched two pairs of eyes. One pair was black and
    the other grey. And while the owners thereof, for the space
    of five seconds, walked past each other, the grey snapped
    at the black and the black riddled the grey.
One looked to say – "The cat."
And the other – "The cur."
But no words were spoken;
Not so much as a hiss or a murmur came through the perfect
    enamel of the teeth; not so much as a gesture of enmity.
If the right upper lip curled over the canine, it went unnoticed.
The lashes veiled the eyes not for an instant in the passing.
And as between the two in respect to candour of intention or
    eternity of wish, there was no choice, for the stare was mutual
    and absolute.
A word would have dulled the exquisite edge of the feeling,
An oath would have flawed the crystallization of the hate.
For only such culture could grow in a climate of silence, –
Away back before the emergence of fur or feather, back to the
    unvocal sea and down deep where the darkness spills its
    wash on the threshold of light, where the lids never close upon
    the eyes, where the inhabitants slay in silence and are as
    silently slain.

The inhabitants of "the unvocal sea" had his deepest sympathy. To them belonged the vast multitude of the inarticulate
who, like children, are unable in rational terms to express their
agonies and desires. He taught *Journey's End* by R. C. Sherriff in
his course on Modern Poetry and Drama and in it is a scene that
appealed to him for its pathos. Captain Stanhope, nerves shot in
the battle-dreary loneliness in the trenches of the First World
War, has had more than he can take and unfairly sends one of his

men packing for his nauseating attempts at gaiety. Second-lieutenant Trotter, more phlegmatic: "Poor little bloke. Never seen him so cheerful before, out here." Stanhope: "I envy you, Trotter. Nothing upsets you, does it? You're always the same." Trotter, bridling: "Always the same, am I? Little you know –." Inexorably, Stanhope. "You never get sick to death of everything, or so happy you want to sing." "I don't know," answers Trotter, "I whistle sometimes."

After all, when it comes down to the ultimate of feelings, words fail and we fall back on the primeval sounds with which we first expressed our emotions – laughter, groans, shrieks, and yes, whistles.

One of the highest peaks of drama he found in *King Lear*, when the old king, forsaken of reason and argument, is confronted by his dead daughter, Cordelia. Compared to the high-flown poetic rhetoric of Cleopatra at the death of Antony, it contains infinitely more grief, for it is but one stage removed from the primitive unarticulated moan. In a slow unwilling realization he is forcing himself to see that she is dead and will not come again. One word suffices, repeated in paralysis like a liturgy, sticking in the despair of its own world of meaning. She will come no more. "Never, never, never, never, never." As creatures of the sea we began, and to the sea we return in times of greatest stress.

The past is wrapped, now, in an envelope of silence as deep as that of the sea. But the sea is also the nourisher of being, and as in the caves of darkness sprout the beginnings of new life so are the seeds of knowledge carried on the mute winds of our heritage. Six years ago none of the members of John Pratt's family had heard of Swaledale, and Gunnerside was no more than a name. But a landscape can strike with sudden shock and from it a crowd of watchers, streaming forth on the wings of invisible trumpets, may bear evidence of things not seen.

Notes

I THE SINGING LAND
1 Ella Pontefract, *Swaledale*, p. 142.
2 p. 10
II SEEDS IN THE MIST
1 Reaney, *A Dictionary of British Surnames*.
2 *Fairbairn's Book of Crests of Families of Great Britain & Ireland*, 4th edition, London, 1905.
3 Arthur Raistrick, *Vikings, Angles, and Danes in Yorkshire*, p. 18.
4 T. D. Kendrick, *A History of the Vikings*, 1930, pp. 274-275.
5 *Ibid.*, p. 276.
6 *Ibid.*, p. 279.
7 *Ibid.*, pp. 279-282.
8 P. H. Sawyer, *The Age of the Vikings*, 1962, p. 3.
9 *Ibid.*, p. 148.
10 Sir Henry Ellis, *Introduction of Domesday Book*.
11 Ella Pontefract, *Swaledale*, p. 150.
12 Margaret Batty, *Gunnerside Chapel and Gunnerside Folk*, 1967, p. 20.
13 Arthur Raistrick, *The Romans in Yorkshire*, 1966 (2nd ed.), p. 23.
14 Grinton papers. British Society of Genealogists.
15 The North Riding Record Society, II, 7.
16 Dodsworth MSS, 46:99. Assize Roll 8-9 Edw. I.
17 The North Riding Record Society, IV, 23.
18 *Ibid.*, IV, 26.
19 *The Chartulary of the Augustinian Priory of St. John the Evangelist of the Park of Healaugh*, Record series, vol. XVII, p. 170. Translation mine.
20 The North Riding Record Society, vol. 1, new series, 1894, pp. 226 and 227.
21 Parliamentary Surveys. Yks. No.

26. Unpublished manuscript.
22 Grinton Papers. Letters Patent to Richard Wiseman.
23 Pontefract, *Swaledale*, p. 122.
24 *Ibid.*, pp. 121-122.
25 The North Riding Record Society, vol. 1, new series, 1894, pp. 226, 227.
26 Grinton Papers. Min Aces L. R. 1328. 28-29 Henry VIII.
27 Grinton Papers.
28 *Ibid.* Exchequer Bills & Answers, James I, York, No. 1345, Simpson v. Hutchinson.
29 *Ibid.*, Charlesworth v. Broderick (10) 30 Eliz. part 6.
30 *Ibid.*, James I, part. 26.
III FROM GRINTON TO GUNNERSIDE
1 Arthur Raistrick, *Old Yorkshire Dales*, p. 146.
2 *Ibid.*, p. 89.
3 Pontefract, *Swaledale*, p. 136.
4 *The Registers of the Parish Church of Grinton in Swaledale*, The Yorkshire Parish Register Society, privately printed, 1905, p. 67.
5 *Ibid.*, p. 66.
6 *Ibid.*, p. 67.
7. *Ibid.*
8 *Ibid.*
9 *Ibid.*, p. 146.
IV UNTIL THE HARVEST
1 Wesley Bready, *England Before and After Wesley*, London, 1938, p. 147.
2 Sir F. M. Eden, *The State of the Poor*, vol. II.
3 Elizabeth Burton, *The Georgians at Home*, p. 210.
4 *Ibid.*
5 *Ibid.*, 211.
6 *Ibid.*, 212.
7 *Ibid.*, 194.
8 John Ward, *Methodism in Swaledale*, p. 23, and Margaret Batty,

Gunnerside Chapel and Gunner-side Folk, p. 7.

9 From a clipping in a Bradford paper on the occasion of the Golden Wedding of Christopher and Jane Pratt, now in possession of Ewart Pratt, St. John's.

10 John Ward.

11 John Wesley, *Journal,* I, 237.

12 *Ibid.*

13 *Ibid.,* II, 18.

14 Ward, *Methodism in Swaledale,* p. 74.

15 Pontefract, *Swaledale,* pp. 56-57.

16 Batty, *Gunnerside Chapel,* p. 7.

17 Wesley, *Journal,* II, 186.

18 Bready, *England Before and After Wesley,* pp. 255-6.

19 Arthur Young, *Six Months Tour Through the North of England,* vol. I, letter xii.

20 Wesley, *Journal,* II, 129.

21 Batty, *Gunnerside Chapel,* p. 9.

22 Ward, *Methodism in Swaledale,* pp. 82-83, and Batty, *Gunnerside Chapel,* pp. 9-10.

V THE DARKENING HILLS

1 Batty, *Gunnerside Chapel,* p. 12.

2 *Ibid.*

3 Leonard Pratt, *Yesterday Our Ancestry,* p. 9.

4 *Ibid.,* p. 15.

5 *Methodist Magazine,* 19 Feb. 1822.

6 Batty, *Gunnerside Chapel,* p. 18.

7 *Ibid.,* p. 43.

8 Ward, *Methodism in Swaledale,* p. 82.

9 *Ibid.,* pp. 82-83.

10 *Yesterday Our Ancestry,* p. 21.

11 *Ibid.,* p. 16.

12 *Ibid.*

13 Christopher Pratt & Sons. Mimeographed sheet.

14 Pratt, *Yesterday Our Ancestry,* p. 21.

15 Raistrick, *Old Yorkshire Dales,* p. 90.

16 "Christopher Pratt & Sons."

17 *Ibid.*

18 *Ibid.*

19 *Ibid.*

20 A granddaughter of Christopher Pratt.

21 *Ibid.*

22 "Christopher Pratt & Sons."

23 Batty, *Gunnerside Chapel,* p. 18.

24 *Ibid., p. 19.*

25 *Ibid., p. 31.*

26 Letter in possession of Mrs. John Ball, Christchurch, N.Z.

27 Pontefract, *Swaledale,* p. 79.

28 Batty, *Gunnerside Chapel,* p. 33.

VII THE TEA FORTUNE

1 Ward, *Methodism in Swaledale,* p. 25.

VIII A PARCEL OF WILD PEOPLE

1 Batty, *Gunnerside Chapel,* p. 51.

2 The story of James Pratt comes from *Yesterday Our Ancestry,* pp. 21-22.

3 "Christopher Pratt & Sons Ltd."

4 *Ibid.*

5 *Ibid.*

6 *Bradford Chamber of Trade Journal,* August 1923, p. 489.

7 *British Medical Journal,* March 5, 1960.

8 "Christopher Pratt & Sons Ltd."

9 *England Before and After Wesley,* p. 415.

10 p. 128.

11 p. 77.

12 pp. 131ff.

13 Remembered by Dr. Cluny Macpherson.

14 Remembered by Mrs. Sarah Colechin.

THE POETRY OF E. J. PRATT

1 *The Iron Door.*

2 John Sutherland, *The Poetry of E. J. Pratt: A New Interpretation,* 1956, p. vii.

3 *Ibid.,* pp. 12 and 14.

4 *Ibid.,* p. 16.

5 Henry W. Wells and Carl F. Klinck, *Edwin J. Pratt: The Man and His Poetry,* 1947, p. 135.

6 *Collected Poems,* Introduction, p. xiv.

Pratt Genealogies

Family No.	Parents & Children	Marriage	Birth*	Death*
94-1†	*Thomas of Grinton*			
95-1	Thomas		29 Feb. 1651*	25 Oct. 1689*
	John		6 Aug. 1654*	
95-2	Anthony		26 June 1659*	
95-3	Michaell		12 June 1661*	8 Oct. 1717*
	Isabell		21 Feb. 1663*	
	Ralph		16 April 1666*	
95-4	William		11 Aug. 1667*	
	George		18 Dec. 1669*	24 April 1670*
	Elizabeth		6 Oct. 1672*	
95-1	*Thomas of Grinton*			
	Deborah		15 Jan. 1680*	
96-1	Thomas		22 July 1683*	
	James		29 Nov. 1685*	1729
	Thristin		Mar. 1687*	
95-2	*Anthony of Grinton*			
	Ann		5 March 1692*	9 June 1709*
	Elizabeth		27 June 1697*	10 May 1707*

*Asterisks indicate baptisms and burials
†Only ongoing families have been given numbers

Ref	Name	Marriage	Birth/Baptism	Death
95-3	Michaell of Kearton			
	Elizabeth		2 March 1689*	
	Elizabeth		2 March 1690*	
	James		9 June 1706*	
95-4	William of Healah			
96-2	Anthony	Mary	10 April 1698*	13 June 1762*
				26 Aug. 1788*
96-1	Thomas of Grinton			
	Thomas		26 Dec. 1715*	
	Jeffrey		6 Feb. 1717*	
	Thomas		29 Dec. 1724*	
	Deborah		23 Sept. 1708*	
96-2	Anthony and Mary of Feetholme			
	Jane		12 April 1730*	
	Sara		12 Nov. 1732*	
	Mary		23 March 1734*	15 March 1758*
	William		7 Jan. 1738*	
97-1	William	5 May 1766	29 March 1741*	
		Mary Clarkson	11 July 1736*	
	Ruth		29 April 1744*	19 June 1766*
97-2	James	4 July 1768	17 May 1747*	18 April 1824*
		Elizabeth Raw	24 June 1744*	24 June 1790*
97-3	Thomas	15 April 1765	26 Feb. 1748*	19 Aug. 1796*
		Ann Lawson		
97-4	Anthony	10 April 1775	1750	23 June 1834*
		Phillis Wharton	1751	25 Dec. 1842*

Family No.	Parents & Children	Marriage	Birth*	Death*
	Hannah	19 May Richard METCALFE	22 Jan. 1758*	
97-1	William and Mary of Barfend			
	Anthony		31 Jan. 1767*	
	Joseph		17 Jan. 1769*	
	William		26 Jan. 1771*	14 Jan. 1779*
	Betty		20 Jan. 1774*	14 Jan. 1779*
	Jemmy		18 Sept. 1776*	
	Betty		19 Feb. 1779*	
97-2	*James and Elizabeth of Gunnerside*			
98-1	Anthony	9 Aug. 1791 Dorothy Chapman	24 June 1769*	7 March 1820*
98-2	James Doley	27 Sept. 1803 Dorothy Reynoldson	12 Jan. 1771*	19 Aug. 1839*
			12 March1785*	29 May 1862*
	Agnes		15 July 1772*	
98-3	William	30 April 1799 Annas Metcalfe	2 April 1779*	5 May 1824*
			1781	12 March1862
	Isabel	18 April 1809 John POUNDER	22 Jan. 1786*	
			27 March1774*	
	Samuel and Thomas		5 Dec. 1789*	
97-3	Thomas and Ann of Feetholme			
	Nanny		27 July 1766*	

198

Ref	Name	Marriage	Baptised / born	Died
	Anthony		20 Dec. 1772*	
98-4	Betty	3 Nov. 1795 William SPENSLEY (bapt. 8 Nov. 1767)	3 July 1774*	
	Anthony		21 Jan. 1776*	
	Mary		19 April 1778*	
	Ruth		7 May 1780*	7 April 1782*
	Thomas		7 April 1782*	
	Dinah	23 Dec. 1806 Joseph WHITFIELD	25 May 1783*	
	Thomas		4 Dec. 1785*	
	Nancy		4 July 1788*	

97-4 Anthony and Phillis of Winterings

Ref	Name	Marriage	Baptised / born	Died
	Mary		28 Sept. 1776*	
	Nanny		13 Aug. 1779*	
	Phillis		29 Oct. 1781*	9 Feb. 1783*
98-5	Hannah		2 June 1785*	
98-6	Anthony	19 March 1811 Ann Kearton	13 April 1789	22 Oct. 1826*

98-1 *Anthony and Dorothy of Gunnerside*

Ref	Name	Marriage	Baptised / born	Died
99-1	*James*	6 July 1813 Sarah Bell[1] (bapt. 25 Dec. 1801*)	31 July 1792	17 July 1858
	Jinny		22 Aug. 1793*	
99-2	Phillis	20 Sept. 1836 Thomas KITCHEN	19 Dec. 1795*	25 April 1876

[1]Baptised at four, she was born in 1797.

Family No.	Parents & Children	Marriage	Birth*	Death*
	Harry		23 April 1797*	
	Nanny	5 July 1821 Thomas HUNT	25 Nov. 1799	23 Nov. 1800*
	Ruth		18 Feb. 1802*	
			22 July 1798*	
			12 April 1802²	
	Ann		1 Sept. 1806*	7 Oct. 1812*
	Mary		27 Jan. 1812*	14 May 1813*
	Alice		2 May 1814*	
	Henry		27 April 1817*	
	Anthony			
98-2	James Doley and Dorothy of Gunnerside and Lodge Green			
	Dolley		1805	22 Jan. 1805*
	William		8 Feb. 1806*	
	Ann		10 Sept. 1808*	
	George		21 July 1810*	25 May 1837*
	Elizabeth	15 Jan. 1833 John WATTERS	19 June 1813*	
	James³		13 May 1820*	
	Isabella	10 March 1840 James LOWES	13 May 1820*	
98-3	William and Annas of Potting			
	James	16 April 1822 Hannah Coates	11 Jan. 1800 / 14 March 1801*	30 Nov. 1867

²The date is probably an error and should be 1803.
³Baptised at age 3.

Ref	Name	Marriage / Event	Birth date	Birth year	Death date	Death year
99-3	Betty (Eliza)	26 July 1826 Charles BRADBURY	7 July	1804*		
99-4	Thomas	25 Nov. 1823 Ann Calvert	18 Jan.	1805		1875
		9 July 1822	11 Aug.	1806*		1868
99-5	Anas	Joseph BUXTON and Mr. BELL	26 May	1807*		
99-6	Ruth[1]	26 Sept. 1837 George PRATT and 20 June 1852 Anthony MILNER	24 Sept.	1795		
			13 Oct.	1809*		
				1816*	21 May	1848*
99-7	Mary	3 Oct. 1831 James THWAITES	7 Jan.	1812*		
99-8	William	Ruth Pratt	12 June	1814*		
99-9	Robert		1 Sept.	1816*		
99-10	Christopher	15 April 1842 Jane Cheesborough	10 Feb.	1819	28 Jan.	1903
				1821		1898
	Anthony		11 Jan.	1821		
	Agness		10 Jan.	1823		
99-11	Jane	Mr. WRIGGLESWORTH	27 Jan.	1824		1863
98-4	William and Betty SPENSLEY of High Whitaside					
	Susannah		4 Oct.	1806*	26 May	1807*
	John		21 Dec.	1807*		
98-5	Hannah of Gunnerside					
	Hannah		21 April	1810*		

1 See also 99-12.

Family No.	Parents & Children	Marriage	Birth*	Death*
98-6	Anthony and Ann of Gunnerside			
99-12	George²	26 Sept. 1837 Ruth Pratt	13 Oct. 1816*	21 May 1848*
	Elizabeth	6 April 1841 John THOMPSON	13 May 1820* 1817	
	Anthony		15 Nov. 1823	30 Jan. 1825*
99-1	James and Sarah of Barfside and Dyke Heads			
	Anthony		31 Oct. 1814*	5 Feb. 1819*
	John		13 Oct. 1816*	
	Anthony		1819	
	James		6 Feb. 1821	23 Feb. 1821*
100-1	Dorothy	20 May 1840 William BELLIS	16 June 1822	
	James		27 Sept. 1824	
100-2	Metcalf	1850 Hannah Wardle	30 Nov. 1826*	26 Dec. 1891
100-3	William	6 June 1848 Mary Calvert	24 Feb. 1828*	c. 1898
	Anthony		7 May 1835*	
100-4	Sarah Ann	8 July 1857 A. ALDERSON, Mr. WHARTON	9 March 1837	12 March 1915
100-5	John	4 July 1877 Fanny Knight	28 Aug. 1839 18 Nov. 1851	15 March 1904 20 Dec. 1926

² See also 99-6.

100-6	Thomas	14 Sept. 1866 Sarah Bell Stoddart	6 April 1843 6 Dec. 1838		25 Nov. 1918 21 Nov. 1921
99-2	Phillis and Thomas KITCHEN of Gunnerside				
	Hannah				
100-7	Anty	9 May 1843 Margaret Neesham	13 May 1820* 18 June 1822* 1822		1873 11 Sept. 1881
99-3	Elizabeth and Charles BRADBURY of Lodge Green				
	William		26 Feb. 1830*		
	Joseph		6 Oct. 1833*		
99-4	Thomas and Ann of Gunnerside				
	Agness	15 Feb. 1841 George BUXTON	15 March 1824		
	William	17 Dec. 1861 Martha Neesham	9 May 1826*		11 Dec. 1866
	Mary	21 Oct. 1847 John BUXTON	11 July 1830*		
	Ann (Nanny)	25 May 1850 John MATHERS	24 Feb. 1833*		
100-8	John	23 April 1859 Mary Sunter	3 Sept. 1835		
100-9	Elizabeth	26 Feb. 1859 Thomas WAGGET	1840		

203

Family No.	Parents & Children	Marriage	Birth*	Death*
	Jane	16 March 1867 George MILNER	10 Feb. 1843	
	100-10 Thomas	3 March 1877 Jane Raw	25 Nov. 1849	15 May 1909
	Hannah	17 Sept. 1867 Thomas URWIN	1837	
99-5	Anas and Joseph BUXTON			
	100-11 Thomas			
99-6	Ruth and George PRATT and Anthony MILNER of Gunnerside			
	William	11 Sept. 1858 Tamar Neesham	6 Oct. 1833*	
	100-12 Anthony		1838	
	Agnes		17 June 1841*	25 July 1841*
	100-13 James	6 Oct. 1866 Ann (Nanny) Rutter	22 July 1842	
			1839	5 March 1881
	Mary Ann		19 Dec. 1844	21 June 1848*
	Ralph (Milner)			
99-7	Mary and James THWAITES of Lodge Green			
	Adam		28 Dec. 1831*	
	100-14 William		22 June 1833*	
	Mary Ann	Mr. KENDALL	9 May 1835*	
	Aggnon		16 Oct. 1836*	

99-8   William and Ruth

    William
    James   1887
    Anthony

99-9   Robert of Bradford

    Robert
    William
100-15 James   Miss Robinson
    Thomas   Rachel Annie Fanthorpe
100-16 Sarah   Alfred NEWSHOLME
    George
    Harold
100-17 Ruth   J. BUNYARD
    Jane Ann
    Lizzie   Mr. JEFFERSON

99-10 Christopher and Jane of Bradford

Name	Married	Spouse	Born		Died
100-18 William	1876	Emma Greenwood	1843	14 June	1914
100-19 Mary	1865	John PROCTOR	1845		
Elizabeth			1847		
100-20 Agnes	1874	William Goodhugh DAWSON	1850		1919
Ruth			1852		1919
100-21 Benjamin	1885	Mary Newsholme and Edith Ball	1853	9 Aug. / 7 June	1931
100-22 Thomas	1 Oct. 1884	Elizabeth Annie Webster	1855	4 July / 14 Aug.	1923
	1 Oct.		1863		1957

205

Family No.	Parents & Children	Marriage	Birth*	Death*
100-23	Job Cheesborough			22 May 1895
		Clara Roberts	1858	
99-11	Mr. WRIGGLESWORTH and Jane			
	Mary			
	John William			
	Albert			
99-12	George and Ruth (see 99-6)			
100-1	William and Dorothy BELLIS			
101-1	Edwin		1848	
		Ellen Gill	1849	
100-2	Metcalf and Hannah of California and Nevada			
	Charles H.		May 1856	29 July 1859
	S. Jane		Oct. 1857	23 Dec. 1858
	Charles W.		25 Sept. 1859	6 April 1950
	Elizabeth	29 July 1887 Edwin F. DOOLITTLE	14 Aug. 1865	7 May 1897
	Margaret	Edwin F. DOOLITTLE	c. 1869	23 May 1907
	John		c. 1872	1914
101-2	Oliver Metcalf	5 June 1902	1876	
		Annie McBride	23 Nov. 1884	24 Jan. 1911

Ref	Name	Married	Born	Died
100-3	William and Mary of Kettlewell and Burnley			
	Sarah Ann		1850	
	Isabella		4 March 1851	
101-3	James	Miss Ashworth	12 June 1854	1932
101-4	Dorothy	John DRIVER	27 Oct. 1856	1917
	Elizabeth		30 June 1858	Feb. 1912
	Mary Jane (Polly)	John William ROBERTS	1863	
100-4	Sarah Ann and Anthony ALDERSON and Mr. WHARTON of Burnley			
101-5	Moses	1882 Maria Heys	21 Dec. 1854	4 Jan. 1913
101-6	Jane (Alderson)	c. 1884 James CALVERT	15 April 1856	Nov. 1925
101-7	Sarah Ann (Alderson)	Frank BRUNT	16 June 1858	8 Jan. 1939
			1840	Sept. 1919
	Lily (Alderson)			
	Rosamond (Alderson)			
	James (Wharton)	Lily		
	George (Wharton)	Polly	c. 1877	c. 1957

Family No.	Parents & Children	Marriage	Birth*		Death*	
				1878	Dec.	1924
100-5	*John and Fanny of Newfoundland*					
	William Knight		2 June	1878	Dec.	1924
		Blanche				
101-8	James Charles Spurgeon (Jim)	15 Aug. 1906	26 June	1880	4 Aug.	1956
		Marion (Minnie) Kerr	3 June	1884	20 Oct.	1967
101-9	Edwin John Dove (Ned)	20 Aug. 1918	4 Feb.	1882	26 April	1964
		Viola Leone Whitney	23 Feb.	1892		
	Charlotte Pitts (Lottie)	24 Aug. 1908	11 June	1884	8 Sept.	1954
		George HARRIS			28 Jan.	1954
101-10	Arthur Milligan	28 April 1924	15 April	1886	25 Jan.	1961
		Maud Bertha Legg	6 June	1899		
101-11	Calvert Coates	6 July 1915	6 Oct.	1888	13 Nov.	1963
		Agnes Horwood	7 Aug.	1888	13 July	1952
	Florence Sophia		31 Oct.	1892		
	Nellie Beatrice		31 March	1896	24 May	1966
100-6	Thomas and Sarah of New Zealand					
	Sarah Elizabeth	1886	28 May	1867	27 Nov.	1933
		Hugh McFARLANE		1855	c.	1905
	Ruth	8 Aug. 1896	14 Feb.	1869	6 Aug.	1940
		David HALL		1836		
101-12	Hannah	14 Sept. 1891	26 March	1871	8 April	1949
		James McCAFFREY	8 Feb.	1853	Sept.	1936
100-7	Anthony and Margaret of Modesty					
	Margaret	16 March 1867		1845		
		James HARKER				

ID	Name	Born	Died
	Hannah		
	Phillis		
	James	1848	
	Martha	1850	
	Mary Ann	1852	27 March 1853
		1 Jan. 1855	
		27 April 1863	
100-8	John and Mary of Gunnerside		
	Thomas	27 Oct. 1859	
	= Hannah Heslop and Mary Raw 15 Feb. 1890		
	John Thomas WISEMAN		
101-13	Dorothy	3 Jan. 1862	7 April 1931
101-14	Ann	21 July 1864	Dec. 1953
	= Matthew BELL		
101-15	George	21 March 1866	8 May 1941
	= Margaret Bowes		
101-16	William	7 Feb. 1868	19 May 1947
	= Margaret Hall		
	John	2 May 1870	12 Oct. 1961
101-17	James	2 May 1870	27 April 1913
	= Mary Elizabeth Miller		8 May 1938
	Elizabeth	5 Feb. 1872	April 1951
	Christopher	11 March 1880	1947
100-9	Elizabeth and Thomas WAGGET		
	John		
	William		
	= Cherry		
	Ann		
	= TERRY		

Family No.	Parents & Children	Marriage	Birth*	Death*
100-10	Thomas and Jane of Melbecks			
	Thomas William		18 June 1877	
	James		24 Aug. 1879*	
	John		30 Sept. 1881*	
	Ann Elizabeth		26 Sept. 1884*	
100-11	Thomas BUXTON			
	101-18 Joseph	Lily		
	Elizabeth			
	Mary Ann			
	Richard			
	Thomas			
100-12	Anthony and Tamar of Gunnerside			
	Ruth		2 Jan. 1859	23 Sept. 1863*
	Elizabeth		14 Jan. 1861	
	Mary Ann		25 May 1863	
	William		5 Feb. 1867	
	Agnes Ellen		25 Aug. 1869	6 Feb. 1870*
	Ruth		6 May 1870	
	Anthony		7 March 1874	
	George		1865/6	28 Jan. 1866*
100-13	James and Ann (Nanny) of Gunnerside			
	101-19 George		20 Sept. 1868	
	Mary Ann		7 July 1870	

100-14 William THWAITES
- John
- John William
- Anthony
- Ruth
- Nancy

100-15 James and Miss Robinson
- John   23 Feb. 1872
- James   26 Jan. 1874

- Harry   25 Oct. 1875
- Agnes   23 June 1879*
- Ruth   23 June 1879*
- Elizabeth (Lizzie)

100-16 Sarah and Alfred NEWSHOLME
- Robert Harold

100-17 Ruth and Mr. BUNYARD
- Agnes   Mr. JACKSON

- Ruth   27 Feb. 1876*
- Elizabeth (Lizzie)   23 Dec. 1879*
- Winnifred

100-18 William and Emma
- Christopher Arthur
- Jane Elizabeth   Mr. RUSSELL

- Harold Victor

Family No.	Parents & Children	Marriage	Birth*	Death*
	Randolph			
	Rosamond			
	Kate Greenwood			
100-19	Mary and John PROCTOR			
	101-20 Harry	Mr. INGHAM		
	Bernard			
	William	Mr. HILL		
	101-21 John			
	Martha			
100-20	Agnes and William Goodhugh DAWSON			
	101-22 Percival Goodhugh	Jane Elizabeth Carson		
	101-23 Winnifred Agnes	Harold Felvus WALKER		
	101-24 William Goodhugh	Margaret Emily Gledhill	1879	26 Aug. 1937
	101-25 Christopher Goodhugh	B. Waterhouse and N. A. M.		
	101-26 Leonard Goodhugh	Freda Hollis		
100-21	Benjamin and Mary Newsholme and Edith Ball of India			

Name	Born	Died
101-27 Henry Pratt NEWSHOLME	27 Aug. 1885	
Kathleen Denness Cooper		
1916		
Henry Harness HARPER		
1917		
101-28 Constance Ruthnam	18 Feb. 1888	
101-29 Harold Evelyn	12 May 1889	May 1968
Margaret Bridge	9 Nov. 1893	Nov. 1970
101-30 Hugh Baldwin	17 Dec. 1891	
Madeleine Heath and Patricia	12 Sept. 1901	
Barbara Weston		
Edmond Alan	11 Aug. 1893	17 Aug. 1894
Geoffrey Lancaster	15 Oct. 1900	Labor Day 1963
24 Aug. 1926		
Florence Amelia Ross	12 April 1901	
100-22 Thomas and Elizabeth Annie of Bradford		
101-31 Leonard Webster	28 Feb. 1886	1 Jan. 1934
1924		
Marie Emmeline Alton		
6 June 1918		
101-32 Christopher	3 June 1887	23 March 1964
Mary Petch	27 Sept. 1892	
1932		
101-33 Geoffrey Cheesborough	3 Oct. 1888	
Jean Thompson		
1926		
101-34 Wilfred Ellington	11 Dec. 1890	
Sarah Smith		
101-35 Thomas Dawson	3 May 1893	Jan. 1960
1 July 1923		
Mary Thornborrow Wilkinson	7 Jan. 1894	1963
Henry Webster	16 Dec. 1895	
Agnes Dorothea (Dol)	31 Oct. 1896	
Basil James Anthony	18 Feb. 1898	
19 Sept. 1936		
Winnifred Buzzard		

Family No.	Parents & Children	Marriage	Birth*		Death*	
101-36	Alfred Stewart Redvers	1925 Kathleen Florence Bedford	28 Feb.	1900	Oct.	1966
	Edward Cecil Handley		5 April	1902		1966
	Ruth Josephine			1906		1906
100-23	Job Cheesborough and Clara					
	Ralph					
101-1	Edwin and Ellen BELLIS of Birstal					
	Horace					
	Eva					
	Elizabeth Ann	John DRIVER	7 June	1879		
	Amy	CLEGG				
101-2	Oliver and Annie of Nevada					
102-1	Oliver F.	1 March 1927 Edna Rose Walker	5 June	1903		
		15 April 1925 Howard A. Miles	24 April	1908		1929
	Annie		28 March	1905		
102-2	John W.	4 June 1927 Agnes Billett	28 Dec.	1907		
			6 Sept.	1910		
101-3	James and Miss Ashworth					
102-3	William Ashworth	1914 Nellie Salter Jago	18 Nov.	1889	13 Nov.	1940
		Thomas ABBOTT		1885	April	1969
	Alice Emma					
	Dora					
	Adelaide					

101-4 Dorothy and John DRIVER of Burnley

	Marriage	Born	Died
Mary		Feb. 1883	1900
102-4 William		22 Feb. 1885	21 May 1958
Mary Ibbotson	5 Sept. 1913	15 March 1885	21 April 1959
102-5 James Herbert		18 April 1889	
Emily Hitchen	5 Sept. 1914	15 March 1891	
102-6 Sarah (Sallie)		28 Dec. 1891	
Charles COLECHIN	10 Jan. 1922	7 Oct. 1893	24 July 1969

101-5 Moses and Maria of Burnley

	Marriage	Born	Died
102-7 William Henry		8 April 1887	July 1957
Ada Longstaff	1916		
102-8 Gladys		27 April 1890	1932
John Taylor WHITAKER	1926		
102-9 Herbert		15 Sept. 1892	
Elizabeth Jackson	6 Aug. 1921	20 April 1894	
102-10 John		21 Aug. 1894	
Lizzie Wallbank	Oct. 1921	Oct. 1893	
Edward		31 July 1896	
Gertrude Edmonson	1929	1898	

101-6 Jane and James CALVERT of Burnley (and Kettlewell)

	Marriage	Born	Died
102-11 Edgar		11 May 1885	
Elizabeth (Lizzie) Holgate	Aug. 1915		

Family No.	Parents & Children	Marriage	Birth*	Death*
	James Anthony (James Anty)			1965
		Gertrude Gleason	15 March	
	George Ernest			1969
		Eliza Baldwin		
102-12	Sarah Ann (Cissie)	George STANSFIELD and	2 March 1893	
		John (Jack) RENNIE		
102-13	Jane Elizabeth			1964
		Arthur RUNDLE	Dec. 1896	9 March 1923
	Rosamond			9 Oct. 1917
		Walter WILD and		1947
		Gwyder Winslow ROSE		
102-14	Doris	12 June 1928	9 April 1899	6 June 1960
		Albert ANGUS	20 Dec. 1897	
101-7	Sarah Ann and Frank BRUNT of Burnley			
102-15	Thomas	Jane Beatty		
102-16	Francis			
101-8	Jim and Minnie of Newfoundland			
102-17	Julia Gwenyth	1 Sept. 1938	13 June 1907	
		Harold George (Hal) PUDDESTER	31 Dec. 1905	
102-18	John Kerr (Jack)	25 Oct. 1934	8 May 1909	
		Christine Emily Dawe	4 March 1909	

Maxwell James	16 Sept. 1939	24 Jan. 1911	
Daphne Lorraine	Jean MacKenzie Sterling	29 Sept. 1914	
	21 Sept. 1957	6 Feb. 1916	
102-19 Arthur Douglas	William John HOUSE	25 Sept. 1920	12 April 1963
	24 June 1947	15 Oct. 1922	15 Nov. 1968
	Minnie Gladys Parsons	10 Dec. 1919	
101-9 Ned and Vi of Toronto			
Mildred Claire	18 March 1921		
101-10 Art and Maud of Wallasey			
Eleanor Maud		9 March 1925	31 May 1927
Gerald Arthur Legg		10 Dec. 1926	
102-20 John Andrew Legg	6 Oct. 1962	5 Jan. 1928	
	Diana Enid Middleton	12 May 1932	
102-21 Margaret Isabella	6 Aug. 1966	29 March 1931	
	Eric Royston PUTNAM	6 Aug. 1931	
102-22 Florence Gertrude	25 Aug. 1958	5 Jan. 1934	
	Alan Johnstone BLAND	17 June 1926	
101-11 Cal and Agnes of Newfoundland			
102-23 Ewart Arthur	30 Oct. 1943	20 March 1919	
	Mary Kathleen Yvonne Rorke	4 June 1922	
102-24 Calvert Coates	26 Apr. 1947	23 Dec. 1921	
	Mary Archibald Rorke	8 Feb. 1924	
101-12 Nan and James McCaffrey of New Zealand			

Family No.	Parents & Children	Marriage	Birth*	Death*
102-25	Ada Sarah	23 April 1923	25 July 1892	
		John William Goss BALL	26 June 1891	
	John Thomas	6 July 1933	17 Sept. 1894	4 April 1949
		Ruth		
	James		5 July 1896	21 Aug. 1896
102-26	Hugh	18 Dec. 1923	4 March 1898	
		Violet Bruce	7 Sept. 1900	
102-27	Thomas	1939	4 Oct. 1899	1 Feb. 1955
		Effie Neville		
	Francis		6 May 1901	17 Oct. 1901
102-28	Arthur Stuart	Sept. 1929	29 June 1903	
		Esther Alice Meredith Hopwood	17 July 1905	
	Ruth Elizabeth		25 Nov. 1906	29 Nov. 1906
	Stella Ruth		21 July 1908	29 July 1908
101-13	Dorothy and John Wisemen of Swaledale			
	Christopher	May 1935	1892	June 1962
		Gladys Rowlands		
	Mary		June 1893	1963
			1890	
	Annie	John KITCHING	17 Aug. 1894	1 Aug. 1964
		June 1925	1894	
		Ernest HERON		
	Dorothy		31 March 1897	
	Elizabeth		5 Feb. 1899	
	Isabella Emilie	June 1926	25 March 1904	
		Harry GAINES-BURRILL	July 1903	1964

101-14	Ann and Matthew BELL of Swaledale		
	102-29 Mary	James KENDALL	
101-15	George and Margaret		
	Dorothy		
	Robert Wesley		
	Mary		(in childhood)
	Margaret Ellen (Peggy)	Mr. DAWSON	
	Elizabeth	Harry CALVERT	
		Hubert HARRISON	
	John	Beryl Last	
	Lydia	Mr. WHITING	
	Anne	Mr. HOWLETT	
	Georgina	Donald LAST	
101-16	William and Margaret of Sabden		
	Mary	Mr. HARGREAVES	March1895
101-17	James and Mary Elizabeth		
	John Calvert		

219

Family No.	Parents & Children	Marriage	Birth*	Death*
	Joseph Pierson			
	Mary Sunter	Mr. TURNBULL		
	Elizabeth Oates	Mr. TULIP		
102-30	Margaret Miller	C. LAWSON		
	Rhoda Hird (Daisy)	Frank LEATHLEY		
101-18	Joseph and Lily BUXTON			
	Earl Russell			
101-19	George			
	Edith			
	Mary Ann			
	William			
101-20	Harry PROCTOR			
	John			
	William Arthur			
101-21	John PROCTOR			
	Alfred			
	Clifford			
	girl			

101-22	Percival and Jane Elizabeth DAWSON	
	102-31 Robert Carson	Sylvia Shaw
101-23	Winnifred Agnes and Harold WALKER	
	Agnes Elise	
	Richard Felvus	
	102-32 William Dawson	D. H. Shiach
	102-33 Winifred Ruth	Thomas CLEGHORN
	102-34 Leonard Geoffrey	Rosemary Salamon
101-24	William and Margaret Emily DAWSON	
	102-35 Winifred Mary	Wilfred M. CRAVEN
	102-36 Josephine Mary	John Walker ROBERTS
101-25	Christopher and B. and N.A.	
	Eileen	
	Robert	Martha
	Peter	
	Barbara	

221

Family No.	Parents & Children	Marriage	Birth*	Death*
101-26	Leonard and Freda DAWSON			
	102-37 Richard	Betty F. Matthews		
	102-38 Ruth	Ilay MARTIN		
	102-39 Molly	Hugh MARTIN		
101-27	Henry and Kathleen NEWSHOLME			
	102-40 Arthur Deness	Jane Keenlisides		
	102-41 George Adam	Rosemary Bishop	18 May 1921	
	102-42 Kathryn Mary	W. John TURNER	1926	
	102-43 Christopher Mansford	Mary Ford	13 Feb. 1929	
	102-44 Helen Felicity	Harry HASTRIP	16 May 1934	
101-28	Con and Henry HARPER of Vancouver			
	102-45 John Harness	20 June 1948 Jean Blackie	16 Sept. 1918	
	102-46 Catherine Margaret Harness	20 Feb. 1946 Alexander MacKENZIE	20 June 1927 14 Aug. 1921	

102-47 Edith Barbara Harness	Aug. 1949	Mason Yorston RAMSAY	26 Sept. 1925 March 1922		March 1966
101-29 Harold and Margaret of Okotoks and Vancouver					
Jean Margaret	1 April 1945	James Bryce MILNER	14 Aug. 1919 9 Feb. 1918		5 June 1969
102-48 Christopher Gratrix	24 Nov. 1948	Marguerite Mary Warlow	24 May 1924 17 Feb. 1926		
101-30 Hugh and Madeleine					
Alan Heath			15 Jan. 1922		1955
102-49 Denis Hugh		Dorothy O'Brien	17 Jan. 1928		
101-31 Leonard and Marie					
Catherine Rosamond					
102-50 Leonard Geoffrey Alton		Leslie Ann Danbury			
101-32 Christopher and Mary of Well					
102-51 Ruth Christina	14 July 1946	Harold EVANS	21 Dec. 1922 25 Oct. 1916		
102-52 Christopher Barwick (Barry)	20 Sept. 1958	Ursula Bottomley	6 Aug. 1924 1 Sept. 1927		
102-53 David Webster	7 June 1958	Margaret Pierson	14 Sept. 1932 1 Sept. 1937		
101-33 Geoffrey and Jean of Well					

223

Family No.	Parents & Children	Marriage	Birth*	Death*
	102-54 Timothy Jean Geoffrey	Pamela Ann Blake		
101-34	Wilfred and Sarah			
	Joan Mary			
101-35	Thomas and Mary			
102-55	Thomas Leonard Chees-borough	17 July 1948 Mary Winifred Allen	22 Oct. 1920 14 July 1915	
102-56	Patricia Ann Elizabeth	19 July 1964 John FRYER	6 Dec. 1924	
101-36	Redvers and Kathleen			
102-57	Kathleen Erica	Douglas Baldock GILLERT		
	102-58 Joyce Elizabeth	Kenneth HARRISON		
102-1	Oliver and Edna of Carson City			
103-1	Oliver F.	9 Oct. 1949 RoseMarie Satti	31 Oct. 1927	
	Gordon Neil	Leontine Favell	6 Feb. 1931	
	Shirley Ann	5 Dec. 1952 Ryland CUNNINGHAM	25 June 1934	
102-2	John and Agnes of Ely			

	Pauline		28 March 1931
	Dale W.		14 Oct. 1932
	James R.		25 July 1934
102-3	Ashworth and Nellie		
	Wycliffe Cyril Ashworth		1916
	Alicia Doreen Ashworth		1918
	Bramwell D. Ashworth		1920
	William Ashworth		1925
102-4	William and Mary DRIVER of Burnley	23 Jan. 1955	
103-2	William Harry	Freda M. Bunney	
102-5	Herbert and Emily DRIVER of Rossendale		
103-3	Dorothy	24 Dec. 1940	24 July 1916
		William BOARDMAN	18 Feb. 1918
102-6	Sarah and Charles COLECHIN of New Zealand		
	Fae Elizabeth (Hall)[1]	21 Dec. 1941	16 Jan. 1922
		Richard Arthur Bernard CLIFF	1918
103-4	Ruth	11 Nov. 1953	1 Nov. 1930
		Donald Sidney GIBLIN	Sept. 1932
102-7	William Henry and Ada		
	Edward		
	William		

[1] Adopted.

FamilyNo.	Parents & Children	Marriage	Birth*	Death*
102-8	Gladys and John WHITAKER			
	103-5 Sheila			
102-9	Herbert and Elizabeth of Burnley			
	103-6 Muriel Joyce	23 July 1944 Gordon Bannister HALL	6 Dec. 1924 18 Sept. 1925	
102-10	John and Lizzie			
	Geoffrey			
102-11	Edgar and Elizabeth CALVERT of the West Indies			
	Penelope Marjorie	30 July Derek SKEET	21 July 1916 25 Dec. 1923	
	103-7 Rosemary	11 Aug. 1950 Brian John MURRAY	15 Aug. 1921 19 May 1918	
102-12	Sarah Ann and George STANSFIELD and Jack RENNIE			
	Florence Mabel Eileen Monica Stanley			
102-13	Jane and Arthur RUNDLE of Australia			
	103-8 Doris	Stanley Gray LLOYD		

Patricia

Robert Geoffrey BOWNESS

102-14   Doris and Albert ANGUS of Winnipeg

    Beatrice[1]

        James   10 Nov. 1921   14 June 1908

    103-9 Albert

        Alona   21 July 1929   29 Dec. 1929

    103-10 Doris

        Gordon   6 March 1932 16 Feb. 1921

102-15   Thomas and Jane BRUNT of Burnley

    Thomas

102-16   Francis BRUNT of Burnley

    Lily

102-17   Gwenyth and Hal PUDDESTER of Newfoundland

    103-11 Harold James (Jamie)   25 Feb. 1967   8 May 1946

    Margaret June Hudson   27 June 1945

102-18   Jack and Chris of Newfoundland

    103-12 John Christopher Maxwell 14 Sept. 1957   9 Dec. 1935

    Mary Frances West   15 Mar. 1935

    Philip Michael Douglas   16 Feb. 1946

[1] Stepdaughter.

227

Family No.	Parents & Children	Marriage	Birth*	Death*
102-19	Arthur and Minnie of Newfoundland			
	Douglas Roger		8 March 1948	
	Gerald John		25 Oct. 1952	
102-20	John and Diana of Scotland			
	Jennifer Mary		11 Oct. 1963	
	Catherine Jane		26 June 1968	
102-21	Margaret and Roy PUTNAM of Romiley			
	Christopher Mark		5 Dec. 1967	
	Sarah Anne		14 Aug. 1970	
102-22	Florence and Alan BLAND of Hoylake			
	William Arthur		6 Feb. 1962	
	Christine Elizabeth		26 March 1964	
102-23	Ewart and Yvonne of St. John's			
	Kathleen Agnes[1]		27 Feb. 1948	
	James Rorke		6 Aug. 1949	
102-24	Calvert and Mary of St. John's			
	Calvert Coates		5 May 1948	
	Robert Tucker		20 Dec. 1950	
	Douglas Rorke		3 Sept. 1959	

[1] Adopted.

102-25 Ada and Jack BALL of Christchurch

103-13 John Francis Goss (Frank)   3 Aug. 1953   28 May 1925
       Patricia Cottee
       Nancy Kathleen   28 Feb. 1927
103-14 Winton James   18 Dec. 1957   16 Nov. 1929
       Glenys Bullard

102-26 Hugh and Violet McCAFFREY of Christchurch

103-15 Maureen Nola   18 Feb. 1956   25 March 1932
       Trevor Raymond GARING   20 Sept. 1934

102-27 Thomas and Effie McCAFFREY of New Zealand

       Stella   15 March 1940
       Yvonne   3 July   1944
       Patricia Joy   13 July 1945
       James Thomas   9 March 1948   1 Feb.   1955
       Nancy Hannah   30 Oct. 1951

102-28 Arthur and Esther McCAFFREY of New Zealand

103-16 Rae Esther   21 Jan. 1956   13 May   1932
       Bruce SCAMMELL   2 Jan.   1932
103-17 Rex Arthur   Feb. 1960   26 April 1933
       Doreen Marjorie Bycroft   March   1931
103-18 Dulcie May   23 April 1960 27 Feb. 1939
       Ernest William POWELL   25 Feb. 1933

Family No.	Parents & Children	Marriage	Birth*	Death*
	Vera Marguerite		28 May 1940	
	Gwenyth Caroline		7 Dec. 1948	
102-29	James and Mary KENDALL of Swaledale			
	Mrs. PETTY			
102-30	C. and Margaret LAWSON of Richmond			
	Tony			
	James			
102-31	Robert and Sylvia DAWSON			
	Robert			
	Jennifer			
	Valerie			
	Philip			
102-32	William and D.H. WALKER			
	Philippa			
	Michael			
102-33	Thomas and Winifred CLEGHORN			
	William A.			
	Charles H.			
	John H.			

102-34 Leonard and Rosemary WALKER

    Nigel F.

    Rupert

102-35 Wilfred and Winifred CRAVEN

    Priscilla   John DIGGLE

    Roger Piers   Judith Raines

    Martin

102-36 John and Josephine ROBERTS

    Carol Margaret

    Alison Mary

    John Richard

102-37 Richard and Betty DAWSON

    Timothy

    Nicholas

102-38 Ruth and Ilay MARTIN

    Hugh

102-39 Hugh and Molly MARTIN

    Catherine

    William

    Richard

102-40 Arthur and Jane NEWSHOLME

Family No.	Parents & Children	Marriage	Birth*	Death*
	Christina Mary			
	Frances			
	Sarah			
102-41	George and Rosemary NEWSHOLME			
	Richard George			
	Sally Katharine			
	Dorothy Mary			
102-42	John and Katharine TURNER			
	Jane Katharine			
102-43	Christopher and Mary NEWSHOLME			
	Stephen			
	Timothy			
102-44	Harry and Helen HASTRIP			
	Michael Christopher			
	Noel Timothy			
102-45	John and Jean HARPER			
	Merridith Carolyn		10 March 1949	
	John Keith Harness		20 Jan. 1953	
	David Kevin		6 Dec. 1956	
	Shelagh Kathryn		27 April 1962	

232

102-46	Catharine and Alexander MacKENZIE		
	Brenda Gayle		
	Donald Alexander		
	Margaret		
	Robert Neill		
102-47	Edith and Mason RAMSAY		
	Constance Anne		
	Kenneth Gary		
	Leah Ruth		
102-48	Christopher and Mary of Halifax		
	Mark Christopher	3 Sept.	1951
	Patricia Marguerite	14 May	1953
	Nicholas Sidney	30 Jan.	1957
	Sarah Jane	29 June	1959
102-49	Denis and Dorothy		
	David		
	Sheila		
102-50	Leonard and Leslie Ann		
	Andrew John		
	Jane Elizabeth		
102-51	Ruth and Harold EVANS		
	Elizabeth Mary	28 Dec.	1948
	Peter Gordon	29 Jan.	1952

Family No.	Parents & Children	Marriage	Birth*	Death*
102-52	Barry and Ursula			
	Elizabeth		26 Aug. 1959	
	Christopher		3 Sept. 1961	
	William John		16 Sept. 1963	
	James		16 March 1968	
102-53	David and Margaret			
	David Martin		3 June 1958	
	Josephine		26 Aug. 1960	
	Jane Louise		4 May 1964	
	Timothy Webster		11 March 1966	
102-54	Timothy and Pamela			
	A girl		1965	
	Lucy		Dec. 1967	
102-55	Tom and Winifred of Darlington			
	Helen Mary		24 Feb. 1950	
	Ruth Elizabeth		17 July 1952	
102-56	Pat and John FRYER			
	Alison Mary			
	Rosamund Ann			
102-57	Kathleen and Douglas GILLERT			
	Jennifer Alison			
	Martin Rory			

234

102-58	Joyce and Kenneth HARRISON	
	Judith Ann	
	Robert Charles Redvers	
103-1	Oliver and RoseMarie of Nevada	
	Linda	26 Aug. 1950
	Joseph	5 May 1954
103-2	Ryland and Shirley Ann CUNNINGHAM of Nevada	
	Elaine	7 July 1954
	Larry	14 Dec. 1955
	Coleen	19 March 1957
103-3	Harry and Freda DRIVER of Burnley	
104-1	Margaret	
	Eric	
	Gillian	
103-4	Dorothy and Bill BOARDMAN of Rossendale, Lancs.	
104-2	Jean	
	Brian DOIDGE	
		20 Sept. 1941
		28 May 1933
103-5	Ruth and Don GIBLIN of Christchurch	
	Beverley	23 March 1955
	Stuart	28 June 1957
	Brent	Nov. 1967

Family No.	Parents & Children	Marriage	Birth*	Death*
103-6	Sheila			
	Ian			
	David			
103-7	Joyce and Gordon HALL of Surrey			
	Guy		1951	
	Jonathan		1961	
	Peter Lyndon		4 July 1965	
103-8	Rosemary and Brian MURRAY of Essex			
	Paul Calvert			
103-9	Doris and Stanley LLOYD of Australia			
	Paul			
	Peter			
	Stephen			
	Helen			
	Margaret			
103-10	Albert and Alona ANGUS			
	Janice Gail		5 Dec. 1955	
	Katherine Gail		11 May 1958	
	David Bruce		6 Sept. 1961	
	Robert Scott		24 May 1968	

103-11	Doris and Gordon		
	Gordon Wayne	4 Sept.	1954
	Norman Grant	2 July	1956
	Sandra Kim	22 March	1961
103-12	Jamie and Margaret PUDDESTER of Newfoundland		
	Leigh Harold James	27 Sept.	1967
103-13	Christopher and Mary of Newfoundland		
	William John	30 July	1958
	Anne Elizabeth Sonia	23 May	1960
	Barbara Marian	16 Feb.	1963
	Edwyn James (Ned)	15 Aug.	1964
103-14	Frank and Pat BALL of New Zealand		
	Graham Francis	4 Oct.	1955
	Kathryn Margaret	10 April	1957
	David Christopher	10 April	1960
103-15	Winton and Glenys BALL of New Zealand		
	Peter Michael	4 Feb.	1960
	Carolyn Margaret	5 Aug.	1962
103-16	Maureen and Trevor GARING of New Zealand		

Family No.	Parents & Children	Marriage	Birth*	Death*
	Andrea		3 Nov. 1959	
	Gillian		12 Feb. 1963	
103-17	Rae and Bruce SCAMMELL of New Zealand			
	Ruth		Dec. 1957	
	David		28 April 1959	
	Christine		Dec. 1961	
	Esther		13 Aug. 1963	
103-18	Rex Arthur and Doreen McCAFFREY of New Zealand			
	Kevin Arthur		11 March 1960	
	Stuart Hedley		13 March 1962	
	Clare Suzanne		13 May 1966	Dec. 1963
	Vicki Rachael		Oct. 1967	
103-19	Dulcie and Ernest POWELL of New Zealand			
	Judith May		17 Jan. 1961	
	Lynnette Anne		5 Nov. 1962	
	Ernest Andrew		28 April 1964	
	Neil James		22 Aug. 1965	
104-1	Margaret and Eric			
	Christopher			

104-2   Jean and Brian DOIDGE

Sharon Lesley   6 June   1963
Marcus John   10 July   1965
Brian William   10 Jan.   1967

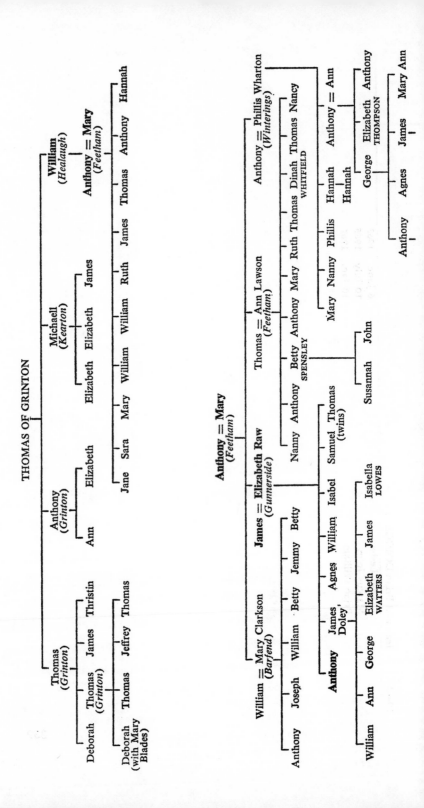

THOMAS OF GRINTON

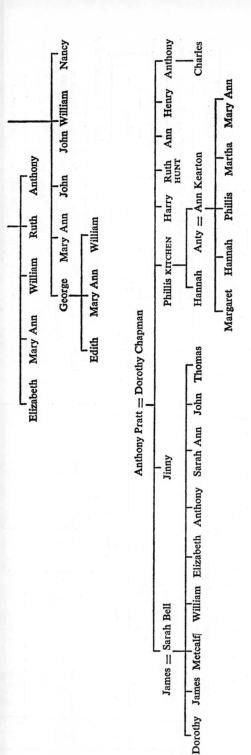
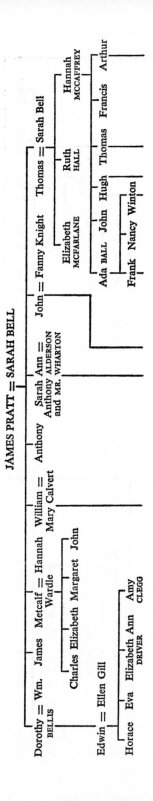

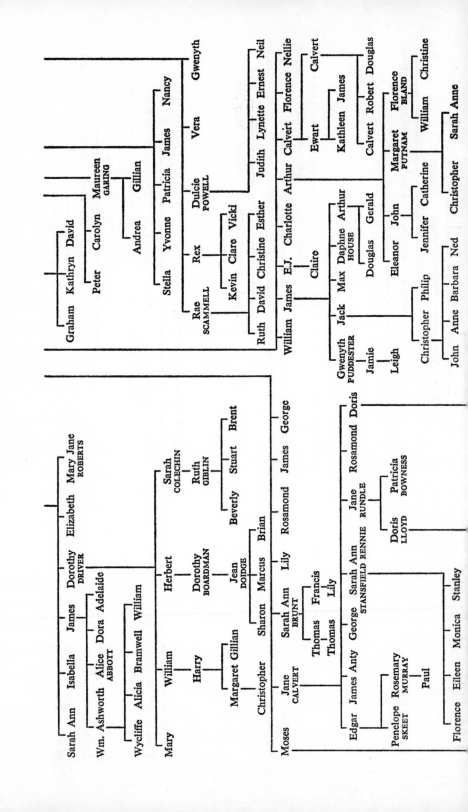

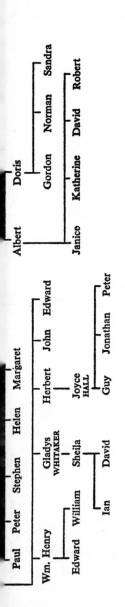

Paul   Peter   Stephen   Helen   Margaret

Wm. Henry

Edward   William

Gladys
WHITAKER

Herbert   John   Edward

Sheila

Ian   David

Joyce
HALL

Guy   Jonathan   Peter

Albert   Doris

Gordon   Norman   Sandra

Janice

Katherine   David   Robert